Crips and Bloods

Recent Titles in
Guides to Subcultures and Countercultures

The Ku Klux Klan: A Guide to an American Subculture
Martin Gitlin

Hippies: A Guide to an American Subculture
Micah L. Issitt

Punks: A Guide to an American Subculture
Sharon M. Hannon

Flappers: A Guide to an American Subculture
Kelly Boyer Sagert

Beatniks: A Guide to an American Subculture
Alan Bisbort

Goths: A Guide to an American Subculture
Micah L. Issitt

Radical Feminists: A Guide to an American Subculture
Paul D. Buchanan

Skinheads: A Guide to an American Subculture
Tiffini A. Travis and Perry Hardy

The Mafia: A Guide to an American Subculture
Nate Hendley

Guides to
Subcultures and
Countercultures

Crips and Bloods

A Guide to an American Subculture

Herbert C. Covey

GREENWOOD™

An Imprint of ABC-CLIO, LLC

Santa Barbara, California • Denver, Colorado

Library of Congress Cataloging-in-Publication Data

Covey, Herbert C.
    Crips and Bloods : a guide to an American subculture/Herbert C. Covey.
        pages cm. — (Guides to subcultures and countercultures)
    Includes bibliographical references and index.
        ISBN 978–0–313–39929–9 (hardback) — ISBN 978–0–313–39930–5 (ebook) 1. Gangs—United States. 2. Gang members—United States. 3. Juvenile delinquency—United States. 4. Street life—United States. I. Title.
HV6439.U5C678   2015
364.106′60973—dc23   2015002592

ISBN: 978–0–313–39929–9
EISBN: 978–0–313–39930–5

19 18 17 16 15   1 2 3 4 5

This book is also available on the World Wide Web as an eBook.
Visit www.abc-clio.com for details.

Greenwood
An Imprint of ABC-CLIO, LLC

ABC-CLIO, LLC
130 Cremona Drive, P.O. Box 1911
Santa Barbara, California 93116-1911

This book is printed on acid-free paper ∞

Manufactured in the United States of America

Contents

Series Foreword

From Beatniks to Flappers, Zoot Suiters to Punks, this series brings to life some of the most compelling countercultures in American history. Designed to offer a quick, in-depth examination and current perspective on each group, the series aims to stimulate the reader's understanding of the richness of the American experience. Each book explores a countercultural group critical to American life and introduces the reader to its historical setting and precedents, the ways in which it was subversive or countercultural, and its significance and legacy in American history. *Webster's Ninth New Collegiate Dictionary* defines counterculture as "a culture with values and mores that run counter to those of established society." Although some of the groups covered can be described as primarily subcultural, they were targeted for inclusion because they have not existed in a vacuum. They have advocated for rules that methodically opposed mainstream culture, or lived by those ideals to the degree that it became impossible not to impact the society around them. They have left their marks, both positive and negative, on the fabric of American culture. Volumes cover such groups as Hippies and Beatniks, who impacted popular culture, literature, and art; the Eco-Socialists and Radical Feminists, who worked toward social and political change; and even groups such as the Ku Klux Klan, who left mostly scars.

A lively alternative to narrow historiography and scholarly monographs, each volume in the *Subcultures and Countercultures* series can be described as a "library in a book," containing both essays and browsable reference materials, including primary documents, to enhance the research process and bring the content alive in a variety of ways. Written for students and general readers, each volume includes engaging illustrations, a timeline of critical events in the subculture, topical essays that illuminate aspects of the subculture, a glossary of subculture terms and slang, biographical sketches of the key players involved, and primary source excerpts—including speeches, writings, articles, first-person accounts, memoirs, diaries, government reports, and court decisions—that offer a contemporary perspective on each group. In addition, each volume includes an extensive bibliography of current recommended print and nonprint sources appropriate for further research.

Preface

I am a gang expert—period. There are no other gang experts except participants.

—Sanyika Shakur (aka Monster Kody Scott),[1] Eight Tray Gangster

Over 25 years ago, I began a journey to better understand street gangs. Back then I was searching for a suitable book topic in crime and delinquency. As part of a book proposal, I discovered that very little academic work was available on street gangs, and much of what was available was outdated. In addition, I realized that scholars had made few attempts to summarize what was then known about youth gangs. Consequently, I invited two colleagues to join me and prepare a text on what was known about street gangs. Three book editions later and after a few joint publications, our friendship and working relationship remain intact. Soon after the first edition of the text, I would be appointed to the Colorado State Juvenile Parole Board, which resulted in my meeting numerous gang-involved youth over a 13-year span. The stories and comments of these gang-involved youth fueled my desire to understand more about their lives within and outside of their gangs. I never imagined that 25 years later I would still be involved with the topic of gangs.

Although gangs have been studied since the 1920s, the volume of literature was very limited until the past two decades. Today this is not the case, as many scholars, journalists, law enforcement agencies, and gang members have contributed to what we think we know about gangs. We know more today than ever before, yet there remains much to be learned. There remain several gaps in our understanding, and mysteries abound as to the true nature of gangs.

This volume tries to shed some light on Crip and Blood street gangs. These two gangs, more than any others, have shaped our perceptions of what street gangs are like throughout the world. However, as this volume will reveal, there are multiple and often contradictory observations and perceptions about both gangs. Scholars, law enforcement professionals, and gang members often have divergent views about both gangs. Part of this disagreement is because what represents a Blood or Crip gang can vary from one set to another and even among members. Apart from some language and subcultural commonalities, a Blood set in one community may have more in common with a Crip set in the same community than it does with other Bloods. Although many members from both gangs are generally committed to their sets and to being violent adversaries of rival gangs, at the end of the day they are more alike than different. From my experience on the parole board and extensive study, I reached the conclusion that youth involved in street gangs share similar backgrounds, hopes, dreams, and experiences as non-gang involved youth. This is not to say that there are no differences, as gang youth tend to offend more, are more likely to be victimized, and engage in negative behaviors, because of their involvement with gangs.

In his study of the Fremont Hustlers, a Crip set located in Kansas City, anthropologist Mark Fleisher observed that much of what gang youth do as members of street gangs is typical of all youth.[2] In fact, many Fremont Hustlers did not even think of themselves as members of a gang. Gang youth form cliques, hang around with others with common interests, and generally are engaged in typical youth behaviors. The difference is how the community responds to these behaviors. Fleisher proposed that negative community reaction to gangs is driven, in large part, because gang behavior is often played out on the streets in full public view. Outsiders, often adults, find gang members' behaviors threatening and alarming, and they typically react in a punitive way, which further alienates already marginalized gang members. The gangs also bring some of this on themselves with their tough and brazen appearances and behaviors.

Although the question is debatable, most observers would agree that no gang has impacted worldwide perceptions of street gangs more than the Crips and the Bloods. Chapter 1 provides a brief introduction to key definitions of subcultures and gangs. It addresses the question of whether Crips and Bloods are true gangs, organized crime syndicates, or subcultures. The chapter notes how difficult it is to determine the extent of Blood and Crip gang presence and activity in the United States. There are inherent challenges in determining just how many Crip and Blood gangs exist and how many members belong. So much of the nature of gangs is defined and shaped by the communities in which they exist. The chapter touches on society's reaction to these gangs with a special emphasis on how they are viewed by and how they view law enforcement personnel.

The history of the Crips and the Bloods is characterized by competing views on why and how they evolved into the gangs we know today. Law enforcement accounts of how both gangs evolved differ from those of the media and of gang members. Memories and "facts" even differ among gang members who were actually present when founding events occurred. Chapter 2 identifies some of these differing views and attempts to unravel what actually occurred.

Chapter 3 identifies Crip and Blood gang characteristics, including common organizational structures, size, leadership, activities, and locations. Typically these gangs have a core membership, regular members, marginal members, claimers, and wannabes. They often have organizationally loose and horizontal structures with few levels of power and authority. Specific roles within the gangs are also identified. The chapter discusses some of the different ways gang members describe their organizational structures and types of members.

Blood and Crip gangs are no different than other gangs in that they need basic processes in place in order to exist and function. Gang processes such as recruiting, making decisions, teaching, joining, controlling, assigning duties, socializing, and exiting are described in this chapter. This chapter notes what gang expert Malcolm Klein concluded years ago, that gangs spend most of their time looking for action and just hanging out.

Chapter 4 identifies characteristics of gang members such as race, gender, socioeconomic status, age, and criminal background. Attention will be paid to how gang members know who is in and who is out of the gang. This chapter also addresses the questions of who joins and why. In addition, the risk factors that influence the chances an individual will join a set are discussed. After joining, membership in these gangs has consequences for individuals, for example, more extensive criminal involvement, more drug use, fewer life opportunities, more involvement in the criminal justice system, and greater chances for criminal victimization.

The Crips and Bloods, more than any other gangs, have shaped gang and general mainstream culture. Their clothing, argot, tattoos, graffiti, music, hand signs, and other cultural features are described in Chapter 5. While each set is unique, it also shares some common cultural characteristics with other gangs. This chapter includes a section on intra-gang communication. Some attention is devoted to how Crip and Blood culture has expanded beyond the gangs to mainstream society.

Crip and Blood involvement in crime and violence is one of the most important and controversial aspects of these two gangs. While accurate measures of the true amount of gang violence are difficult to obtain, it does appear that gang-related violence in general is underreported but is also in decline across the nation, with the exception of a few hot spots. Most of the literature on Crip and Blood gangs stresses their violent nature. The gangs promote their violent image to the outside community to instill fear. To the extent possible, the nature of this violence is described in Chapter 6. Crip versus Blood, Crip versus Crip, and violence against the general non-gang public is covered. Special attention is paid to what gang members have to say about this violence and the reason it occurs. The violent rivalry between the two gangs is discussed, as are attempts to make peace.

Chapter 7 addresses another controversial area, the extent and nature of Crip and Blood involvement with illegal drug use and trafficking. While researchers agree that both gangs are involved at some level in the use and distribution of illegal drugs, especially cocaine, there is little agreement on the nature and extent of this involvement. In contrast, law enforcement agencies concur that both gangs are heavily involved, and some operate well-coordinated and sophisticated distribution networks; for example, a recent national survey on gangs found that 95 percent of responding law enforcement agencies indicated that drug trafficking in their jurisdictions was moderate to severe.[3] Law enforcement agencies view the Crips and Bloods as key players in this trafficking. This chapter reports on the nature and opposing views of this involvement.

Chapter 8 covers the relationship between the media and Crip and Blood gangs. No community is immune from the effects of the media. The media feeds youth desires to join gangs. The bad boy, cultural outcast, tough guy, powerful male image fostered by Crip and Blood members is attractive in some circles of American society. A number of youth have migrated to the Crips and Bloods without any previous contact with local set leaders in part due to media-promoted images of the gangs.

Chapter 9 provides short case descriptions of Crip and Blood gangs drawn from the Internet, research, autobiographies, police documents, and other resources. While autobiographies of Crip and Blood members abound, very little information is available on the characteristics of the sets.

Chapter 10 makes the point that until society is willing to rethink how it approaches these gangs, they will persist. Few intervention programs get at the root causes of why youth and young adults join and continue to participate in these gangs. As long as these gangs meet the needs of marginalized individuals and alternatives are unavailable, they will continue to thrive. This chapter includes a brief section on societal efforts to address these gangs.

These chapters are in no way intended to provide an exhaustive account of what is known about Crip and Blood gangs. They do provide a general overview of both gangs and some representative sets. Local sets have shared subcultural characteristics that help define how to be a Crip or Blood but also are molded with local interpretations.

Notes

1. Sanyika Shakur, *Monster: The Autobiography of an L.A. Gang Member* (New York: Atlantic Monthly Press, 1993).
2. Mark Fleisher, "Inside the Fremont Hustlers." In Jody Miller, Cheryl L. Maxson, & Malcolm W. Klein (Eds.), *The Modern Gang Reader,* Second Edition (Los Angeles: Roxbury, 2001). See also Mark Fleisher, *Dead End Kids: Gang*

Girls and the Boys They Know (Madison: University of Wisconsin Press, 1998); Mark S. Fleisher, "Youth Gang Social Dynamics and Social Network Analysis: Applying Centrality Measures to Assess the Nature of Gang Boundaries." In James F. Short Jr. and Loraine A. Hughes (Eds.), *Studying Youth Gangs* (Lanham, MD: AltaMira, 2006).

3. National Gang Intelligence Center, *2013 National Gang Report* (Washington, DC: Federal Bureau of Investigation, 2013), 11.

Acknowledgments

I want to acknowledge my spouse, Marty Covey, for all of her encouragement and support for my writing projects over the years. She has been an unwavering source of assistance and encouragement, especially during those times when I ask myself if it is really worth all of the effort. Whenever a thoughtful review is needed, I know she can be counted on to provide helpful comments. I note that our marriage remains intact. Laura Menard provided valuable comments and editorial input on the final version of the manuscript. I appreciate her as a friend and writer. Magendra Varman provided a carefully copyedited version of the manuscript and Erin Ryan the images. Michael Millman with ABC-CLIO has been wonderful to work with on this and other projects. His insights and advice have proven to be invaluable. I know I can count on him for encouragement and needed support. The other editorial and production teams at ABC-CLIO are very professional and easy to partner with.

Timeline

1960s   Some have suggested the Crips began in the late 1960s.[1] According to Christensen, they were established in southeast Los Angeles and quickly gained a reputation as a serious and violent gang

1965   The Watts riot, or rebellion, started on August 11 and ended six days later.

1968   In late 1968 Raymond Lee Washington formed the Baby Avenue Cribs, which soon morphed into the Crips. In the late 1960s other Los Angeles gangs started adopting the Crip name, such as the Eastside Crips and Inglewood Crips.

1971   According to Tookie Williams, the Cribs, or Crips, were started in South Central Los Angeles at Washington High School. There is disagreement on whether this was the actual founding year.

       The first media coverage of the Crips following the death of a black youth who died while in police custody. The resulting public outcry resulted in street fights between white supremacists and black youth. There is no evidence that the Crips were involved in these street conflicts, but the media still credited them for much of the violence that occurred.

1972   In March members of a Crip set beat to death a black teenager, Robert Ballou, son of an attorney, for his leather jacket at the Hollywood Palladium. This gang-related homicide shocked Los Angeles and increased public awareness of the Crips. The media picked up on the story and gave it much publicity, which eventually led the Los Angeles Police Department to increase its efforts to suppress gangs.

1973   Piru Street Boys, a Crip gang at the time, attempt a truce with other Crip gangs but was unsuccessful. They subsequently thus broke their Crip connections and formed the Bloods.

1979   On August 9 Raymond Washington, co-founder of the Crips, was killed a few blocks from his home.

1980s   Crack cocaine trafficking expanded in Southern California and with it, the proliferation of Crip and Blood gangs. With the profitability of illegal drug sales, members of both gangs expanded their involvement in sales of marijuana, PCP, crack cocaine, and LSD. While most observers agree that the 1980s saw increased Crip and Blood involvement in drug trafficking, especially cocaine, some scholars believe they were not so involved (see Chapter 6).

1985   The gangsta rap group NWA (Niggers with Attitude) was formed. This group is credited with being the first gangsta rap group to achieve major commercial success. Three years later the group produced *Straight outta Compton,* which served as a model for other gangsta rap artists.

1988   Rollin 60s Crip Durrell Dewitt Collins accidentally shot Karen Toshima while she stood in line at a movie theater in the wealthy community of Westwood, California, during a Crip and Blood face off. Her death brought greater attention to the existence of gangs in Los Angeles. Before the shooting many people in Los Angeles were unconcerned if gang members killed each other; no one but the gangs and their family members seemed to care about gang-related deaths. As long as gang violence was confined to the poor parts of town, those living outside of those areas were disinterested. With this shooting, gang violence became a broader issue for the city.

1991 Major Los Angeles drug dealer and gang member Rene McCowan was found decapitated, brutalized, and laid out for all to see.

1992 On April 28 a number of gang truces between the Bloods and the Crips were established but were often broken throughout the early part of the 1990s. The most important truce between Crip and Blood gangs became approved the day before the end of the Rodney King trial. Older gang members agreed to the truce because they did not want their children to be victims of the cycle of violence and live in constant fear. In addition, many questioned the value of black on black violence. The truce made it possible for people in the different housing projects, such as Nickerson Gardens and Jordan Downs, to visit their friends and families in projects once controlled by rival gangs.

The Crip and Blood truce led to a community action plan to put $6 billion in private investment into the impoverished and impacted areas of the Los Angeles rebellion (riot). The hope was to create 74,000 jobs over five years. This investment never occurred, and elected officials and the private sector failed to support local improvements. The truce, sometimes referred to as the Watts Truce, lasted the better part of a decade before collapsing, and it resulted in a notable decline in gang-related homicides.

The Los Angeles (also known as the Rodney King or the South Central) riots, or rebellion, started on April 29 and ended on May 4. On March 3, 1991, Rodney King was brutally beaten by Los Angeles police officers, and the episode was caught on video and widely distributed. The police brutality captured on the video could not be ignored, or so some people thought. The police involved in the incident were tried for assault and excessive use of force. On April 29 the police officers were acquitted. This jury decision triggered riots in Los Angeles that lasted from that date and finally ended on

May 4. Because the beating was captured on film, the world became aware of what many blacks already knew—police could be brutal to people of color. The beating and the events surrounding it led some Crips and Bloods to realize that they were facing a common foe, a racist and segregated white society. Some gang members realized that they had been victimizing each other and that killing their own people did not make sense.[2]

1993   The United Blood Nation on the East Coast formed within the New York City prison system on Riker's Island. Omar Portee, better known as OG Mac, and O.G. Deadeye (Leonard Mackenzie) are credited with creating the United Blood Nation in response to the Latin Kings, who victimized black men incarcerated at Riker's Island.

Sanyika Shakur published his autobiography, *Monster: The Autobiography of an L.A. Gang Member*. This autobiography would become very influential in defining the Crip subculture, especially for those not involved in gangs.

1996   Tupac Shakur, the famous rapper and gang member, was shot to death in a Las Vegas drive-by. Three days later three Crips were killed in Compton, California, breaking a two-year truce between the Crips and the Bloods. Implicated in the drive-by shooting was Notorious B.I.G., a famous East Coast gang member and rapper. Notorious allegedly paid a Crip $1 million to kill Tupac. Tupac gained more fame and financial success following his death than while he was living.

1997   Notorious B.I.G., aka Biggie Smalls or Biggie, a known gang member and famous rapper, was shot to death on March 9 in New York six months after being implicated in Tupac's murder.

2005   Stanley Tookie Williams, co-founder of the Crips, was executed by the state of California in spite of public pleas against his execution and his extensive writing related to keeping youth away from gangs. He was executed on December 13 at the age of 51 after serving 24 years on death row for the murder of four people in two robberies committed in 1979.

Branden Bullard, the leader of the Grape Street Crips, was gunned down. This led to a prolonged gang war that resulted in multiple shootings and eight gang-related deaths.

Notes

1. Loren W. Christensen, *Gangbangers: Understanding the Deadly Minds of America's Street Gangs* (Boulder, CO: Paladin, 1999), 47.
2. Donovan Simmons and Terry Moss, *Bloods and Crips: The Genesis of a Genocide* (Bloomington, IN: Authorhouse, 2009).

CHAPTER ONE

Introduction

Being a Crip gang member, man, is beyond anything you cherish in life. You know, you got a mother. You cherish her to the most respect. But a Crip gang, a Crip, being a Crip, is something that you constantly seeking out for unity every day, power. 'cause you never get enough of it. Man, it's like a mother f***ing fever.[1]

—Unidentified Crip

The Bloods and the Crips, two predominantly African American gangs, are the two most widely known and recognizable gangs operating in the United States and perhaps in the world. Originating in the Los Angeles area, Blood and Crip gangs have come to represent the archetype of what it means to be a street gang. They are the iconic representation of what a street gang is and what it should be. While there are other major street gangs, such as 18th Street, MS 13, Black Gangster Disciples, and Latin Kings and Queens that have a major presence, none of these have had the impact on American and world culture more than the Crips and Bloods. For example, in Sierra Leone and other African nations, black youth gangs embrace names of the Crips and Bloods and what they understand to be the subcultures of both gangs.[2] The Crips were the first African American gang to emerge as a major force in street gangs.[3]

What was once a small Los Angeles gang of less than a dozen members, what many members refer to as a set, is now a loosely affiliated group of gangs (sets) spread throughout the world. Bloods and Crips often prefer the term *set* over *gang* to describe their groups. They are present in a number of urban areas across the United States, including Los Angeles; Oakland; New York; Portland, Oregon; Denver; Minneapolis; Akron; Cleveland; and Omaha. Rather than being a tight and well-defined affiliation or network, both gangs are clusters of local gangs that share the same name, some basic cultural values, and a sense of lore.

One might ask what distinguishes the Crips and Bloods from any other gang or group. It is true that the Crips and Bloods share many characteristics with other gangs. Bloods and Crips, similar to other gangs, socialize most of the time with each other, party together, look for something to do, hustle money, have barbeques, verbally combat each other, and are involved in all aspects of the gangster lifestyle. Yet they also are unique in ways that are recognizable throughout the world. The answer can be found in their distinct subcultures and related symbols, values, images, behaviors, attitudes, and meanings.

Subcultures

This volume refers to culture as a set of beliefs, customs, art, and so on of a particular society, group, place, or time. Societies typically have (common) beliefs along with ways of life and thinking called culture. Culture is diffuse and not dependent on face-to-face contact between all members. Within the larger societal culture can be smaller subcultures. Subcultures are unique groups of individuals with shared beliefs, values, ways of life, and thinking that are different from the larger societal (mainstream) culture. American culture is comprised of multiple subcultures, such as Latino, Southern, street, wealthy, Italian, skinhead, and gang.

A subculture is a group of people within a culture that separates themselves from the larger culture. The *Oxford English Dictionary* defines the term as "a cultural group within a larger culture, often having beliefs or interests at variance with those of the larger culture."[4] Because most members of the Crips and Bloods are adolescents or young adults, Campbell and Muncer's definition of youth subculture seems appropriate. They define youth subculture to be a geographically diffuse societal movement of teenagers and young people who share a common set of values, interests, and a tacit ideology but who are not necessarily dependent on face-to-face interaction with other members and do not have any rigid criteria of entry, membership, or obligation.[5] Subcultures are important frames of reference that youth and adults use to interpret and relate to their social worlds. Gangs fit the definition of being subcultures because of their shared values, norms, and behaviors. Youth gangs constitute a unique subculture in modern society. Like other subcultures, gangs are distinct from but also part of mainstream American culture. In other words, while they have much in common with the wider society, they also have their own unique set of values, norms, lifestyles, and beliefs.[6]

The concept of subculture is useful for understanding gangs. Gang experts James Diego Vigil and Steve C. Yun observed, "Gangs are a stark subset of youth subcultures in a complex society, making up a dark side of Los Angeles in particular and urban America generally."[7] It is important to note that subcultures lack the organization present with gangs and do not have the face-to-face interaction that characterizes gangs.[8] Individual Crip and Blood gangs form within larger Crip or Blood subcultures. So at one level both gangs may be organized ethnically, politically, linguistically, or economically along similar subcultural lines to other Crip or Blood gangs. Each gang (set) at the street level has unique characteristics that separate it from others belonging to the same Crip or Blood subculture. Put differently, a Crip does not equal a Crip and a Blood does not equal a Blood in all circumstances. There are both shared and unique characteristics of both gangs. There is no single Crip or Blood gang; rather, there is a group of street gangs that label themselves as either Crip or Blood gangs.

An alternative perspective on gangs is to view them as urban tribes. Some have characterized modern street gangs such as the Bloods and Crips as the new urban tribes.[9] *Tribe* used in this sense is a group of people who use a common language, culture, and territory. The bonds that hold tribes together are shared attitudes members have toward each other and the behavioral patterns of cooperation and mutual assistance that reflect those attitudes. Many of the characteristics of Crip and Blood gangs would support them being urban tribes.

Definition of a Gang

Gangs have been defined in a variety of ways. Among scholars and law enforcement agencies, there is little agreement about how to define gangs.[10] Gang members define gangs effortlessly. Some have suggested that gang members themselves play a key role in defining what it means to be in a gang.[11] Most definitions note that a gang is a group of people who have face-to-face interaction, have a common name or identifier such as a symbol, claim a territory, have a sense of membership, share a set of goals and/or values, and engage in criminal or antisocial behavior. Street gangs are often territorial, making it quite difficult for the 1,400 gangs in Los Angeles to coexist peacefully, including the Crips and Bloods. The Crip and Blood gangs seem to have all of these features.

According to the National Institute of Justice, most researchers accept the following criteria for classifying groups as gangs:[12]

- The group has three or more members, generally aged 12–24.
- Members share an identity, typically linked to a name, and often other symbols.
- Members view themselves as a gang, and they are recognized by others as a gang.
- The group has some permanence and a degree of organization.
- The group is involved in an elevated level of criminal activity.

There are several reasons why defining gangs is difficult.[13] Gangs have a wide variety of organizational structures and take multiple forms, so they can be difficult to classify and describe.[14] Because gang culture, such as mannerisms, language, and clothing, can be appealing to some individuals not involved in gangs, they can physically appear like they are in gangs when they are not. Legal and societal definitions of gangs can differ from region to region. Some definitions place more emphasis on the criminal side to gangs than others, ignoring the fact that most of a gang's energy goes into socializing. Those involved in and some writing about gangs use terms interchangeably such as *nations, tribes, cliques, crews*, and *sets*.

Law enforcement agencies tend to view the Bloods and Crips as being similar to organized crime. There have been major Blood and Crip arrests in New Jersey, Los Angeles, and North Carolina that indicate that in some situations, the two gangs are quite similar to organized crime to the extent of being prosecuted on multistate racketeering charges.[15] These and other gang prosecutions indicate well-organized and hierarchical gang structures. However, many academics disagree that the Bloods or Crips are very organizationally sophisticated and well structured. They conclude that it is wrong to assume that Crips or Bloods are anything similar to organized criminal organizations. The National Drug Intelligence Center, which conducted a survey of states, concluded:

> It is important to note that when a gang has claimed affiliation with the Bloods or Crips, or a gang has taken the name of a nationally known gang, this does not necessarily indicate that this gang is a part of a group with a national infrastructure. While some gangs have interstate connections and a hierarchical structure, the majority of gangs do not fit this profile.[16]

The center cautioned that just because a gang labels itself as a specific gang, such as Bloods or Crips, does not necessarily mean there are organizational links.

Most Blood and Crip activities are highly localized and occur at the street level. While some of these gangs share common identities and may on occasion band together in criminal or social activities, Bloods and Crips for the most part lack the hierarchical features common to organized crime or criminal syndicates. Rather than a tightly knit organized crime syndicate, it is more accurate to describe Blood and Crip gangs as having horizontal and seemingly weak alliances based more on lore than fact. They have a degree of shared subcultural characteristics but are not, as is sometimes conveyed in the media, super gangs or criminal syndicates. They vary by location and share little other than a common name and backgrounds. Numerous gangs throughout the United States and world emulate what they believe to be Crip or Blood subcultures but have no real affiliation other than in name and appearance. There is no evidence of a Crip or Blood nation in California. In Los Angeles it is currently estimated there are over 200 Crip sets and maybe 100 Blood sets, there is no common leader among any of them, and they war on one another.[17] Each gang is completely independent of other gangs; however, there are clear situations when incarcerated leaders have been able to control their gang's activities. To many gang members, it is more important to know what neighborhood or project the gang member is from than whether they are called a Blood or Crip.

At times Bloods and Crips go well beyond the definition of a gang. This is because they have a much more extensive presence in American society and culture than other street gangs. Their influence on society and culture goes beyond the confines of gangs. Just why they have so much influence on each other and on society is not fully understood.

The following diagram illustrates the basic relationship between Crip and Blood subculture, gangs or sets, and subgroups within the gangs. From the top to the bottom, it moves from general to specific. With each level, local interpretations become increasingly important. Crip or Blood subculture is an abstract set of shared ideas, values, set of meanings, and beliefs of what it is to be identified as a Crip or Blood. This means that at a high level all Crips and Bloods share some

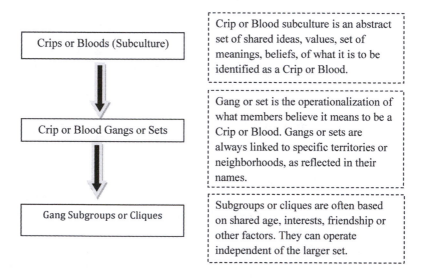

Crip and Blood subculture, gangs, and subgroups within the gangs.

general subcultural characteristics, but this interpretation of subculture takes on a local flavor when translated to actual gangs or sets. So each Crip or Blood is similar but also unique in how it operates. Taken a step further, Blood or Crip gangs may have subgroups of individuals, called sets, who may put their own spin on what their membership means and how the gang operates.

Extent of Crip and Blood Gangs in the United States

The Crip and Blood sets are found in the majority of states. Estimates of the number of Crip and Blood gang members differ greatly depending on several factors. How gangs are defined, imitative behavior by others, law enforcement overidentification, gang attrition, media attention, and fluid membership influence the estimates of the extent of these gangs. Set membership can fluctuate, with members easily moving in and out through fluid boundaries, making counts of who is in or out difficult.[18] How activities, such as crime, are counted can affect our perception of the extent of gang presence. For example, if two known Bloods independently commit a crime without their leadership's approval, does that crime get counted as a gang crime or simply a crime committed by two individuals who also happen to be gang members? Law enforcement would have considerable discretion on how that crime would be interpreted.

Another challenge to estimating the number of Crip and Blood gangs is that there is considerable adoption of their subculture by youth and young adults. It is known that Crip and Blood gang names have been adopted by street gangs throughout the United States and throughout the world. For example, sets in Columbus, Ohio, adopted "big city" gang names, such as the Crips and Bloods.[19] Marcus Felson reported that several gangs adopt language, clothes, colors, names of more powerful gangs to enhance their own images.[20] These copycat gangs share little in common with each other besides a common name. The extent of this phenomenon among street gangs is unknown but thought to be extensive. The reasons Crip and Blood gang names are adopted by other street gangs has a lot to do with the notoriety of the gangs in the media and on the street. Some copycat gangs may think that these gang names give them status, power, and street coolness. If marginal members or affiliates are included, gangs may number in the hundreds, and coalitions of gangs may have thousands of members.[21]

The public fascination with Crip and Blood gangs can be characterized as romantic.[22] The Crip and Blood gang life and subculture represents a romantic adventure for some youth. It is clear is that many youth have adopted Crip and Blood subcultures in terms of dress and identity, thus making the extent of true Crip and Blood activity in the United States impossible to accurately estimate. Many gangs throughout the country attach Crip or Blood to their gang names and identities without any connection between their gangs and the larger Crip and Blood confederations. This practice was found by Sanders in San Diego, where Filipino gangs used African American gang names and colors with no connection to those gangs.[23] This practice occurs in other countries as well. For example, gangs with Crip (les Bleus) and Blood (les Rouges) names are found in Montreal.[24] Richard Swift commented on this phenomenon across the world:

> This is partly because local gangs use the names and symbols of better known gangs (e.g. Crips, Bloods, Maras, Latin Kings) in order to inflate their reputations. But someone who calls themselves a Crip or a Blood in Toronto or a Mara in St. Louis or Amsterdam likely has nothing to do with the home base of such gangs in Los Angeles or El Salvador.[25]

There is also a problem of the media and researchers attributing criminal activity to gangs when they are not involved. There is always a danger that the cultural label of gang, and more specifically Crip or Blood, will be given to groups and activities that in reality are in no way associated with these gangs. Mercer Sullivan illustrates this with some case examples showing how criminal behavior by groups was wrongfully labeled Crip and Blood.[26] It is not that Crips and Bloods do not exist, for they do, but that defining gangs and specifically Crips and Bloods can be imprecise.

In spite of these difficulties, attempts have been made to estimate the numbers of Crip and Blood gangs and members. For example, by the early 1970s, Vigil estimated there were 18 Crip or Blood sets in Los Angeles area.[27] Authorities have made other estimates of the number of gangs and membership in Los Angeles. For example, in 1992 the Los Angeles Police Department estimated that there were about 15,742 Crips in 108 sets and 5,213 Blood members in 44 sets.[28] Another estimate held that there were 30,000 to 35,000 Crips in 600 sets.[29] The Los Angeles Sheriff's Department estimated that in California alone there were over 12,000 members of the Crips and the Bloods in California Youth Association correctional facilities or on parole.[30] Since this estimate there has been a growth in gang membership and although any precise numbers are subject to change, in the Los Angeles metro area alone, there are probably between 80,000 and 100,000 gang members, some of whom are Crips and Bloods. In Los Angeles it is currently estimated there are over 200 Crip sets and maybe 100 Blood sets.[31] Even with these estimates, no one knows for sure how many there are in Los Angeles and across the country.

Self-report studies have found that membership in gangs has remained stable over recent decades. These studies estimate between 10 and 15 percent of all youth report being in gangs. But in some areas, that percentage can increase to around 25.[32] In Los Angeles about 25 percent of black youth between the ages of 15 and 24 might belong to either the Crips or Bloods. The high percentage of Los Angeles youth in gangs is not indicative of other urban areas.

Society's Reaction to the Bloods and Crips

Gang experts such as Malcolm Klein and others have long noted that communities influence and shape gangs within their borders.[33] Gangs are largely shaped and defined by the communities in which they reside. Some communities seem to accept gangs as a normal feature, while others work to suppress and eliminate them. The Crips and Bloods, similar to other gangs, do have supporters on the outside. While they may terrorize their neighborhoods, they also have a degree of neighborhood support and acceptance. For example, Richard Swift noted that the Crips and Bloods are viewed by some to be a lesser evil than racist law enforcement officers, as witnessed by acts of police brutality on Los Angeles.[34]

In much of the literature on the Crips and Bloods, there are frequent references to negative encounters between gangs and law enforcement personnel. From a black perspective, law enforcement in many communities is seen as brutal, prejudiced, and discriminatory. One Crip stated, "The only thing I can say is whenever a person gets stopped by the police, and you're black, they are already going to have a negative attitude towards you."[35] Many Crips and Bloods, when writing their memoirs, recall their encounters with law enforcement as being negative and brutal. In general, people who are black experience law enforcement as adversarial with unjustified violence. Consequently, many blacks see the police as community outsiders and the enemy. Police harassment is a common theme when discussing interactions between blacks and law enforcement personnel. This is especially true when law enforcement encounters young black males, whether gang involved or not, on the street. For example, Stanley Tookie Williams, a first-generation Crip from the west side recalled one of his early encounters with law enforcement personnel:

> In spite of my being the most inconspicuous-looking youth around, the cops swooped down on me because I was a "black youth walking." Two white cops jumped out of the car with their hands poised on their guns and demanded I stand still. One cop asked, "Are you a Panther, boy?" At the time I didn't have a clue what he was talking about. I knew nothing about the revolutionary group called the Black Panthers. I thought the fool was trying to call me an animal, so I responded, "Of course not!" His rough pat-down search was a legendary law enforcement procedure known to virtually all black males living in South Central, involving undue intimate contact in the groin area. Preparing to leave me, smiling, the cop said, "I'll be watching you, nigger." This was his attempt to instill fear of the law in me. I feared neither the law nor him—only his gun.[36]

The tension between law enforcement and Crip and Blood gangs is a constant theme in much of the literature. Law enforcement has attempted to address this tension by using a community policing approach. With community policing, officers become part of the community by befriending citizens, walking the streets, and talking to people in situations other than when a crime has been committed. In short, the approach humanizes both the police and members of the community in an effort to break down the us-versus-them mentality that is common in some communities. The goal is to prevent crime but also to eliminate police brutality. Research has consistently shown that a community policing approach is far more effective when balanced with some degree of gang suppression rather than approaches that simply crack down on gangs, which does more to solidify the gangs.

Bloods and Crips in Prisons and the Military

Most of what we know about the Bloods and Crips comes from the street. However, it is well known that both gangs have members in the military and members who are incarcerated; law enforcement agencies report that the Crips and Bloods have military trained members,[37] and according to multiple sources, Crip and Blood gang members are in all four branches of the military.[38] For example, one study concluded that the Crips, Bloods, and Gangster Disciples had the most representation in military-trained gangs.[39] Some of these military-involved Crip and Blood members have been involved in crimes such as drug trafficking, robbery, assaults, and homicides. To some degree, this is to be expected, as the military often reflects the society from which it stems.

Incidents of gang-related major crimes have occurred at military bases in South Dakota and Washington.[40] Besides concern over the crimes committed by these gangs, there is also alarm over gangs' access to and training with more sophisticated weapons. There are a few documented cases in which Crips or Bloods have enlisted in the military for the purpose of obtaining explosives or weapons to support their drug trafficking efforts.[41] Some military weapons and equipment have ended up in the possession of gangs. In addition to the weapons and training explanation for why gangs are sending members to the military, an alternative reason is that some gang members want to get away from their gangs. Some suggest that the majority of gang members who join the military do so to get away from their gang-infested neighborhoods.[42] The military represents a ticket out of the gangster lifestyle. The military has responded by creating gang intelligence manuals to help curb gang activities among its ranks.

Almost all adult and youth prison and other detention systems have gangs. Racism is often the fuel for prison gang conflicts. The presence of Blood and Crip gangs in the prison system is well documented.[43] In 1993, the United Blood Nation was formed at New York's Rikers Island prison. In California major prison gangs such as the Mexican Mafia (La Eme), Aryan Brotherhood, Black Guerrilla Family, and Consolidated Crips are present and often fight for control.[44] According to ex-Crip Colton Simpson, Bloods have a weak alliance with the Black Guerilla Family in the California correctional system under the umbrella of 415, which is the zip code of the San Francisco Bay area. He also noted in his autobiography that he remembered most prison conflicts were between northern and southern Mexicans and between Crips and Bloods.[45] The Bloods and Crips were reported in 2001 to be gaining strength in the prison system.[46]

Finally, prison gangs seem to have a lot of control over what happens with their gangs on the streets. The question arises, then, of how incarcerated gang members with life or long-term sentences can still control what happens on the streets. There are three reasons this control is possible: messages can be smuggled out to the streets, some gang members are released, and there is always the possibility that gang members or their family members will be incarcerated and subject to punishment from the gangs in the prison system.[47]

Concluding Observations

Noted gang authority Malcolm Klein, in his review of Steven R. Cureton's book *Hoover Crips: When Cripin' Becomes a Way of Life*, noted some basic concerns that are applicable to much of the literature on the Crips and Bloods.[48] He commented that there is very little systematic research on the Bloods and Crips. There are a few autobiographies, journalistic accounts, and law enforcement reports on them, but these can be very limited and biased. The bias is because both gangs remain fairly secretive about what they do, and both members and outsiders often write about impressions rather than facts. The idea that the Crips and the Bloods are noble efforts to right societal wrongs is inaccurate. Both gangs and their individual members are frequently self-serving and do not focus on any higher political objective or cause.

In contrast, law enforcement and government agencies can also be biased against them. They tend to view them as simply criminally motivated and violent groups, ignoring the fact that most of a gang's time is devoted to non-criminal activities. From this perspective, gangs are negative forces in society that should be eradicated. Not everything these gangs do is negative, and they do fill needs of disenfranchised people.

Notes

1. Gangland, "Crips vs Bloods Gangs War Documentary," accessed on September 12, 2014, at: http://www.youtube.com/watch?v=CbGW6R8B_zU.
2. John M. Hagedorn, *A World of Gangs: Armed Young Men and Gangsta Culture* (Minneapolis: University of Minnesota Press, 2008), 107.
3. William B. Sanders, *Gangbangs and Drive-Bys: Grounded Culture and Juvenile Gang Violence* (New York: Aldine De Gruyter, 1994).
4. Oxford English Dictionary. "Subculture," accessed on November 10, 2013, at: http://oxforddictionaries.com/us/definition/american_english/subculture.
5. Anne Campbell and Steven Muncer, "Them and Us: A Comparison of the Cultural Context of American Gangs and British Subcultures." *Deviant Behavior* 10 (1989), 272.
6. Randall R. Shelden, Sharon K. Tracy, and William B. Brown, *Youth Gangs in American Society, Second Edition* (Belmont, CA: Wadsworth, 2001), 69. See also Anne Campbell, Steven Muncer, and J. Galea, "American Gangs and British Subcultures: A Comparison." *International Journal of Offender Therapy and Comparative Criminology* 26 (1982), 76–89.
7. James Diego Vigil and Steve C. Yun, "A Cross-Cultural Framework for Understanding Gangs: Multiple Marginality and Los Angeles." In Ronald C. Huff (Ed.), *Gangs in America III* (Thousand Oaks, CA: Sage, 2002), 162.
8. Harold W. Pfautz, "Near-Group Theory and Collective Behavior: A Critical Reformulation." *Social Problems* 9 (1961), 167–174.
9. Gregg W. Etter, 2012. "Gang Investigation." In Michael Birzer and Cliff Robertson (Eds.), *Introduction to Criminal Investigation* (Boca Raton, FL: CRC Press, 2012), 313–334.
10. Shelden, Op. cit.
11. Beth Bjerregaard, "Self-Definitions of Gang Membership and Involvement in Delinquent Activities." *Youth and Society* 34 (2002), 31–54.
12. National Institute of Justice, "What Is a Gang? Definitions," accessed on February 12, 2014, at: http://www.nij.gov/topics/crime/gangs–organized/gangs/definitions.htm.
13. See Robert J. Franzese, Herbert C. Covey, and Scott Menard, *Youth Gangs.* (Springfield, IL: Charles C. Thomas, 2006) for a literature review and discussion on defining gangs.

14. Malcolm W. Klein and Cheryl L. Maxson, *Gang Structures, Crime Patterns, and Police Responses* (Los Angeles: Social Science Research Institute, University of Southern California, 1996).

15. Federal Bureau of Investigation, *Dozens of Members of Violent Street Gang Charged with Narcotics and Weapons Violation Following Joint Investigation Known as Operation Thumbs Down* (Los Angeles: Author, August 29, 2013). See also Federal Bureau of Investigation, *Twenty-Eight Members and Associates of Patterson Bloods Street Gang Charged in Manhattan Federal Court with Distributing Heroin, Crack Cocaine, and Powder Cocaine and with Firearms Offenses* (Newark, NJ: Federal Bureau of Investigation, U.S. Attorney's Office, February 24, 2014); Federal Bureau of Investigation, *Four United Blood Nation Members Convicted of Racketeering Charges Following a Six-Day Trial* (Charlotte, NC: Federal Bureau of Investigation, U.S. Attorney's Office, May 9, 2013). Other governmental examples exist throughout the United States.

16. National Drug Intelligence Center, *National Gang Survey Report* (Johnstown, PA: Author, 1996), v.

17. James C. Howell, *Gangs in America's Communities* (Thousand Oaks, CA: Sage, 2012), 33.

18. Franzese, Op. cit.

19. Jody Miller, "Gender and Victimization Risk among Young Women in Gangs." *Journal of Research in Crime and Delinquency* 35, no. 4 (1998), 437.

20. Marcus Felson, *Crime and Nature* (Thousand Oaks, CA: Sage, 2006).

21. Irving Spergel, "Youth Gangs: Continuity and Change." In Michael Tonry and Norvil Morris (Eds.), *Crime and Delinquency: An Annual Review of Research*, Vol. 12 (Chicago: University of Chicago Press, 1990).

22. Mercer L. Sullivan, "Are 'Gang' Studies Dangerous? Youth Violence, Local Context, and the Problem of Reification." In James F. Short Jr. and Lorine A. Hughes (Eds.), *Studying Youth Gangs* (Lanham, MD: AltaMira, 2006), 15.

23. Sanders, Op. cit.

24. Karine Descormiers and Carlo Morselli, "Alliances, Conflicts, and Contradictions in Montreal's Street Gang Landscape." *International Criminal Justice Review* 21 (2011), 297–314.

25. Richard Swift, *Gangs* (Toronto: Groundwork, 2011), 18.

26. Sullivan, Op. cit.

27. James Diego Vigil, *A Rainbow of Gangs: Street Cultures in the Mega-City* (Austin: University of Texas Press, 2002).

28. Peter Patton, "The Gangstas in Our Midst." *Urban Review* 30 (1998), 50.

29. U.S. Department of Justice, "Crips." In *Drugs and Crime* (Washington, DC: U.S. Drug Intelligence Center, November 2002).

30. Franzese, Op. cit., 56.

31. Howell, Op. cit., 33.

32. Shelden, Op. cit., 29.

33. See Malcolm W. Klein, *Street Gangs and Street Workers* (Englewood Cliffs, NJ: Prentice Hall, 1971); Malcolm W. Klein, *The American Street Gang* (New York: Oxford University Press, 1995).

34. Swift, Op. cit., 21.

35. Yusuf Jah and Sister Shah'Keyah, *Uprising: Crips and Bloods Tell the Story of America's Youth in the Crossfire* (New York: Touchstone, 1995), 60.

36. Stanley "Tookie" Williams, *Blue Rage, Black Redemption: A Memoir* (New York: Simon and Schuster, 2007), 57–58.

37. National Gang Intelligence Center, *2013 National Gang Report* (Washington, DC: Federal Bureau of Investigation, 2013), 29.

38. Gregory Vistica, "Gangstas in the Ranks." *Newsweek* 126 (July 24, 1995), 48.

39. Carter F. Smith and Yvonne Doll, "Gang Investigators' Perceptions of Military–Trained Gang Members (MTGM)." *Critical Issues in Justice and Politics* 5 (2012), 1–17.

40. Vistica, Op. cit.

41. Bureau of Organized Crime and Criminal Intelligence, *Crips and Bloods Street Gangs* (Sacramento, CA: Bureau of Organized Crime and Criminal Intelligence, n.d.), 7.

42. Ibid., 8.

43. Wayne S. Wooden, *Renegade Kids, Suburban Outlaws: From Youth Culture to Delinquency* (Belmont, CA: Wadsworth, 1995), 136. Crips and Bloods have also been identified in prison systems outside of the United States.

44. Karen Umemoto, *The Truce: Lessons from an L.A. Gang War* (Ithaca, NY: Cornell University Press, 2006), 81.

45. Colton Simpson and Ann Pearlman, *Inside the Crips: Life Inside L.A.'s Most Notorious Gang* (New York: St. Martin's Griffin, 2005), 98.

46. Mark S. Fleisher and Scott H. Decker, "An Overview of the Challenge of Prison Gangs." *Corrections Management Quarterly* 5 (2001), 1–9.

47. For a journalistic overview of how prison gangs control the streets, see Ross Kemp, *Ross Kemp on Gangs Los Angeles* (London: British Sky Broadcasting, 2008).

48. Steven R. Cureton, *Hoover Crips: When Cripin' Becomes a Way of Life* (Lanham, MD: University Press of America, 2008).

CHAPTER TWO

A History of the Crips and Bloods

There's a lot of BS that has been said on how the Bloods started and how the Crips started.[1]

—Angelo, Blood

Today California is the most populous state, having more manufacturing and wealth than any other. The state has the largest agricultural producer of food, and its tourist economy is unsurpassed. California's economy would place it among the top 10 largest countries in the world. It is known for having a wonderful climate and being a great place to live. It is a state you would not think of as the birthplace of the Crips, Bloods, and other gangs that include the Mexican Mafia, Nuestra Familia, Hell's Angels, Aryan Brotherhood, and Sur Trece.

However, California incarcerates more adults and juveniles in its correctional systems than any other state. These systems are so large that they are unmanageable and contribute to the formation of serious prison gangs. The state's crime rates are high, and pockets of poverty are spread throughout many areas of the state. California is woefully in debt, and thus the financial resources to adequately address educational needs are not available. California experienced some of the worst inner-city rebellions in American history. California now has the lead, although Illinois and specifically Chicago is becoming comparable, in having more gang and drug-related violence than any state. Ex-gang member Luis Rodriguez appropriately asked, "What gives?"[2]

Background: The Marginalization of People of Color in Los Angeles

Street gangs in Southern California have been around for decades. The history of black street gangs in the Los Angeles area can be traced back to the 1920s.[3] Social marginalization of black and other ethnic minority populations from mainstream Southern California society has led to them being excluded from full participation. Black youth, facing discrimination, segregation, joblessness, single parent households, poverty, poor housing, lack of opportunity, and an overall shortage of social capital, formed social groups called street clubs for mutual support. Mostly social, these clubs focused on providing members with support and a sense of acceptance and belonging not available in mainstream society. Over time, with attacks by white racist gangs and negative reactions from white society, these clubs evolved into street gangs.

During World Wars I and II, blacks and other minorities worked in the factories and industries of California.[4] General Motors, Ford, Firestone, Bethlehem Steel, Michelin, American Can, and others had large operations that employed people of all backgrounds. Blacks and other minority groups migrated in great numbers from rural areas of the United States to Southern California searching for a better life. Blacks believed Southern California offered new opportunities for jobs along with less racism and segregation than many areas of the country, especially the Deep South. This brought new wealth to black and other people of color throughout California. The first generation of migrant blacks fared well compared to where they originated.

What this prosperity did not bring was social equality. Many blacks found financial success but also marginalization from mainstream society. Blacks and other people of color were openly segregated in well-defined neighborhoods of Los Angeles, as Latinos had been before them. Where blacks and Latinos could live was limited by restrictive residential covenants.[5] The area open to blacks was South Central Los Angeles along a narrow corridor running from

Alameda Avenue to the harbor. Three low-income housing projects—Nickerson Gardens, Jordan Downs, and Imperial Courts—all within a mile of each, other coexist within this area. These projects can best be described as slums.

The boom and opportunities for blacks during the two world wars would eventually end following World War II. As the industries supplying the war effort disappeared, jobs were lost, especially those held by minorities. The percentage of unemployed black men skyrocketed to between 40 to 60 percent.[6] Putting this into context, at the height of the Great Depression, unemployment peaked at close to 25 percent. The layoffs and reduced job opportunities ensured that unemployment would be a permanent fixture for young black men and other people of color in Southern California. The lack of jobs and investment in the community, and the decline in household incomes contributed to a rapid descent for many black neighborhoods.

Following World War II, from the late 1940s and early 1950s, gangs of white youth came into black neighborhoods and assaulted people. In response, black youth formed car clubs and gangs for defense. In the 1940s, groups such as the Avenues, Black Cobras, Blood Alley, Brims, Businessmen, Del-Vikings, Denver Lanes, Flips, Huns, Farmers, Gladiators, Rebel Rousers, Slausons, Sir Valiants, and Watts were formed by young black teenagers for protection from white racist teenage groups such as the Spook Hunters.[7] These black groups were the precursors to the Bloods and Crips.[8] Over time, they would become increasingly involved in robberies, thefts, gang fights, automobile thefts, and other street crimes.

In the mid-1960s living conditions continued to worsen, and black neighborhoods were ripe for protest and rebellion. One of the most dramatic events was the Watts riot, or rebellion, that started on August 11, 1965, and ended six days later. The Watts rebellion resulted in 34 deaths; over 3,400 related arrests; and $40 million dollars in property damage. It was triggered by what happened to Marquette Frye, a 21-year-old black man. Frye was pulled over for suspicion of driving while intoxicated. The highway patrol officer, convinced Frye was intoxicated, ordered the vehicle impounded. When Frye's mother, the owner of the car, arrived on the scene, the situation escalated and became physical when pushing started. Police backup was called and arrived to find that a large hostile crowd had gathered. In the eyes of the black community, the stop and overreaction provided just another example of police brutality and mistreatment of people of color. Conflict at the scene escalated and spread quickly throughout the neighboring area.

A glimmer of hope occurred in parts of the country, and specifically South Central Los Angeles, with the rise of black political movements such as the Black Panthers and Student Nonviolent Coordinating Committee (SNCC) in the late 1960s. Following the Watts rebellion, political action groups such as PUSH and the Black Panthers became very active in the Los Angeles area. The Panthers believed the way to obtain black liberation was through revolution.[9] It should be noted that the Panthers set up and sponsored positive programs in their communities, such as child daycare. These black power movements provided disenfranchised black youth with a mechanism for community organizing and social change. In the film *Crips and Bloods Made in America* (2009), director Grace Peralta noted that gang activity was at an all-time low when these political action groups were active. Some believe that the lesson about organized political violence provided by Watts would play an instrumental role in the development of early Crip culture and ideology. One ex-Crip member, who goes by the name Danifu, suggested, "The Crips and other gangs were being nurtured in that type of environment where black people were basically rebelling and expressing themselves."[10]

Government and law enforcement agencies such as the Federal Bureau of Investigation (FBI) viewed black political action groups as a security risk and actively worked to eliminate them. In the late 1960s FBI director J. Edgar Hoover created COINTELPRO (Counter Intelligence Program) to eliminate dissident black political groups such as the Black Panthers.[11] A number of armed conflicts occurred between the Panthers and police. Eventually government efforts led to the demise of the Panthers and other political action groups. These conflicts and clashes between the police and Panthers were widely covered in the media. Black youth found the Panthers' response to the police and their display and use of firearms attractive and a means of power against the repressive system.

Following the elimination of several black power groups in the late 1960s and 1970s, alienated and angry black youth looked for other outlets to fight their oppressors.[12] The former political action groups had been a viable alternative to street gangs. However, with the elimination of these political groups, a vacuum was created that street gangs were able to quickly fill. Alex Alonso summarized:

> The response was a defensive reaction formation that triggered the formation of gangs. Such gangs did not form as a result of lower class culture, mother-centered households, deindustrialization or middle class flight. Nor did they form in response to pressures to conform to middle class values. Rather they arose in response to much less subtle dynamics: White violence and intimidation, and the deepening racialization of inner-city youths.[13]

These street gangs did not have the same commitment to the community or the larger issue of social justice.[14]

Some have suggested that the earlier black political power groups inspired and influenced founding members of black street gangs such as the Crips. Crip co-founder Raymond Washington and his associates are thought to have modeled themselves after the militant stance promoted by local black radicals. In fact, Washington's recipe for the formulation of the Baby Cribs was borrowed from the Black Panther cadre and the spirit of the Watts uprising.[15]

In addition to the elimination of black political movements, other forces worked to create an ideal situation for the Crips and Bloods to develop. *At a time that economic opportunity was disappearing from South Los Angeles, the Crips were becoming the power resource of last resort for thousands of abandoned youth.*[16] Massive and inequitable funding cuts to schools and social programs for the poor under California's 1978 Proposition 13 further aggravated the situation for the increasingly impoverished population. Public funding for schools with students of color was a fraction of that available to white students. Poor educational opportunities and few jobs helped make gangs an option for many black youth. William Dunn wrote:

> . . . conditions were perfect for the combustion of kids into youth gang behavior. Parents had been emasculated, with no voice in government. Economics were terrible, no jobs for high school grads. And schools had no resources for after school programs; youngsters had nothing to do after school.[17]

Over the years Crip and Blood gangs have agreed to a number of truces to halt gang violence. One such truce occurred between the Bloods and Crips in Carson, California, on July 29, 1988. At a truce gathering a Crip and Blood shake hands and call for alternatives to gang membership, such as jobs and education. (AP Photo/Ira Mark Gostin)

In addition to the Watts rebellion, another tipping point for Los Angeles' black community was the Rodney King incident on March 3, 1991. King, a black man, was brutally beaten by Los Angeles police. Because the beating was captured on videotape, the world would learn what many blacks already knew, that some police encounters were brutal to people of color. The videotape and corresponding story were spread worldwide by the mass media. The officers involved were tried for assault and the excessive use of force. On April 29, 1992, the jury acquitted them and in doing so sent a message to blacks and other people of color that it was okay to brutalize minority and marginalized people. To the black community, this was an unacceptable decision, and something needed to be done. The Los Angeles (also known as the Rodney King or the South Central) rebellion was triggered the day of the jury's decision and ended on May 4, 1992.

In the end, 53 deaths and over 2,000 serious injuries resulted from the rebellion. An estimated $1 billion worth of damage occurred from arson, theft, and vandalism. While some view the rebellion as racially motivated, others have suggested that the riots were based on social class differences. Blood and Crip gangs participated in the looting and violence, but the larger black community was also involved in the rebellion.

The day before the Los Angeles rebellion began, the Crips and Bloods had declared a gang truce. Several hundred gang members on both sides gathered near Nickerson Gardens with the hope of a cease-fire. A gang truce was declared by OGs from both gangs. One unidentified gang member present at the scene told a reporter, "I do drive-by shootings, I kidnap babies, I kill people, so what? I'm an active gang member." One man, who asked not to be identified at the time, said, "I'm going to stop."[18] Not everyone thought the truce would hold, but gang homicides did drop over the following year. Those naysayers were right, and after the better part of a decade, the rivalry and violence would begin again.

The Rodney King beating and the events surrounding it led some Crip and Blood gang members to realize that they were facing a common foe, a racist and segregated society. Some gang members realized that through gang violence they were actually victimizing each other and killing their own people, and this did not make sense.[19] The common enemy for some became law enforcement.

Formation of the Crips

There are competing accounts of how and why the Crips were formed. Since the group's inception, there have been attempts to link the Crips to black political movements. Some have suggested that the Crips emerged with the demise of the Black Panther Party, as some eventual Crip members were involved with political action groups, including the Panthers.[20] For example, Steven Cureton's research concluded that the Crips evolved from the Black Panthers when Bunchy Carter and Raymond Washington formed the Crips in 1969.[21] Cureton noted that they did so out of disappointment with the Panthers' failure to achieve its political objectives. He concluded the original Crips were more of a community action group, but with the death of Bunchy Carter and the profitability of drug and gun sales, the gang shifted to a more criminal orientation.

In 1969 Raymond Lee Washington formed a gang called the Baby Avenues Cribs, which was named after an older and established African American gang named the Avenues, or Avenue Boys. Washington was a great recruiter and soon convinced Thomas Ligon, Elvis Dexter, Craig Cradduck, Alden Jones, Vertis Swan, Jimel Barnes, Greg Davis, Michael Conception, and others to join his gang.

There is considerable street lore and debate about the formation of Crip gangs.[22]

A 1973 interview in the *Los Angeles Sentinel* echoes the idea that the breakup of the Avenues was the start of the Crips. According to "Eric," a member of the Avenues:

> Three years ago I didn't have nothing to do, so I used to hang around 103rd and Avalon, I was an Avenue then ... The Avenues gang evolved into ... the Crips ... The (Crips) gangs ... were born in the most dangerous part, in the bricks (projects).[23]

Another early and important member who is often credited as being a co-founder of the Crips was Stanley "Tookie" Williams. Washington and Williams are both credited with starting the first Crip gang in 1969, although Williams disagrees with the founding year.[24] According to some sources, he identified the beginning being in 1967.[25] These two leaders of east and west side neighborhood gangs in South Central Los Angeles decided to unite to fight other local gangs. Originally the gang was promoted as a group dedicated to protecting their neighborhoods from outside threats from white and black gangs. Another motivation for forming the Cribs was defense against rival neighborhood gangs. It should be noted that Washington had already formed the Baby Avenues, and some have noted that Williams may have been involved with a street gang named the Denker Boys.[26] Both certainly had been active in crime and gangs before forming the Crips.

According to Tookie Williams, Raymond Washington and an associate approached him at Washington High School and asked if he wanted to form an alliance with them because, similar to Williams, they were facing issues with gangs in their neighborhood. Tookie recalled in his memoirs that the two men who approached him wore clothing similar to what he was wearing; thus he viewed them as sharing the same views. Some have challenged this version of events, suggesting that Williams wrongly associated the event with Washington High School and thus downplayed the fact that the gang was actually formed on the streets.[27]

There is even more lore about the origin and meaning of the name Crip, and there are several street explanations for how the name Crip evolved. One version has it that originally the Crips were called the Cribs (referring to baby crib) because of the young ages of the members, which was about 17 years. Another version suggests the name Crip comes from the combination of the word *crib* with *RIP* (rest in peace).[28] Jimel Barnes, an early member of the Crips, explained his view of how the name came about. He recalled that Raymond Washington came to him, pulled out a picture of a baby's crib, and said:

> This is what I'm going to call our gang, Crips—like Cribs. It's from cradle to grave, C-RIP, may you rest in peace. Chitty chitty bang bang, nothing but a Crip thang, Eastside Cuz.[29]

Others have suggested that the reference to crib is related to people's homes or residences being referred to as their cribs.[30] Over time, Crib evolved into Crip. Tookie Williams's memoir recalled an early meeting with Raymond Washington and the naming of the gang. Williams said, "Raymond suggested the Cribs."[31] In a later meeting, the names Black Overlords, Assassins, and Cribs were suggested. The group voted, and Cribs became the name of the gang. This name would not last long and because members often mispronounced it as Crips, the latter became the name of the gang.[32] According to Williams and unlike later street lore has suggested, there was no political or community agenda attached to the name or original gang.[33]

According to another source, Crip co-founder Raymond Washington started a black political action group named the Community Revolutionary Inner Party Services (CRIP) in 1969.[34] It also has been suggested that the name Crip is linked to the name Common Revolution in Progress, but there is little to no evidence to support this claim.[35] In his autobiography, co-founder Tookie Williams denies any political affiliation or agenda.[36]

An alternative account of the origin of the name holds that because some of the members carried canes with them on the street to symbolize being pimps, Crib was changed to Crip, which was short for cripple. Yet another explanation is that one of Washington's older brothers had a leg injury and walked with a limp because of a bad ankle and bowed legs. In a similar vein, another account places emphasis on gang members' use of canes. According to this account, Washington named the gang after a member who walked with the aid of a stick, hence the name Crip, which was short for cripple.[37] Washington's brother allegedly wrote on his sneaker, "Crip," short for cripple, and the name was adopted by the gang.[38] This explanation has also been verified by one of Raymond Washington's associates.[39]

Others have suggested that Crip comes from the gang's crippling of victims. Yet another explanation links the name Crip to a misprint in the *Los Angeles Examiner* attributing a crime to some young men with canes, and the name stuck. Yet a different version is that the name Crip was adopted by a street gang named the Cribs from the horror movie *Tales from the Crypt*.

More recently, some have attempted to characterize or recast the Crips as a political action group. Some have interpreted the name Crip as reflecting a political agenda. Juan Francisco Esteva Martínez and Marcos Antonio Ramos provide some examples of how the name Crip has been modified to reflect a social change agenda in recent years:

> Today in Los Angeles, Crip Young Gangsters have begun to recognize and celebrate these roots by redefining the word Crips as (1) Community Revolution in Progress, (2) Community Resources for an Independent People, (3) Community Reform in progress, (4) Continuing Revolution in progress, and (5) Clandestine Revolutionary International party.[40]

In all, there are almost a dozen accounts for the origin of the name Crip. In the end, with all of the competing stories, we may never know the truth behind the name Crip. Regardless of what the truth is, the name Crip has stood the test of time and is widespread throughout many regions of the world. Part of the subculture of the gang is the value of having debatable lore that members can discuss as being the true origin and subculture of the gang.

Formation of the Bloods

There is general agreement that the Crips were formed earlier than the Bloods. The Huns, Slausons, Businessmen, and other hustler street gangs were the precursors to the Pirus, Brims, and Bishops that eventually served as the forerunners to the Bloods. Hustler gangs were not known for their violent activities but rather selling drugs, pimping, and other less serious street crimes. The formation of the Bloods is linked to Piru Street in Compton, California. The earliest Blood gangs originated around Piru Street Boys in Compton; hence they were called Piru gangs.[41]

In the late 1960s Crips began attacking some of these hustler gangs, specifically the Pirus. Many of the conflicts occurred at local high schools or public parks in South Central Los Angeles. The east side was seen as more impoverished than the west side, thus Crips and similar east side sets would make forays into the west side to target black youth, some of whom were Pirus. According to OG Red, "When Crips started out, we were taking leather coats, because at that particular time the eastside of Los Angeles was on a lower poverty level."[42]

Sylvester "Puddin" Scott and Vincent Owens co-founded the Piru Street Boys and are also credited for establishing the Bloods.[43] In 1969, after some one-sided and losing confrontations with the larger Crips gang, Scott and Owens and their Pirus joined forces with other area gangs to form the Bloods. Others have placed the year the gang formed as 1968.[44] The gangs thought that by being united local sets could more strongly respond to the dominating Crips. There simply were more Crips than Pirus, and it made sense to gain numbers by joining forces with other local sets that also had issues with the Crips. The Compton Pirus combined with the L.A. Brims, Denver Lanes, Inglewood Family, Bishops, and other local sets.[45] The Brims were particularly eager to form an alliance because one of their members had been killed by the Crips. The death of Lyle Joseph Thomas was a triggering event in the formation of the Bloods. Thomas, nicknamed Bartender, is generally thought to be one of the original founders of the Pirus. He was killed by a group of Westside Crips.

East Coast Blood gangs are thought to have links to the United Blood Nation (UBN) that developed in New York City's Rikers Island prison. Bloods on the East Coast are often referred to as the United Blood Nation (UBN). The UBN was created to protect black inmates from the Latin Kings and Netas, powerful Latino gangs. The Latin Kings targeted blacks in the prison. Some of the more violent black inmates organized and formed the UBN for protection and modeled it after the Blood gangs on the West Coast. In 1993 Omar Portee, better known as OG Mac, and OG Deadeye (Leonard Mackenzie) are credited for creating the UBN while at Rikers Island in 1993. OG Deadeye got his nickname for his cloudy right eye that looked dead. West Coast Bloods did not view the East Coast Bloods as legitimate because they had not sanctioned the eastern upstarts. Later in the 1990s saw the formation of another Blood gang, the Double ii Bloods. The *ii*s were a reference to Inglewood, California, and Ill town in New Jersey. This gang was accidently started when two West Coast Bloods visited New Jersey, and locals adopted the Blood subculture from them. Eventually, the Double ii's would be led by Tehwan Butler, who would eventually be sentenced to a long prison term.

East Coast Bloods follow the subculture of the Bloods gang in terms of colors, clothing, and tattoos; however, their membership and criminal activity are primarily local.[46] In addition, the UBN tends to be more organized than the Los Angeles–based Bloods. The UBN sets share a comprehensive philosophy, expressed in an oath, a prayer, a song, a motto, a concept of war, and 31 common rules.[47] UBN sets tend to be more racially diverse than their West Coast counterparts, and they are most active in the northeast and mid-Atlantic regions of the country. Once very organized, the UBN became fractionalized when OG Mac was sentenced to long-term incarceration.

As is the case with the Crips, the Bloods have different accounts as to how the gang name Bloods evolved. One account is that the name stems from the Vietnam War when black American soldiers referred to each other as "blood" or "bloods." There was a long-time southern practice of blacks referring to each other as blood. This use implies a sense of brotherhood, sisterhood, or blood-related family. Others have noted that black males used the word *blood* as street slang for each other in Los Angeles before the formation of Blood gangs.[48] Put differently, the term *blood* used on the street referred to "brothers" of the same racial background.

In another version, in the early 1970s some Crips referred sarcastically to the Pirus as Roosters, and the Pirus referred to the Crips as Crabs. Increasingly, anti-Crip gangs embraced the name Blood. The original Blood gangs would divide into smaller sets and geographically spread throughout the Los Angeles area, all adopting the Blood name.

Concluding Observations

There have been multiple stories surrounding the creation of the two notorious Los Angeles street gangs the Crips and the Bloods.[49] There is currently no definitive history of the Crips and Bloods, but there are a few points that seem to be consistent. The Crips evolved from existing gangs and were influenced by the black political movements of the late 1960s. While the political objectives of the Crips are subject to debate, it is undeniable that the poor quality of life and opportunities available for young black males were driving forces in the rise of the Crips, Bloods, and other street gangs. Their growth was also fueled by repressive and discriminatory law enforcement practices characteristic of the time. There is also agreement that the Bloods were formed out of a coalition of existing street gangs in response to the Crips. On the East Coast, the formation of the Bloods was largely in response to attacks from other prison gangs such as the Latin Kings. On the West Coast, they were largely a response to attacks from rival gangs, such as the Crips, on the streets.

The difficulty in reconstructing the history of both gangs is due to two factors. One is the large amount of street lore and legend passed from one member to another that surrounds both gangs. The second is the spread of their subculture that has resulted in reinterpretations of their history. The wide adoption of their subculture has caused local gangs to spin and alter that history over time.

Notes

1. Yusuf Jah and Sister Shah'Keyah, *Uprising: Crips and Bloods Tell the Story of America's Youth in the Crossfire* (New York: Touchstone, 1995), 67.
2. Luis Rodriguez, "The End of the Line: California Gangs and the Promise of Street Peace." *Social Justice* 32, no. 3 (2005), 12.

3. Bureau of Organized Crime and Criminal Intelligence, *Crips and Bloods Street Gangs* (Sacramento, CA: Author, n.d.), 3.

4. James Diego Vigil and Steve C. Yun, "A Cross-Cultural Framework for Understanding Gangs: Multiple Marginality and Los Angeles." In C. Ronald Huff (Ed.), *Gangs in America III* (Thousand Oaks, CA: Sage, 2002), 163.

5. Rodriguez, Op. cit., 15.

6. William Dunn, *The Gangs of Los Angeles* (New York: iUniverse, 2007), 183.

7. Stacy Peralta, *Crips and Bloods Made in America* (Cinedigm, Los Angeles, a film by Docuramafilms, 2009); Randall G. Shelden, Sharon K. Tracy, and William B. Brown, *Youth Gangs in American Society, Second Edition* (Belmont, CA: Wadsworth, 2001), 10; Alex A. Alonso, "Radicalized Identities and the Formation of Black Gangs in Los Angeles." *Urban Geography* (2004), 25, 658–674.

8. Bill Valentine, *Gang Intelligence Manual* (Boulder, CO: Paladin, 1995), 45.

9. Dunn, Op. cit.

10. George Percy Barganier, III, *Fanon's Children: The Black Panther Party and the Rise of the Crips and Bloods in Los Angeles* (Ph.D. dissertation, University of California, Berkeley, 2011), 64.

11. Jeff Chang, *Can't Stop Won't Stop* (New York: St. Martin's, 2005), 48.

12. Wayne Caffey, *Crips and Bloods* (Los Angeles: Los Angeles County Sheriff's Office, 2006), 2.

13. Alonso, Op. cit., 25, 7, 671.

14. Richard Swift, *Gangs* (Toronto: Groundwork Books, 2011), 84.

15. Barganier, Op. cit., 63.

16. Mike Davis, *City of Quartz: Excavating the Future in Los Angeles* (New York: Vintage, 1990), 300.

17. Dunn, Op. cit., 185.

18. Frank Stoltze, "Forget the LA Riots: Historic 1992 Watts Gang Truce Was the Big News" (April 24, 2012), accessed on September 12, 2014 at: http://www.scpr.org/news/2012/04/28/32221/forget-la-riots-1992-gang-truce-was-big-news/.

19. Donovan Simmons and Terry Moses, *Bloods and Crips: The Genesis of a Genocide* (Bloomington, IN: Authorhouse, 2009).

20. Shelden, Op. cit., 11.

21. Steven R. Cureton, "Something Wicked This Way Comes: A Historical Account of Black Gangsterism Offers Wisdom and Warning for African American Leadership." *Journal of Black Studies* 40 (2009), 347–361.

22. Shelden, Op. cit., 11.

23. William Dunn, *The Gangs of Los Angeles* (New York: iUniverse, 2007), 89.

24. Stanley Tookie Williams, *Blue Rage, Black Redemption: A Memoir* (New York: Touchstone, 2004).

25. Tom Hayden, "Williams, Stanley Tookie." In Louis Kontos and David C. Brotherton (Eds.), *Encyclopedia of Gangs* (Westport, CT: Greenwood, 2008), 274.

26. Dunn, Op. cit., 187.

27. Dunn, Op. cit.

28. Juan Francisco Esteva Martínez, "Bloods." In Louis Kontos and David C. Brotherton (Eds.), *Encyclopedia of Gangs* (Westport, CT: Greenwood, 2008), 43.

29. Jah, Op. cit., 152.

30. Richard W. Bailey, *Speaking American: A History of English in the United States* (New York: Oxford University Press, 2012).

31. Williams, Op. cit., 91.

32. Dunn, Op. cit.

33. Williams, Op. cit., 92.

34. Simmons, Op. cit., xi.

35. Valentine, Op. cit., 47.

36. Williams, Op. cit.

37. Shelden, Op. cit., 11.

38. Nate B. Hendley, *American Gangsters, Then and Now: An Encyclopedia* (Santa Barbara, CA: ABC-CLIO eBook Collection, 2009).

39. Robert Walker, "Crips and Bloods History," accessed on October 15, 2013 at: http://www.gangsorus.com/crips_bloods_history.htm.

40. Juan Francisco Esteva Martínez and Marcos Antonio Ramos, "Crips." In Louis Kontos and David C. Brotherton (Eds.), *Encyclopedia of Gangs* (Westport, CT: Greenwood, 2008), 46.

41. Loren Christensen, *Gangbangers: Understanding the Deadly Minds of America's Street Gangs* (Boulder, CO: Paladin, 1999), 48.

42. Jah, Op. cit., 53.

43. United Gangs of America, "Crips," accessed on December 2, 2013 at: www.UnitedGangs.com.

44. Gregg W. Etter, "Gang Investigation." In Michael L. Birzer and Cliff Robertson (Eds.), *Introduction to Criminal Investigation* (Boca Raton, FL: CRC, 2012), 324.

45. Martínez, Op. cit.; Shelden, Op. cit., 11.

46. Washington/Baltimore High Intensity Drug Trafficking Area (HIDTA), "Bloods," accessed on January 18, 2014 at: http://www.hidtagangs.org/GangLibrary.aspx.

47. Ibid.

48. Simmons, Op. cit., xii.

49. Jasmine B. Randle, "Los Angeles County's Criminal Street Gangs: Does Violence Roll Downhill?" (Electronic Theses, Projects, and Dissertations, Paper 10, 2014), 9.

CHAPTER THREE | Characteristics of Crip and Blood Gangs

When I am with my homeboys I feel powerful. It's like I can do anything because they got my back. I'm covered, no matter what.[1]

—Bopete, Crip

Much has been written about Crip and Blood gang culture and individual members, but there is surprisingly little information on the organizational characteristics of these two gangs. Although both gangs have existed since the late 1960s, very few descriptions of their size, structure, operations, and other organizational characteristics exist. The Crips and Bloods are what James Diego Vigil would label "established" gangs because they have been around for decades and persist from generation to generation.[2] We should know more given their longevity but for whatever reason, few researchers and outsiders have penetrated either gang. Consequently, we are left with accounts from past and present members along with occasional journalistic depictions. We have a considerable amount of information about Crips and Blood subculture but know comparatively little of their true organizational nature or characteristics.

Size

Estimates on the typical number of members in a Crip or Blood set vary. For example, in the early 1970s the largest Crip and Blood sets in Los Angles had around 500 members.[3] Today estimates range from a low of 5 to as high as 1,000 members.[4] Other estimates place the range from 10 to 40 members.[5] In Columbus, Ohio, most sets had fewer than 30 members.[6] Other studies report that the gangs' median sizes range from 45 to 66 members, with the smallest having 8 and the largest having 230 members.[7] Typically, Blood and Crip gangs have a small core of 5 to 25 members who are the most active in gang activities and from whom the leadership of the gang is drawn. Then there is a group of peripheral or marginal members that are less strongly involved with the gang and less committed to gang activities.

There is little doubt that Crips outnumber Bloods by a considerable margin. There are more Crip gangs and members than Blood gangs and members. According to one source, Crips outnumber Bloods in Los Angeles about three to one.[8] Bloods are assumed to be more violent in inter-gang conflicts with Crips to make up for their numerical disadvantage, but this has never been proven.

Gang Structure

There are several ways to characterize gangs, for example, by size, types of activities, values, roles within the gang, leadership, and structure. Gangs have both vertical and horizontal organizational structures. Vertical structure refers to the gang's organizational hierarchy, that is, gangs have members with different degrees of power and authority arranged in different levels. For example, some gangs give more authority to members who are older or who have the strongest commitment to the gang. These members sit higher up in the gang's structure.

Horizontal structure refers to relationships of members within the gang. Horizontal can also refer to relationships among different sets. If members have relatively equal status within the gang, such as few different levels of power, authority, and status, then the gang is considered to have a horizontal, or flat, structure. Crip and Blood sets, similar to most other street gangs, have fairly level, horizontal organizational structures. Crip and Blood gang structures tend to be flexible, loose, informal, and non-hierarchical.[9]

While most Crip and Blood gangs fit this pattern, some observers have reported that these gangs are highly structured organizations.[10] For example, one source noted that East Coast Crips tend to be more formally organized with a well-defined chain of command than West Coast Crips.[11] The United Blood Nation (UBN) once had multiple levels from top to bottom, with OGs at the top, followed by superiors, ministers, captains, lieutenants, and finally soldiers. Each one of these levels had different levels of authority, status, responsibilities, and power within the gang. This pattern, according to some law enforcement gang experts, may differ by region. These chains of command can resemble corporate or mafia-like structures.

Highly structured Blood or Crip gangs are more the exception than the rule, as most are unstructured. The absence of structure allows them to be very adaptive to situational factors that the gang may face. Individuals and cliques within the gang can do their own thing as long as it does not bump up against the basic principles of being a Blood or Crip. Both gangs are typically comprised of several independent sets that share some characteristics but are also unique. Each set may have cliques or crews.[12] These smaller subgroups may act autonomously and even have conflicts with other individual members or subgroups of the same set or gang. Sets have names that usually refer to the geographical area where they operate and have some degree of control. Each set has differing degrees of criminal influence where it operates. Many gang members refer to their gang as their set rather than gang.

Gangs frequently differentiate between age cohorts, with younger members associating more with other younger members and older with older. The younger cohort is always ranked lower in status within the gang than the older cohort. Most Crip and Blood gangs have age-graded structures, that is, members tend to engage within the gang with members about their same age (cohort).[13] These age cohorts, or peers, share many of the same experiences, interests, and characteristics. The age cohorts tend to hang out together more extensively and tend to commit crimes together. They can and sometimes do operate fairly independent of the larger set. For example, a cohort may sell drugs on the side or commit crimes without the knowledge or approval of set leadership.

Some Bloods and Crips prefer the term *hood* to identify their gang or set. Some seldom use the word *gang* to describe themselves but prefer *set* or *nation*.[14] To them, a hood refers to a gang that controls a specific neighborhood or area. Hoods can be subdivided into a number of sets (gangs) or street-level groups that outsiders would inaccurately label gangs. The importance of the hood is evident in the names both gangs use to identify their sets. Crip and Blood sets typically name themselves with references to neighborhood locations, such as street numbers, parks, avenues, or housing projects, for example, the Grape Street Crips, E 52nd Street, Compton Crips, Hoover Street Crips, and Piru Street Bloods are all named after specific locations. The importance of neighborhood or territory to these sets should not be overlooked. A Blood shared his view of the importance of the hood (territory):

> The hood meant life or death. It was that deep. If you said, F six-Deuce, I'd try to kill you. It was that deep. Don't come in the hood with a blue rag, or we'll try to kill you.[15]

Crips and Bloods often refer to their gangs at the street level as sets and the neighborhoods they operate in as hoods. Both gangs are territorial, but territory is sometimes linked more to drug trafficking than to identification with particular neighborhoods. However, comments made by well-known Eight Trey Crip leader "Monster" Kody Scott (Sanyika Shakur) to journalist Léon Bing illustrate this concept well.[16] He shared that a set member's neighborhood often matters more than whether he is a Crip or Blood.

Crip and Blood Affiliations

The media has depicted the Bloods and Crips as being similar to organized crime. Because Crip and Blood subculture has been embraced by gang and non-gang, this has been interpreted as evidence of both gangs being syndicates with long-reaching criminal tentacles. The adoption of Blood and Crip names and subculture has led the public to assume that these gangs are organizationally linked. Some gangs assume that by adopting Crip or Blood gang names they become more legitimate to outsiders.[17] Contrary to the well-organized monoliths the media portray the gangs as, they share a common name, some general subcultural aspects, and little more.[18] Even though they have embraced the Blood and Crip subcultures, these gangs maintain their independence and their local leadership structures. They often chose to affiliate with local gangs.

It is tempting, because of their reputation and the perceived presence of Crip and Blood gangs, to conclude that both are highly organized with structures similar to drug cartels or organized crime syndicates. This would be inaccurate, as most Crip and Blood gangs do not work together in any unified or coordinated manner. They are simply not that organized and do not have a well-established chain of command. Even within a set, there can be cliques or subgroups that commit crimes for personal benefit, not for the set or gang.

So are Crips and Bloods aligned with other street gangs at the international and national levels? Well, there are horizontal alliances that are referred to as nations, as in People, Folk, Blood, and Crip. In the minds of members, these nations are real, but operationally they are not. Bloods are known to have formed an alliance with the People Nation and the Crips with the Folk Nation. The People and Folk Nations are East Coast and Midwestern alliances of gangs and corresponding sets. David Allender wrote about the Crips and the Bloods:

> In the 1980s, West Coast black gangs formed two loose confederations—the largest, the Crips, and their rivals, the Bloods. Contrary to what many believe, there is neither one Crip nor one Blood gang. Rather, numerous sets of each have joined together to either protect themselves or facilitate their criminal activities. These represent two of the Four Nations. The other two originate from Chicago. In the late 1970s, a very large criminal street gang, known as the Gangster Disciples, formed a coalition with several other street gangs to maximize drug profits and protect their members from violence perpetrated by rivals. The consolidation called itself the Folk Nation. Other gang sets in Chicago felt the need to form an alliance to ensure their share of the drug market. Led by the Vice Lords and the El Rukins, this band dubbed them the People Nation, thus creating the big four street gang nations, in no particular order of influence, the Crips, Bloods, Folks, and People.[19]

David Kennedy has provided an accurate description of how Crips and Bloods are organized that captures the importance of locality:

> The essentially local nature of groups is profound and extends to issues of larger gang affiliations which are present much more in appearance than in fact. Where there are apparent associations with national "supersets," such as Los Angeles's Bloods and Crips and Chicago's People and Folks, such "claiming" is typically in name only, without any lines of reporting or authority, or in fact any connection at all, to the root gangs in Los Angeles and Chicago. Local groups "claiming" Bloods will, for example, fight with other blood sets and do business with Crip sets without any regard for allegiance and hierarchy.[20]

To underscore his point, Kennedy also shared an observation from longtime respected Los Angeles Crip Aqeela Sherrils:

> A lot of people think that there is a level of sophistication within the gang culture like the Mafia. Not at all. There's no organization, there's no nothing.[21]

In the final analysis, Crips and Bloods do have horizontal alliances with other gangs with the same names but are more locally focused than their shared names would imply.[22] There are groupings of Crip and Blood gangs that have a local or neighborhood orientation. The focus of the gang is more on local gang culture and relationships than any broad-based gang organization. The term *supergang* that some observers have used to characterize both gangs and imply a well-organized and heavily coordinated organization does not accurately apply to Crips and Bloods. Sets within each of the gangs generally operate independently of each other.[23]

It is important to note that some Crip and Blood gangs and members may be hybrids.[24] Some hybrid members may claim multiple affiliations with different gangs. Some have described these gangs as hybrid gangs that have the same names but not the same characteristics of more traditional Blood or Crip sets.[25] Subcultural boundaries of gang membership may change with hybrid gangs. Specifically, they are considered hybrid because they willingly adopt non-traditional cultural aspects of other gangs and blend them into their Crip or Blood set. For instance, a hybrid Crip gang may use red clothing and embrace Blood symbols, which would be unacceptable to traditional Crips in Los Angeles. Being a hybrid set also affects how some members are known. They may be considered a Blood in one community and a Disciple in another. Their gang affiliation shifts with wherever they find themselves. Hybrid sets, whether Crip or Blood, may cooperate with rival gangs in other areas to commit crimes or socialize.

Blood and Crip Gang Migration

One of the more controversial topics regarding Crip and Blood gangs is whether they migrate to other cities or locations. The expansion of gangs to new communities across the United States is called gang migration. Gang migration is the purposeful movement of gang members to different geographical locations to establish new bases of operation with the objective of increasing set power and influence. Law enforcement personnel and researchers have focused much attention on gang migration. When a Crip or Blood gang appears in a new location, a frequent conclusion drawn by locals is that the gang has migrated from an established location to expand its operations. One gang member expressed this view of gang migration:

> It started in California; it's like an organization of colors. It's all colors. I guess they named it the Crips. They have been Crips for about seven years now but they just hit St. Louis about five years ago, 'cause that's the number one gang in L.A.[26]

It is easy to understand why migration would occur because by all outside appearances, Crips look like other Crips and Bloods like other Bloods. Research has shown that while in some instances migration is the case, most of the time a new Crip or Blood gang can be attributed to local youth adopting Crip or Blood subcultures rather than outside gang members moving into the area.[27] This view was expressed by a Midwestern gang member when he noted the local origination of gangs: "In Columbus, Crip and Blood sets were homegrown rather that the product of migration from other cities."[28]

More evidence is found in Scott Decker and B. Van Winkle's study of black gangs, which found that only 16% of those interviewed thought that gangs emerged in Saint Louis because of the migration or efforts of gangs in Los Angeles.[29] They concluded that most gang formation could be attributed to local neighborhood issues and disputes that were influenced by media images and popular culture rather than from the actual movement of Los Angeles–based gangs into the area. Gang expert Cheryl Maxson also investigated the evidence for gang migration of Crip, Blood, and other gangs.[30] In her summary, she wrote that although migration occurs, it does not do so to any great extent. The presence of Blood or Crip gangs in locations other than Southern California does not indicate that these gangs are migrating or that they have strong organizational links. The pattern is more likely that local gangs adopt and imitate Crip or Blood names and gangster characteristics and in doing so give the impression that there is a calculated expansion of these gangs across the United States. Emphasizing gang migration grossly underestimates the nature of street gangs as grassroot entities.[31] The research strongly suggests that most Crip and Blood gangs are homegrown and not migrant because most of these gangs simply lack the organizational ability and structure to systematically expand into other cities or regions. Expansion within metropolitan areas, however, is quite possible for some gangs, as witnessed by seemingly perpetual gang conflicts over territory.

However, law enforcement agencies are working cases that indicate migration is occurring. For example, two West Coast Bloods indirectly promoted Blood gang subculture in New Jersey by being embraced by local youth, consequently leading to the formation of the Double ii Bloods gang.[32] Results from the 2013 National Gang Survey of law enforcement agencies indicate that agencies see gang migration occurring to expand illegal drug operations or to help gang members find legitimate employment to supplement illicit revenue.[33]

Are Bloods and Crips Franchises?

Related to the question of gang migration is that of gang franchising. Some have suggested that Bloods and Crips actively seek out new markets in which to franchise their names. Some experts conclude that

Crip and Blood sets establish franchises in new neighborhoods.[34] For example, Gregg Etter wrote in 2012, "Gangs in this country often operate somewhat like fast food franchises, each bearing the corporate logo of Crips or Latin Kings but independently owned and operated."[35] The sets, for a fee, provide protection and selling rights to street drug dealers. Some observers have concluded that the Bloods form franchises, pointing to the Rolling 20s and how this group served as a parent gang for several other gangs to counter the Rolling 30s Crip gang.[36] However, some research rejects this idea. For example, in 1996 Spergel and colleagues noted that most new gangs were not franchises.[37] While there may be exceptions, this observation was reaffirmed by others.[38]

Types of Membership

It is generally agreed that there are different types of membership in Crip and Blood gangs. Various classification schemes have been proposed to describe these different types of members. For example, the Bureau of Organized Crime and Criminal Intelligence indicated the following hierarchical structure and types of members for Blood and Crip sets.[39] At the lowest level are the youth that are hired as lookouts for the sets. The next level up were members who serve as runners assigned to transport drugs and supplies across locations. Gang leaders believe younger members are ideal for these lower- and high-risk roles because criminal penalties are less severe for them than for adults. The dealers are the next higher level up. They sell drugs for the gang on the street. The final and highest level is what the bureau labeled the "godfathers." These gang members oversee the gangs' operations and make all important decisions. They serve as gang leaders. Gangs use other terms to label members at this high level, such as shot callers and OGs. Some Blood sets may have first ladies who serve as managers and secretaries.

There are alternative ways to characterize the levels and types of gang members. In one scheme, regular members are referred to as soldiers. Typically in their mid-teens to early twenties, soldiers carry out much of the gangs' criminal and violent activities. Some observers and insiders have suggested that they are the most dangerous of all members because they are willing to do almost anything to build a reputation and gain the respect of older gang members. Their sense of commitment to the wishes of the gang is strong and unwavering. Associates are gang members who are less committed than soldiers to gang objectives. Associates are not considered full members, but they do participate in some criminal activities and identify as being with the gang. At the top are the leaders, most frequently called OGs or shot callers. They represent the core membership of the gang because they make all major decisions and remain engaged with the organization over the long run.

An alternative classification scheme organizes members according to age. Moving from the youngest to the oldest are the tiny gangsters (TG), original tiny gangsters (OTG), baby gangsters (BG), original baby gangsters (OBG), original gangsters (OG), double OG (OOG), and triple OG (OOOG). For example, Big Phil recalled being a Baby Crip and the distinctions made within his gang:

> So we were original Baby Crips. We were baby homeboys. There are double O.Gs. too, because we were the babies running with them, and we were packing, doing their dirty work. Those were our big homiez, our big brothers. We had to watch their backs. Whatever we did, we did it for them, the love.[40]

Why would OGs want to include younger members in their gangs—after all, they are the ones who make decisions and typically are the most involved with actual gang operations? One reason is these youth are more open to following instructions from older members and following the gang's code. Taylor noted that younger members are less likely to denounce their gang when confronted by rival gangs or law enforcement.[41]

Some Blood and Crip gang structures are believed to be headed by OGs, and beneath them are the governors. Governors are trusted core members of the gang that do not receive the same respect as leaders that OGs do, but they still hold considerable power. Governors control drug trafficking and other criminal activities as directed by the OGs. Below the governors are the regents. Regents typically take a more direct role in overseeing the drug-selling operations in specific locations called spots. The regents also supervise the first and second chairs who are similar to lead workers in the street, and they also over-see security for drug sales at the spots. They do this through the use of enforcers who control the gang's activities at the local level. Those who actually sell drugs on the street are called shorties or gang bangers; Peter Patton likens them to being the infantry of the gang.[42]

Ex-gang member Ice T suggested that there are three levels of gang membership.[43] He identified the hardcore members who are warriors focused on violence. They are always in attack mode. At the second level are members who are highly involved in the gang, are willing to stand up for it, are usually involved in running the gang, but are mostly involved for social reasons. At the third level are affiliates who know gang members, wear the colors and abide by the rules, and occasionally direct the gang. Affiliates are members who go along to get along.

Other gang labels for the different types of members include wannabe, core, fringe, associate, original young gangster, baby young gangster, baby gangster, and hardcore. Some Blood sets refer to rank and file members as brims or hats. It should be noted that Crip and Blood members will associate with non-gang individuals, but they do not consider them important.[44]

Depending on the gang, organizational structure can be elaborate, as previously described, or very simple. For example, some Crip and Blood gangs in Montreal have very simple types of membership comprised of rookies and veterans.[45] So, at a minimum, Crip and Blood gangs do recognize different types of membership but may label them slightly differently. Almost all Crip and Blood members refer to the central gang leaders as OGs.

Leadership

There is little question the OGs make the important decisions for their respective sets and play significant leadership roles. In spite of being identified as leaders, leadership in Blood and Crip gangs is typically neither formal nor well organized.[46] Crip and Blood gangs typically do not formally acknowledge single gang leaders, though this is not to suggest leaders are not present. Leadership qualities are possessed by a number of gang members, so leadership roles can be fluid depending on circumstances.[47] The lack of a formal structure facilitates gang needs for situational leadership. That is, because a single leader cannot be everywhere at the same time, it is valuable to have members who can rise to the occasion when specific leadership needs arise.

Some have concluded that both gangs are characterized by having floating leaders that depend on the situation.[48] That is, gang leadership is very much in the moment depending on which gang members are present. This makes sense because all members of these gangs are seldom in the same place at the same time, and street situations vary. Other factors, such as possession of a gun or weapon, who else is present, and transportation may influence who steps into a leadership role.

Leaders tend to be drawn from the OGs of the set and may vary depending upon what leadership roles need to be filled. Gangs identify leaders for a number of reasons, including their influence, ability to fight, toughness, commitment to gang values, street courage, longevity, charisma, or whatever characteristics members believe are important. Both gangs need guidance and leadership, which typically come from older gang members, who are typically in their twenties to thirties and sometimes even older.

Blood and Crip gang leaders are typically selected from members with the more extensive criminal backgrounds. There is seldom, if ever, any formal selection process; rather, a chain of events leads to a member emerging as a gang leader. Members with the biggest reputations for violence, criminal activity, and charisma tend to evolve into leadership roles. Self-assertion and ruthlessness can also be important factors in the emergence of a gang leader. Much of it adds up to the individual's reputation on the street and within the gang. This all suggests that some members are more likely to be leaders than others.

Although they share the common labels of Crip or Blood, the gangs within each larger "organization" operate independently of each other under local set leaders. Unlike organized crime, which has crime bosses, historically these gangs have not had hierarchical or formal leadership structures. There are individuals who have received national attention, such as Stanley Tookie Williams, Raymond Washington, Tupac Shakur, Notorious Biggie, and Sanyika Shakur, but none have been national leaders of all Crips or Bloods.

Old gangsters (OGs), or shot callers, always play leadership roles. Typically the gang member with the most money, women, drugs, and other desired objects receives the most respect from other gang members. Gang members with the most respect and power are sometimes said to have juice. These gang leaders have proven themselves on the street, and many have served time behind bars. Angelo shared his view on how it works, saying, "I'm an OG to the guys that are up under me, and there are guys over me that I consider O.Gs. So it's a level of leadership or seniority which you have in the neighborhood."[49]

Gang researchers have studied how the inner-city environment shapes sets' leadership and organizational structure. For example, Sánchez Jankowski focused on the intense competition for and conflict over scarce resources that exist in gang areas. He argued that gangs are organized and leadership is structured around this competition and their economic interests.[50] Others, such as Vigil, stress the role culture conflict has on shaping the structure of gangs and leadership.[51] The media and larger community reaction to gangs may also shape gang leadership and structure.[52] In the end, for most Crip and Blood sets, leadership is defined by local circumstances. Those members who are most committed to set objectives and values and who are in the right place at the right time tend to emerge as leaders of their sets.

Territory

Territory (turf) is important to most street gangs, and Crip and Blood gangs are no exception. When some gang members speak of their territory, they say they represent their hood. Both gangs emphasize their respective territories regardless of where they are located in the United States. South Central Los Angeles was the initial territory for both gangs. In Los Angeles initially Central Avenue was the dividing line for the early Crip gangs but over time the dividing line between Eastside and Westside Crips became the Harbor Freeway.

Blood and Crip gangs typically have well-defined territories they think of as their own. They, similar to other street gangs, incorporate their neighborhoods, territories, housing projects, communities, cities, street, street numbers, and other indications of where they are from into their gang names. For example, the Rolling 30s are so named because the gang claims the east side of town beginning at east 30th Street; the Eight Tray Gangsters are so named because their northern boundary is 83rd Avenue.

This sense of territory is very important to these gangs.[53] It is strongly linked to gang identity and can be almost impossible to separate. The fact that both gangs incorporate neighborhoods and locations into their names underscores the importance of territory. Illustrating this point, one gang member shares:

> As far as names, every gang has come up with different names from their area. A lot of gangs are named after streets. Almost every gang gets its name from its area.[54]

Claiming territory is a way gangs establish a presence in mainstream society, which denies them opportunity to expand outside of these boundaries. Gangs think of territory as a social claim for existence and will sometimes die to maintain the claim. Ironically, set members are willing to die for their territories, although they really have very little at stake other than love of the hood. For example, Big Phil, a Crip, noted the irony of defending territory:

> Really, we don't even own a damn thing, but we think it's our territory. I mean, we feel that this is our neighborhood; this is where we lay our heads down. We feel if you come over here with drama, you're disrespecting us.[55]

Bloods and Crips are committed to protecting their turf from rival gangs. Both groups protect and control these territories for a number of reasons, for example, controlling criminal activities, including drug sales, or community security from criminal intrusions by other gangs. Some view their role as being similar to law enforcement in providing a degree of neighborhood security. To this end, both gangs have developed ways to identify each other based on appearance, such as wearing colors, bandanas, jackets, hats, sweatshirts, and other apparel to ensure that individuals are correctly identified as gang members or outsiders. They also mark their territories with graffiti that identifies the neighborhood gang and warns others not to violate the gang's boundaries.

Gang Activities

What do gangs do with their time? Crips and Bloods, similar to most street gangs, spend most of their time hanging out looking for action and socializing. Most of their time is spent simply being together. The social bonding that occurs within the gang is an important underlying theme in much of the literature.[56] Hanging out, or "chillin," may involve drinking, partying, using drugs, talking, hawking females, watching television, joking around, barbequing, looking for action, and looking for ways to make quick money. Typically this hanging out occurs in designated public parks or on the streets. Certain street corners or other areas of neighborhoods are well-known places where they hang out. Contrary to what some—such as the mass media—may believe, they do not spend most of their time committing crimes or being violent. As one gang member stated, "We mostly got drunk and talked to women."[57] As well-known Crip Tookie Williams recalled in his memoir:

> On Sundays, the park was swarming with Crips strolling with their pit bulls, playing football, gambling, getting loaded, hawking females, breaking out, or just kicking back and snacking on barbecue.[58]

The spontaneity of hanging out together strengthens the need to belong to the gang because of members' desire for social gratification. Gang members prefer activities that provide them with immediate gratification.[59] Being in the presence of other gang members with similar values and perspectives on life is both personally gratifying and immediate. It is a social bonding experience in a world in which they feel rejected by and alienated from the mainstream. The gang is a way to quickly benefit members, partially because many do not have long-range goals. Or if they have long-range goals, the ways to achieve them are either not available or closed.

One activity gang members engage in is carrying out crimes in the name of the set. Gang members are expected to put in work for their set. Putting in work generally refers to doing a set's dirty work. For some, this is usually a criminal act. Gang members, especially new ones, indicate that they will do anything to fit into their gang. One Blood said it this way:

> I was a Ninja who would do anything to fit in, felt accepted by my peers. I wanted that attention, recognition, fame, that street respect and all that came with it.[60]

Recruitment

As with other gangs, both Crips and Bloods need to have processes to ensure that they continue to operate and function, such as attracting and keeping members, making decisions, sharing gang values and objectives, and having ways for members to leave. Each local set has developed its own processes to ensure that the gang continues to operate. These processes are typically tailored to meet local conditions where the sets have a presence.

Bloods and Crips, similar to all gangs, need to add new members to stay viable. There are a variety of ways they recruit or attract new members. Gangs often want to expand membership to increase their neighborhood influence and power. They believe there is strength in numbers and are always looking for new members who can be trusted and are loyal to the gang. For some gangs, there is little need to recruit because there always seems to be a group of youth wanting to join. The gangs seem like magnets that some youth gravitate toward. Some refer to these gang-aspiring youth as wannabes. The Bloods and Crips draw some of their membership from wannabes who are typically younger adolescents seeking the gangster lifestyle. According to a national survey of law enforcement agencies, the Bloods are doing well in absorbing local gangs and recruiting new members. Compared to other gangs, "The Bloods street gang was identified as the most prolific organization, recruiting 25 percent of the total number of neighborhood based gangs absorbed by national gangs."[61]

It is important to note that as many Latino gangs do, another way to gain members is linked to family ties. It is not uncommon to find inter-generational gang involvement. Children sometimes follow their fathers, mothers, brothers, sisters, and/or extended family members into the Crips or Bloods. Older brother or sister gang-involved individuals may serve as role models for their younger siblings.

Some sets use force to get some youth to join. The set will assault the individual over and over until he or she joins or joins a rival set for protection. The victim's motivation is to simply stop the attacks and have some level of self-protection. Moving from the neighborhood in response to such attacks could be another option but is not realistic for many impoverished youth, so the intense pressure to join a gang fosters their involvement.

School grounds or areas near schools have been used to recruit members. It is known that some Crip gangs hang around high schools to recruit new members.[62] During the 1980s, Bloods began to actively recruit members from local schools and public areas such as parks. It was during this time that the cocaine trade became profitable, and adding new members helped with drug trafficking. Another pattern of recruitment is to absorb existing gangs, crews, or criminal groups into Crip or Blood gangs. Initially both gangs expanded their membership by combining existing gangs to form new and larger gangs.

With the expansion of social media, the nature of gang recruitment is changing. If one uses a search engine to search Crips or Bloods, it will result in multiple websites and references (hits) to both gangs. Some of these websites are controlled and maintained by the gangs themselves. In a study of Blood and Crip presence on social media sites, David Décary-Hétu and Carlo Morselli found that from 2010 and 2011 Crip and Blood involvement in social media sites dramatically increased.[63] Décary-Hétu and Morselli concluded that these websites are not used directly for member recruitment but may, by virtue of promoting gang subculture, may be appealing to youth at risk of joining gangs.[64] New gang members are almost always from the local neighborhoods and are known by current members. Bloods and Crips do not recruit directly via the Internet (as with a dating service). They suggest that the intent of these websites is to build up the gangs' reputations. In addition, the websites reinforce the general public perception that the Crips and Bloods are tough and powerful. These are two perceptions that some youth find appealing and want to emulate. Not related to attracting new members, the websites also are used to threaten rivals or gang enemies.

Initiation into the Gang

Street gangs sometimes have initiation rituals for new members who are being accepted into the gang. Such initiation rituals go beyond accepting the individual into the gang. They establish a common bond among members that is intended to induce the individual to support other members in the name of the gang even at the risk of his or her own their lives. Initiation rituals test whether new members' commitments to the gang are sincere. These initiation rituals can vary from gang to gang and are typically informal and often involve committing a crime, fighting another member, or attacking a rival gang member.

Some Crip and Blood sets, similar to most other street gangs, have informal initiation rites for those wanting to belong. These initiation rites are sometimes referred to as being jumped in or courted in. An example of being jumped in is having the approved candidate pass through a double line of gang members who hit, beat, kick, and otherwise assault the candidate into the gang. East Coast Bloods beat a new member in for 31 seconds, symbolized by 031: 0 means Blood, 30 is for the 30 rules Bloods must obey, and 1 is Blood members' symbol for each other.[65] It can also mean "I have love for you Blood."

While some members must be jumped in, others are quoted in, which requires them to fight established members of the gang. Weapons, such as clubs, are sometimes used in these initiation rites. If the initiate makes it through the gauntlet and demonstrates toughness and commitment, he or she is admitted into the gang. Some gangs expect the individual to fight back to show toughness.[66] At the end, it is not uncommon for those who were kicking and hitting the candidate to embrace the new member. Females can also be beaten in (beat in) or sexed in, which involves having sex with one or more members of the set.

Some gangs totally reject the concept of jumping a member in and find that the idea of fighting or beating down fellow members does not make sense. Rather, they prefer that the candidate take on a challenge against rivals. Crip Tookie Williams wrote, "In lieu of the archaic gang tradition of 'jumping in' a new member, I instituted an initiation by battle, requiring a new member to test his mettle against the opposition—not against his own homeboys."[67]

For some Blood and Crip sets, those seeking to belong are expected to carry out certain risky acts as part of their initiation into the gang. Some of these sets require new recruits to go on missions for the gang. A mission could be committing some violent crime. Other requirements might include committing crimes in the name of the gang or attacking a member of a rival gang. Initiation into some Blood gangs can involve some type of ritual involving blood. Razor or knife attacks carried out during the commission of other crimes, such as robberies or assaults, have been linked to Blood initiation, but there is no evidence that this practice is universal. The UBN on the East Coast, for example, slash rivals' or complete strangers' faces with razors as part of their initiation rituals. They refer to the practice as "a buck 50" because the slash would require 150 stiches if done correctly.[68]

An alternative way to gain entry is vouchering, that is, having a current gang member vouch for an individual who wants to be accepted into the gang. To ensure accountability, the member who vouched for the initiate is held responsible for the actions of the latter. Some Crip and Blood gangs do not have any initiation rituals for new members; as some gang members are third generation, some suggest that gang members are not jumped in but are literally born into their gangs.[69]

Leaving the Gang

Upon joining a gang, some members believe and proclaim they are members (down) for life. This commitment to the gangster lifestyle is emphasized by the media but is not necessarily supported by the evidence. For some members, leaving the gang is an option they can take without facing repercussions from their gang.[70] However, some members believe that once they are a Blood or Crip, they will always be one and that applies to other members, too. Similar to joining, some gangs may have processes—formal or informal—for members to leave the gang. One Crip explained it, "Ain't no getting out ... That's, that's not even in the Crip book."[71] Another Crip spoke of the possibility of leaving the Crips, noting that once you are a Crip you never get out: "You may slow down, but you'll never get out."[72]

The difficulty of getting out varies locally from gang to gang. Some gang members simply quit hanging out with other gang members, others move away, and some are beaten out. Others just quit and walk away. Some simply say they are out, but others have to endure some form of exit ritual. For instance, some gangs require the individual to fight other members of the gang.[73]

Breaking away from all association with the gang can be difficult for ex-members. There are several reasons for this, including the fact that the individual may continue to live in the same neighborhood where the gang is present; thus encounters with prior gang associates are common and invite exchanges. Peter Patton provides an example from one ex-gang member's comment, "Some of my old homies still give me a hard time because I don't run with them anymore. Some even hit me up for money and stuff."[74]

Another difficulty in leaving is rival gangs who will remember the ex-gang member's past. If there are scores to settle, even though the individual is no longer engaged in the gang, it will not matter to those seeking revenge. One ex-gang member shared this comment: "Every so often, some dude from another gang will remember me from my past days, and then all the bullshit starts. They try to intimidate me or try to sucker me into a fight."[75]

So why do members leave their gangs? A three-year study of street gangs that included Crips and Bloods living in Saint Louis found that members leave for a variety of reasons. One reason is to avoid future violence and victimization. When asked why he quit his gang, one gang member shared, "Because I was put in the hospital."[76] He added that Hoover (Crips) used a bat to hit him in the head. Others leave because they find work, burn out, want to take care of their families, or simply mature out. Some are incarcerated for long sentences and find maintaining links and involvement in their gangs to be difficult. When they are released they sometimes find that the gang they knew at the time of their incarceration has different members who are likely to be younger and view them as no longer in step with the times. The prospects of possible additional incarceration makes continued gang involvement less appealing to some.

Concluding Observations

Crip and Blood gangs are similar to other street gangs in many regards. Both gangs are organized like other street gangs. They have leaders, tend to be informal with horizontal structures, and have distinguishable informal and formal roles, procedures for getting in, ways of making decisions, and so forth. What separates Crip and Blood gangs from others is the ways in which their structures are expressed. For Bloods and Crips, much of their organization is demonstrated through their respective subcultures. Their mannerisms, ways of dressing, language, and appearance organizationally separate them from other street gangs.

There is considerable debate on just how organized both gangs are. Law enforcement authorities typically characterize them as highly structured groups with Mafia-like structures and operations. In contrast, researchers and gang members believe the degree of structure is overstated and see gangs and corresponding sets as highly fractionalized. Unlike organized crime syndicates, most Blood and Crip sets have a local orientation with a focus on neighborhood rather than regional concerns, that is, Crip and Blood sets have little in common other than their names and elements of their subcultures.

Notes

1. Léon Bing, *Do or Die: America's Most Notorious Gangs Speak for Themselves* (New York: HarperCollins, 1991), 50–51.
2. James Diego Vigil, "The Established Gang." In Scott Cummings and Daniel J. Monti (Eds.), *Gangs: The Origins and Impact of Contemporary Youth Gangs in the United States* (Albany: State University of New York Press, 1993).
3. James Diego Vigil, *A Rainbow of Gangs: Street Cultures in the Mega-City* (Austin: University of Texas Press, 2002).
4. Operation Safe Streets, "L.A. Style. A Street Gang Manual of the Los Angeles County Sheriff's Department." In Malcolm W. Klein, Cheryl L. Maxson, and Jody Miller (Eds.), *The Modern Gang Reader* (Los Angeles: Roxbury, 1995).
5. Gregg Etter, "Gang Investigation." In Michael L. Birzer and Cliff Robertson (Eds.), *Introduction to Criminal Investigation* (Boca Raton, FL: CRC Press, 2012), 323.
6. Jody Miller, "Gender and Victimization Risk among Young Women in Gangs." In Jody Miller, Cheryl L. Maxson, and Malcolm W. Klein (Eds.), *The Modern Gang Reader, Second Edition* (Los Angeles: Roxbury, 2001), 233.
7. Karine Descormiers and Carlo Morselli, "Alliances, Conflicts, and Contradictions in Montreal's Street Gang Landscape." *International Criminal Justice Review* 21 (2001), 302.
8. Yves Lavigne, *Good Guy, Bad Guy* (Toronto: Random House, 1993).
9. Etter, Op. cit., 323.

10. Peter L. Patton, "The Gangstas in Our Midst." *Urban Review* 30 (1998), 1.

11. PoliceOne, "Gangs: East Coast Crips," accessed on September 12, 2014 at http://blutube.policeone.com/gang-videos/3222043850001-gangs-east-coast-crips/.

12. Wayne Caffey, *Crips and Bloods* (Los Angeles: Los Angeles County Sheriff's Office, 2006), 5.

13. David Starbuck, James C. Howell, and Donna J. Lindquist, "Hybrid and Other Modern Gangs." In *Juvenile Justice Bulletin, December 2001* (Washington, DC: Office of Juvenile Justice and Delinquency Prevention, 2001).

14. Patton, Op. cit., 56.

15. Yusuf Jah and Sister Shah'Keyah, *Uprising: Crips and Bloods Tell the Story of America's Youth in the Crossfire* (New York: Touchstone, 1995), 174–175.

16. Bing, Op. cit., 244.

17. Starbuck, Op. cit., 3.

18. Malcolm W. Klein, *The American Street Gang* (New York: Oxford University Press, 1995).

19. David Allender, "Gangs in Middle America." *FBI Law Enforcement Bulletin* 70, no. 12 (2001), 6.

20. David Kennedy, "Violence and Street Groups: Gangs, Groups and Violence." In James Hawdon, John Ryan, and Marc Lucht (Eds.), *The Causes and Consequences of Group Violence* (Lanham, MD: Lexington, 2014), 54.

21. Daniel Duane, "Straight Outta Boston." *Mother Jones* (January 1, 2006), accessed on September 1, 2014 at http:/www.motherjones.com/print/15100.

22. Randall G. Shelden, Sharon K. Tracy, and William B. Brown, *Youth Gangs in American Society, Second Edition* (Belmont, CA: Wadsworth, 2001), 40.

23. Etter, Op. cit., 315.

24. Shelden, Op. cit., 47.

25. Starbuck, Op. cit.

26. David G. Curry and Scott H. Decker, "What's in a Name? A Gang by Any Other Name Isn't Quite the Same." *Valparaiso University Law Review* 31 (1997), 507.

27. Starbuck, Op. cit., 4.

28. Miller, Op. cit., 233.

29. Scott H. Decker and Barrick Van Winkle, *Life in the Gang* (New York: Cambridge University Press, 1996).

30. Cheryl L. Maxson, "Gang Members on the Move." In *Juvenile Justice Bulletin* (Washington, DC: Office of Juvenile Justice and Delinquency Prevention, 1998).

31. Tom Hayden, *Street Wars: Gangs and the Future of Violence* (New York: New Press, 2004), 15.

32. Gangland, "One Blood" (September 14, 2013), accessed on September 7, 2014 at: https://www.youtube.com/watch?v=WHKYiE-zjE8.

33. National Gang Intelligence Center, *2013 National Gang Report* (Washington, DC: Federal Bureau of Investigation, 2013), 25.

34. Juan Francisco Esteva Martínez and Marcos Antonio Ramos, "Crips." In Louis Kontos and David C. Brotherton (Eds.), *Encyclopedia of Gangs* (Westport, CT: Greenwood, 2008), 44.

35. Etter, Op. cit., 315.

36. Juan Francisco Esteva Martínez, "Bloods." In Louis Kontos and David C. Brotherton (Eds.), *Encyclopedia of Gangs* (Westport, CT: Greenwood, 2008), 14.

37. Irving Spergel, David Curry, Ron Chance, Candice Kane, Ruth Ross, Alba Alexander, Edwina Simmons, and Sandra Oh, "Gang Suppression and Intervention: Problem and Response." In *OJJDP Summary, Office of Juvenile Justice and Delinquency Prevention* (Office of Justice Programs, U.S. Department of Justice, February 1996).

38. Maxon, Op. cit.

39. Bureau of Organized Crime and Criminal Intelligence, *Crips and Bloods Street Gangs* (Sacramento, CA: Bureau of Organized Crime and Criminal Intelligence, n.d.).

40. Jah, Op. cit., 27.

41. Stanley S. Taylor, "Why American Boys Join Street Gangs." *African Journal of Law and Criminology* 2, no. 1 (2012), 62.

42. Patton, Op. cit. 56.

43. Ice T, "The Killing Fields." In Malcolm Klein, Cheryl Maxson, and Jody Miller (Eds.), *The Modern Gang Reader, Second Edition* (Los Angeles: Roxbury, 1995).

44. Bing, Op. cit., 13.

45. Descormiers, Op. cit., 302.

46. Loren W. Christensen, *Gangbangers: Understanding the Deadly Minds of America's Street Gangs* (Boulder, CO: Paladin, 1999), 48.

47. Malcolm W. Klein and Cheryl L. Maxson, *Street Gang Patterns and Policies* (Oxford: Oxford University Press, 2006).

48. Bill Valentine, *Gang Intelligence Manual: Identifying and Understanding Modern-Day Violent Gangs in the United States* (Boulder, CO: Paladin, 1995), 48.

49. Jah, Op. cit., 67.

50. Martin Sánchez Jankowski, *Islands in the Street: Gangs and American Urban Setting.* (Berkeley: University of California Press, 1991); Felix M. Padilla, *The Gang as an American Enterprise* (New Brunswick, NJ: Rutgers University Press, 1992).

51. See James Diego Vigil, *Barrio Gangs* (Austin: University of Texas Press, 1988); James Diego Vigil, "Cholos and Gangs: Culture Change and Street Youth in Los Angeles." In C. Ronald Huff (Ed.), *Gangs in America* (Newbury Park, CA: Sage, 1990).

52. See Malcolm W. Klein, *Juvenile Gangs in Context* (Englewood Cliffs, NJ: Prentice-Hall, 1967); Malcolm W. Klein, *Street Gangs and Street Workers* (Englewood Cliffs, NJ: Prentice-Hall, 1971); Marjorie Zatz, "Chicano Youth

Gangs and Crime: The Creation of a Moral Panic." *Contemporary Crisis* 11 (1987), 129–158.

53. Patton, Op. cit., 58.

54. Jah, Op. cit., 68.

55. Jah, Op. cit., 35.

56. For example, see Geoffrey Hunt, Karen Joe, and Dan Waldorf, "Drinking, Kicking Back and Gang Banging: Alcohol, Violence and Street Gangs." *Free Inquiry in Creative Sociology* 24 (1996), 123–132.

57. Donovan Simmons and Terry Moss, *Bloods and Crips: The Genesis of a Genocide* (Bloomington, IN: Authorhouse, 2009), 75.

58. Stanley Tookie Williams, *Blue Rage, Black Redemption: A Memoir* (New York: Simon and Schuster, 2007), 181.

59. Patton, Op. cit., 65.

60. Eugene L. Weems and Clarke Lowe, *America's Most Notorious Gangs: A Concise Approach to Gang Prevention and Awareness* (Dixon, CA: Universal Publishing, 2013), 4.

61. National Gang Intelligence Center, *2013 National Gang Report* (Washington, DC: Federal Bureau of Investigation, 2013), 11.

62. Valentine, Op. cit., 46.

63. David Décary-Hétu and Carlo Morselli, "Gang Presence in Social Network Sites." *International Journal of Cyber Criminology* 5, no. 2 (2011), 876–890.

64. Ibid.

65. Gangland, "Bloods," Op. cit.

66. Taylor, Op. cit., 61.

67. Williams, Op. cit., 108.

68. Gangland, "Bloods," Op. cit.

69. Michael Krikorian, "War and Peace in Watts," accessed on February 15, 2014 at: www.laweekly.com/2005-07-14/news/war-and-peace-in-watts/full/.

70. Scott H. Decker and Janet L. Lauritsen, "Leaving the Gang." In C. Ronald Huff (Ed.), *Gangs in America III* (Thousand Oaks, CA: Sage, 2002).

71. Gangland, "Crips vs Bloods Gangs War Documentary" (June 17, 2014), accessed on September 12, 2014 at: http://www.youtube.com/watch?v=CbGW6R8B_zU.

72. Ibid.

73. Patton, Op. cit., 72.

74. Ibid., 73.

75. Ibid., 73.

76. Decker and Lauritsen, Op. cit., 57.

CHAPTER FOUR

Characteristics of Crip and Blood Members

[I] joined the gang not only for protection, but for the love for the unity, to be part of the family. I got my first gun when I was 13 years old.[1]

—Shaka, Blood

The characteristics of Blood and Crip gang members are no different from many other street gangs. Often Blood and Crip members have similar characteristics with each other and other gangs that include a history of school failure, criminal involvement, dysfunctional families, low-income households, behavioral problems, and shared ethnicity.

Although ethnicity and race seem to be becoming less important to modern gangs, the fact remains that most gangs are comprised of members with similar ethnic, racial, and socioeconomic backgrounds. It has been noted that modern gang culture continues to model much of the historical structure of early gangs. Racial identity and ethnicity have remained important to social standing throughout history. Christopher Adamson noted that race and ethnicity remain an important role in the creation of gangs and in some cases can be the main reason for gang rivalries.[2]

Most Crip and Blood gang members have African American ancestry (black). As Blood and Crip gangs developed across the United States, people of other ethnic heritages such as Anglos (white or European), Latinos, Native Americans, and Asian Americans became members.[3] Recently the press has reported that affluent European American youth are joining established African American gangs, including the Crips and the Bloods.[4] This later pattern is most likely copycat behavior and not reflective of true Crip or Blood gangs. In Maryland and Virginia some whites and Asian Americans are Crips.[5] However, the overwhelming majority of members are of African American ancestry.[6] It is not so much ethnicity that distinguishes Crips and Bloods from other gangs as it is the subculture of what it means to be a member. There are other gangs, such as the Black Gangster Disciples, Black Gorilla Family, and Vice Lords that have a predominantly black memberships. These gangs ethnically are similar but have distinctive gang characteristics that set them subculturally apart from the Crips and Bloods.

The fact that most gang members come from single parent households has been documented by several studies.[7] Most Crip and Blood members come from homes in which a father figure is not present. Consequently, they are raised by women such as mothers, grandmothers, aunts, or other female relatives.[8] Some of them report that they were emotionally impacted by not having fathers in their lives. For example, one Crip shared his feelings of abandonment and hatred for his biological father:

> If I could, I'd go see him. 'Cause he's my real father. I wouldn't go now, not right now, 'cause I got hostility towards him. He just left, he left my mama for nothin'. I don't know why. . . . If I could change things, I'd make him not leave. But if I see him now, boy, I'd probably try to kill him or something.[9]

Some connect the absence of fathers to their joining a gang because they view some of the members of the gang as substitutes for their absent fathers. Hence they sometimes refer to their gang as their family.

Some of the gang members mention that their families are dysfunctional because of excessive drug and/or alcohol use by parents or other family members. It is also common to hear of one or both parents spending time in and out of jail or prison. An underlying theme is the lack of adequate care being provided by caretakers who are working through their own issues and challenges. Describing gang members in the California correctional system, one ex-gang member and staff member expressed the family backgrounds of the gang members he worked with:

> You find a gang member who comes from a complete nuclear family, a kid who has never been exposed to any kind of abuse, I'd like to meet him. Not a wannbe who's a Crip or a Blood because that's the thing to be in 1990, I mean a real gang banger who comes from a happy, balanced home, who's got a good opinion of himself. I don't think that kid exists.[10]

In sharp contrast are gang member references to parent or parents, grandparents, or extended family members trying to provide good care. Some gang members observe that family members did everything they could to raise them right, even under tough circumstances.

Both gangs' members tend to be adolescents or young men. Reports of members as young as eight or nine years of age exist, and some observers have noted that some people identify newborns who may grow up to be members.[11] Crip and Blood members tend to be younger than those of other street gangs.[12] Some observers have reported that individuals join a gang between 11 and 15 years of age, with some exceptions being between 16 and 20 years old.[13] One study found gang members between the ages of 13 and 40 years, with a median age of 22.5 years.[14] One study of Bloods and Crips in Montreal, Canada, found the youngest age to be 12 and the average age of gang members to be between 15.5 and 17.3 years.[15] The oldest member in that study was 40 years old.

Although these gangs sometimes attract members from grade school–aged youth, some authorities have found that some gang members may continue their affiliation well into their forties.[16] As one Crip from Watts stated:

> If they start late [in adolescence], they are more likely to tell what they know and cooperate with police, or not follow the code of the streets. It's because guys that turn [to gangs] after high school are not really experienced. When a younger member passes these

kinds of tests from junior high to his early 20s, he gains a name for himself, has a reputation to protect.[17]

Currently, much of the research and literature on gangs in general states that gang members stay involved with their gangs longer than they did in the past. If this is true, one reason for continued involvement with gangs, including the Crips and Bloods, could be the absence of alternatives for gang members. The loss of jobs has limited the number of life options available for gang-involved individuals.

Educationally, Crip and Blood members tend to drop out or have been expelled from school.[18] Most gang members see school as a waste of time and boring. To them, an education affords them no benefits in life. Having an education does not guarantee a job or the success in life that it might have a few decades ago. As one gang member named Angelo put it:

> Brothers are not dumb and stupid; there's a lot of brothers out here that are intelligent, that want to go back to school, but they say, "What am I going to go back to school for, I'm not going to get a job anyway."[19]

B-Dog, a Blood, expressed his belief that education offers no value to poor black youth trying to survive on the streets:

> The schools these days, they only teach little shit, anyway. To me, the street gangs're better than school. Lemme say it this way—little motherfuckers be out there, they gotta learn how to survive. School ain't gonna teach 'em how to do that.[20]

Consistent with other street gangs, Crip and Blood gangs are mostly comprised of males. Of all street gang members, 94% were male in 2000.[21] However, both gangs have female members or associates, for example, Jody Miller found female members of Crip and Blood gangs in Columbus, Ohio.[22] As in other gangs, females historically have served in support roles such as holding weapons, serving as mules for drug transportation, prostituting themselves, and providing lodging and/or sex for gang members. There is growing evidence that their roles have been expanding over the years.[23] They are increasingly serving as soldiers, fighters, and leaders and in other roles indicative of equal and full gang membership.[24] A 19-year-old female Los Angeles Crip illustrated this point when she was asked about female roles within the set and responded, "It depends on the female."[25] She then commented that roles depended on how far the female wanted to go in the set.

Crip co-founder Tookie Williams remembered the formation of a female gang of Crips in 1971 called the Criplettes.[26] The original Criplette member, Bonnie Quarles, was Tookie Williams's girlfriend. The Criplettes modeled themselves after the Crips as much as they could. They violently victimized both sexes, used drugs, and had personal relationships with some of the male Crips. Eight Tray Gangster Crip leader Sanyika Shakur (Monster Kody Scott) was ambushed by a group of females who were associates of the Rollin 60s Crips. They lured him to a house, where he was shot seven times but managed to survive. In a sense, Criplettes are a female auxiliary to the Crips but act independently. Females help support the gang through prostitution, drug sales, and other criminal activities.

The Blood equivalent of the Criplettes are the Bloodlettes.[27] Bloodlettes (or if associated with the Pirus, the Ru'lettes) are the female version of the Bloods. They are rivals with Crips and Criplettes. Their organizational structure is similar to the Criplettes, and they have been known to ambush Crips.

Individual Risk Factors Related to Joining

A number of studies have investigated risk factors related to gang membership, that is, individual characteristics that make certain individuals or groups more prone to joining gangs such as the Bloods and Crips. Risk factors increase the chances that an individual will join and belong to a gang. These risk factors are essentially the same for all gangs, including the Bloods and Crips.

- Family characteristics such as the absence of a father figure increase chances for gang involvement. Family dysfunction is often related to the absence of a father in the household. The poorer a family and the more dysfunction present, the greater the likelihood that a youth will be involved with gangs.[28] Substance abuse within the family also matters. One Blood put it this way: "I know people who have mothers and fathers, but they need shoes, they need clothes, because their mother or father would rather go out and get beer, wine, weed, or dope."[29]

- School factors such as low school achievement increase the risk of gang involvement. An individual's commitment and attachment to school and education appear to matter. Poor school performance and the absence of academic achievement and success increase the risk of gang involvement. In a similar vein, no or few positive activities or interests outside of school increase the risk. Those youth with no pro-social activities such as school sports, clubs, or similar after-school activities are more likely to get involved with gangs.

- Impoverished areas where arrest rates are high, social disorganization is rampant, and low-income households are abundant have an increased presence of street gangs and consequently give youth more opportunities to join.

- Having friends, peers, and/or family members who are delinquent and/or gang involved is a risk factor.[30] If an individual's family members are involved with gangs or associates, the likelihood for gang involvement increases. If an individual's peers are involved in delinquent or criminal activities, this increases chances for involvement in gangs. Research has shown that those youth who have committed delinquent or criminal acts are more prone to joining or otherwise being involved with gangs.

- Lack of positive role models increases an individual's chances of gang involvement. Youth who lack positive role models such as family members, teachers, counselors, neighbors, coaches, religious associates, or supervisors are more at risk. Too often some of the most respected role models for youth are gang leaders who appear to have everything and be successful.

- Individuals with behavioral problems at an early age; negative life events such as the loss of a parent or mental health issues; and delinquent or criminal beliefs are more likely to join or otherwise be involved with gangs.

Any one or all of these risk factors does not guarantee that an individual will join a gang. Having one or a combination of these factors simply increases the chances that an individual will join. If an individual has a large number of risk factors, they may have an additive effect.

There are clear exceptions when individuals seem to act independently of these risk factors.

Why Join the Crips or the Bloods?

One of the central questions asked about street gangs such as the Crips and Bloods is why do individuals join? Why are young adolescents and young adults attracted to gangs? The value of gang relationships is based on the individual's perception of the benefits he or she receives from membership.[31] Gang members identify multiple reasons they joined. Some individuals view gangs as offering physical, emotional, and financial protection.[32] Gang members report that they joined the gang for street protection from other gangs or individuals. They know that once in a gang they will have some degree of protection because of their membership. Typically, they report that others in the gang will cover their back when things get tough.

Gang members perceive great benefit from their involvement with the Crips or Bloods. One Ex-Blood commented, "... who you kick it with largely defines you."[33] For some, belonging to a Crip or Blood set is like having a surrogate family. Similar to a family, both gangs take care of their members by providing shelter, identity, friendship, protection, status, and comfort during difficult times. Gangs provide basic necessities such as clothing, shelter, and safety when families fall short. If a member needs a place to stay, emotional support, food, or whatever, his or her homies often help. A Watts Crip illustrated a common pattern when he explained that when he had no place to live, he ate and slept at the apartments of other gang members and was given money for food.[34]

Gangs often provide social support networks not always available at home. Some gang members even say that their gang provides them with the love absent from their homes and childhoods.[35] It is well documented that gang members frequently come from homes that are strained, disenfranchised, impoverished, and often dysfunctional. Jimel Barnes, one of the charter members of the Crips, stated, "A lot of youngsters don't get love at home from their parents, so they go out in the streets or go to the gang and look for love, and get that bonding."[36] In addition, gangs provide structure that is not available from members' families.[37] External to their families, gangs create their own support systems and nurture members. David Allender noted that gang members, even in the toughest gangs, often talk of how they love one another.[38] Ironically, this support network disappears when a gang member is in detention or prison. Many autobiographies written by ex-gang members comment that none of their homies wrote or called them when they were locked up.

Some individuals believe that being a gangster is necessary for survival. To low-income marginalized youth facing economic and social disadvantage, gangs offer status and at least the appearance of wealth. In some impoverished communities poor youth see gang members as the only successful role models. Some appear to have all the cash, jewelry, cars, women, and status they need. With few options, the gang looks like an attractive alternative. Due to multiple marginalization of youth, some believe that the only way to gain status and respect in their communities is to commit crimes and join gangs. Inequality in the social structure helps promote illegitimate behaviors such as crime and deviance. On the surface the gangster lifestyle appears to be a way to successfully adapt to the hardships of the streets; it is seen as a means by which powerless black males and females can obtain status, success, and power in their neighborhoods.

One reason for an individual to join a gang is the promise, or hope, of economic gain. Crip and Blood members often identify financial gain as the reason they joined.[39] For them, it is about the money. This money is obtained through drug sales, carjacking, theft, armed robbery, hustles, and other crimes. Gang members often support one another financially by posting bail if a member is arrested, providing street protection when they are involved in drug trafficking, and other prosperous illegal activities. Crip co-founder Tookie Williams explained how he became immersed in the gangster lifestyle:

> Like many others I became a slave to a delusional dream of capitalism's false hope: a slave to dysfunction; a slave to nihilism; a slave to drugs; a slave to black-on-black violence; and a slave to self hate. Paralyzed within a social vacuum I gravitated toward thughood, not out of aspiration but out of desperation to survive the monstrous inequities that show no mercy to young or old. Aggression, I was to learn, served as a poor man's merit for manhood. To die as a street martyr was seen as a noble thing.[40]

Another reason for joining is the excitement and fun that come from belonging to a gang.[41] Individuals join gangs to increase stimulation and excitement in their daily routine; belonging can be a rush and socially exciting. According to Allender:

Excitement often represents a motivation for suburban and affluent youths. Gangs composed of these types of individuals usually have very fluid membership, with associates joining and leaving to be replaced by others with a passing interest.[42]

Crip Tookie Williams summed up the appeal of being in a Crip gang in this way:

Up to this point, my life had been possessed by a Crip rage, a lethal momentum hurling me into perilous situations where the odds of living were long. Playing my own version of Russian

Members of the Grape Street Watts Crips, a gang based in the Jordan Downs housing project in Watts, pose with their shotguns and wear their gang's signature Vikings baseball caps. Posing with guns is very common among Blood and Crip gangs. For years, Grape Street had a violent rivalry with the Bounty Hunter Bloods, based in the Nickerson Gardens neighborhood, but over the years this rivalry has declined. (Axel Koester/Corbis)

roulette, I got an adrenaline high from roaming the streets and terrorizing entire communities, as if daring someone, anyone, to fire a bullet that would stop me forever.[43]

OG Red, a Crip, explained what attracted him to being in a gang:

The excitement, to be noticed. You were somebody, you weren't just the average schoolboy. I was mainly attracted to the excitement.[44]

This perception of fun and excitement holds sway even though much of a gang member's time is spent hanging out and looking for something to do. Belonging to a gang is seen as better than simply staying home, being alone, and doing nothing. With a gang, you at least have others to bond and spend time with. Crip Tookie Williams once wrote:

I didn't enjoy getting into trouble. I just found the streets to be more interesting than being at home.[45]

Some gang members say that they joined to be more attractive to the opposite sex. They note that male gang members tend to have more contacts with females because some women find gang members more appealing and attractive. Some females tend to view gang members as adventurous and like to be associated with bad boys.

A sense of belonging to a group or some other entity is an allure of gang membership.[46] Being in a gang offer members a strong sense of belonging. When an individual joins the Crips or Bloods, he or she declares to the outside world through association, clothing, symbols, and other subcultural activities that he or she is a member of a group. Some even believe that other members of the gang would die for them.

Profiles of Crip and Blood Members

There is no single profile that fits all Crips and Bloods, but many share similar histories and characteristics. The following are some example case histories of Blood and Crip gang members. Some are well known and have legendary status in gang tradition, such as Raymond

Washington, Sylvia Nunn, Tookie Williams, and Sanyika Shakur. Others are less well known in gang lore.

Roy (Crip)

Roy is an African American male Crip from Watts. Growing up, his home life was strained because his father was absent due to a long prison sentence. When he was released, his father was killed in a gang-related incident, leaving Roy without a dad. Roy grew up in a single parent household with a mother who was a drug addict. He grew up on the streets and rarely attended school. Roy was characterized as being aggressive, frustrated, and hostile at a very young age. He was a bully when he attended school and took other kids' money. He joined a Crip set and was called on to be a shooter for the gang, which he willfully did.[47]

Sylvia Nunn (aka Rambo; Piru Blood)

Sylvia Nunn was born on June 9, 1962, in Compton, California. She was raised in a black middle-class family. Her father taught her survival skills such as stealing cars and shooting guns so that she could protect herself on the streets of Compton. Her involvement in crime started at the early age of 10 when she helped a group commit an armed robbery of a store. Following the robbery she demanded from the boys her fair share of the money.

She would become one of the most famous Pirus because of her violent and fearless attacks on rival Crips. She was introduced to the Lueders Park Pirus by her brother Marcus. She would find Marcus with multiple gunshot wounds in a park near her home. A Crip set had shot him. He would survive his wounds. Enraged by this event, Sylvia would seek revenge by shooting at groups of people to kill or wound as many Crips as she could; hence she earned the nickname Rambo. She joined the Pirus in 1979 and eventually earned the status of "male." In the 1980s she became involved in drug use and sales and continued to be violent. On June 12, 2008, Sylvia was featured on an episode of the cable series *Gangland* in an episode called "From Girl to Gangster." The show focused on her life and affiliation with the Lueders Park Pirus.[48] Eventually she moved out of California, withdrew from the gang, married, and is an anti-gang activist.

Joseph (Crip)

Joseph is a black male from South Central Los Angeles. His father left home when he was seven years old, which left him with a strong feeling of abandonment. Consequently, he grew up in a single parent household and early in life started associating with boys involved with crime. At age 12, he joined a Crip gang. He bullied classmates and often missed school. After joining the Crips, he took on the gang name of Lil Loc because of his young age. When involved with the Crips, he drank and used marijuana at set gatherings. Commenting about his gang, he noted that he considered it his family.[49]

OG Red (Crip)

OG Red was raised in a fatherless home in Alieso Village in Los Angeles. Red joined a gang when he was 10 years old, in 1971. He used illegal drugs such as PCP and pills, and mostly drank alcohol. He reported being in and out of jail many times and also having prison stays. He identified mental health issues that led to placement in mental facilities during his youth. He worked his way into be being an OG among the Crips.[50]

Raymond Lee Washington (Crip)

Raymond Lee Washington was born on August 14, 1953, in Los Angeles. He was the youngest of four brothers. Washington is credited as being the co-founding father, along with Tookie Williams, of the Crips. Raymond was known as a tough kid and a talented athlete in the neighborhood. With three older brothers, he learned to fight at a very young age. His younger half-brother, Derard, remembered, "I never saw my brother lose a fight, except to my older brothers when he was real young."[51]

Lore has it that he initially fought only to protect himself or other youth in the community. Raymond Washington was reputed to be a warmhearted individual who protected the kids in his neighborhood from the bullying of outside gangs.[52] Others have a different opinion of Washington and his motives and view him as a bully with a mean streak. While growing up, Washington was expelled from several

Los Angeles schools, including Fremont, Locke, Washington, and Fairfax high schools. Washington gained a reputation on the streets as a tough street fighter and soon became involved with crime and gangs. It was on the streets that he became a member of the Avenues gang in his early teens. The Avenues were headed by a muscular and tough teen named Craig Munson. At age 15, Washington beat up Munson's younger brother. In retaliation, Craig Munson beat up Washington.

Following this beating Washington left the Avenues and formed the Baby Avenues. In 1969, at the age of 15 while attending Freemont High School, he began recruiting some of the kids in his neighborhood into an organization initially called the Baby Avenues or Baby Cribs.[53] The Baby Avenue Cribs were named after his previous local set named the Avenues or Avenue Boys. Washington was an excellent recruiter, and it was not long before his gang became large. Washington's talent for hand-to-hand combat served him well in enlisting new gang members.

Over time the name Cribs morphed into Crips.[54] After committing several criminal acts Washington was arrested for second degree robbery and sentenced to prison at the Deuel Vocational Institution in Tracy, California. While there, Washington recruited others into the Crips. He was eventually released in 1970 and returned to Los Angeles.

Washington disliked guns and preferred to solve disputes with his fists.[55] He had always been anti-gun, so he discouraged the use of guns by gang members.[56] First-generation Crip Robert Jones shared, "Raymond believed a real man don't need no gun."[57] Regardless of his thoughts, guns became increasingly popular among gangs during the mid-1970s, much to his disappointment.

As a Crip, he was involved in violence. He saw inter-gang violence and gang-related homicides involving close friends and family members. Unhappy with Crip and Blood violence and infighting, as well as police violence, Washington tried to unite everyone into a single gang to stop the extreme violence. He sought to establish peace among warring sets of gangs. His efforts were not approved by gang members and eventually resulted in his murder. On August 9, 1979, Washington was killed in a drive-by shooting in South Central Los Angeles at age 25. His murder has never been solved.

Ralph Nelson (Blood)

Ralph Nelson was nicknamed Sugar Man because his grandmother thought he was a sweet baby. His negative experiences in school contributed to his decision to become involved with gangs. Ralph was an excellent athlete, especially in football, but was not treated fairly by his high school coach. He tried to do well in school and live by the rules, but things did not work out (even though he did nothing wrong).[58] He graduated from high school and soon found factory work.

Nelson was the recognized leader of the Piru Brothers, a Blood gang. Being the leader provided him with status he could not achieve in school. He did have a brief football career with the National Football League's Washington Redskins and eventually moved away from Los Angeles to become a bus driver.

Stanley "Tookie" Williams III (Crip)

Stanley "Tookie" Williams III (December 29, 1953–December 13, 2005) is widely recognized as one of the co-founders of the Crips. Williams was born in New Orleans and at the age of six moved with his mother to Southern California for a better life. Similar to other gang involved youth, he was raised by a single parent, was poor, was subjected to beatings, and was motivated by greed. He was victimized by black gangs in junior high school, missed a lot of school, and moved around from school to school. When he did attend, he made connections with other youth that he would use to his advantage on the streets. According to his autobiography, Williams was first a gang victim before he was a gang leader. His first encounter with a gang was when he was robbed and beaten by older, larger boys who roamed his neighborhood looking for smaller defenseless targets. After being robbed and beaten, Williams began to hate gangs and vowed never to join one.[59]

His mother worked several jobs to support them and thus left him alone to wander the streets, which is when he was exposed to various negative influences and often had to fight for protection. Over the years Williams gained a reputation as a great fighter and by his teens was famous on the streets. By age 16 he was arrested and placed in detention, where he became involved with weightlifting. In 1971, at the age of 17, he made friends with Raymond Washington. The two immediately hit it off and formed a gang called the Cribs, the name of which was eventually changed to Crips. Williams was from the west side and established the Westside and Compton Crips (led by Mac Thomas); Washington, from the east side, formed the Eastside Crips. According to Williams, in the late 1970s he got hooked on drugs such marijuana, barbiturates, LSD, angel dust, and sherms (cigars or cigarettes soaked in PCP).[60]

He was incarcerated as a juvenile for stealing a car and other crimes. He adhered to the gang value of never snitching to authorities on gang-related matters. Williams was convicted of homicide and robbery in two separate incidents. He was incarcerated in 1981 and received a death sentence. Williams would become a major anti-gang activist while

Michael Scruggs, a former founding member of the Inglewood Village Crips gang, reacts to the news of California governor Arnold Schwarzenegger's denial of clemency to Stanley "Tookie" Williams on Monday, December 12, 2005. While in prison, Williams wrote extensively about the downside of gangs and claimed redemption. Major celebrities such as Snoop Dog, Sean "Puff Daddy" Combs, and Jamie Foxx pled on his behalf, but to no avail, and he was executed on December 13, 2005. (AP Photo/Damian Dovarganes)

incarcerated, writing several books, including some directed toward children to keep them from joining gangs. His most powerful book was published posthumously in 2007 and was titled *Blue Rage, Black Redemption: A Memoir*. This autobiography told of his involvement with gangs and the path he took to reform and reject gangs.

Williams made a series of appeals through the courts, all of which failed. Williams and his legal counsel, having exhausted all legal appeals, then filed a petition for clemency with the governor of California. A campaign was started to urge Governor Arnold Schwarzenegger to grant clemency because of all of Williams's anti-gang efforts while in prison. The basis of the appeal was that Williams had reformed or been redeemed through his anti-gang efforts and new evidence of his innocence. Anti–death penalty and civil rights organizations also rallied around the effort to stop the execution. Numerous celebrities voiced their support for Williams, including Snoop Dogg, Sean "Puff Daddy" Combs, and Jamie Foxx.

In opposition, area law enforcement agencies such as the Los Angeles District Attorney's Office and Police Department actively opposed the clemency petition. They did so because Williams refused to share information about his gangs with authorities. They argued that if he had truly rejected gangs, he would cooperate. In his mind it was important not to snitch on gang members. Not revealing gang-related information to authorities is a common and central value of street gangs. The authorities were not convinced that he had changed, and they had empathy for the wishes of his victims' families. On December 12, 2005, Governor Schwarzenegger denied clemency, and Williams was executed on December 13, 2005. To the very end, Williams claimed he was innocent.

Sanyika Shakur (aka Monster Kody Scott; Crip)

Kody Scott (aka Sanyika Shakur) was born in 1963. His involvement with gangs began at age 11, when he pumped off eight shotgun blasts at a rival gang. Scott changed his name to Sanyika Shakur after reflecting in prison about his life and involvement with gangs. He earned his nickname Monster from robbing and violently assaulting a man for 20 minutes and leaving him in a coma and disfigured. The police said that whoever had committed this crime was a monster, and this name stuck.[61] His autobiography, titled *Monster,* provided an insider's view of how he lived as a Crip. Some have suggested that his book romanticized the gangster lifestyle and placed much of the responsibility for creating street gangs on him.[62] He shared some of his experiences while he was imprisoned at Soledad and befriended by the journalist Lēon Bing.[63]

Shakur was one of the most famous Eight Tray Crips. He believes he was the product of a violent and destructive environment.[64] His involvement with the Crips led to many violent encounters with rival gang members as a victim but also as an offender. He not only victimized rivals, he was also shot and stabbed several times. In one incident when he was only 17, he was shot five times and survived.

Shakur served time in several of California's prisons, including Soledad, Pelican Bay, San Quentin, and Folsom, often in solitary confinement. It was during his time in prison that he moved from being a gang member to being a revolutionary.

Colton "C-Loc" Simpson (Crip)

In the mid-1970s Colton Simpson became involved with the Crips when he was 10 years old. Raised by his grandmother in South Central Los Angeles, Simpson would be initiated into the Crips by running down an alley with gang members shooting at him. He spent much of his life incarcerated first as a youth and then as an adult. Being a Crip had implications for him while incarcerated, as he would be involved with assaults and other gang-related activities and crimes within prison walls.

On the streets Simpson was involved in typical gang activities and crimes. Violence characterized much of the time he spent with the Crips. Eventually Simpson would change his views on gang life and work toward helping people get out of that lifestyle. In 2005 he would tell about his life as a Crip in an autobiography titled *Inside the Crips: Life inside L.A.'s Most Notorious Gang.*

OG Mack (Blood)

Omar Portee (aka Godfather Mack, The Big Homie, or more commonly OG Mack) was born in New York. He committed robbery, his first known crime, at the age of 17. He is credited with co-founding the United Blood Nation in New York City. OG Mack and Leonard "Dead Eye" McKenzie co-established the United Blood Nation while incarcerated at Rikers Island prison in 1993. Upon leaving prison in 1999, he assumed leadership of the East Coast gang the One-Eight-Trey Bloods. Angry with those claiming to be Bloods but not being actual Bloods, OG Mac went to the streets and purged those he saw as imposters. In 2003, at the age of 33, he was convicted of conspiracy to commit murder, illegal possession of an AK-47 military rifle, racketeering, conspiracy to distribute crack cocaine, and other crimes. He was sentenced to a 50-year sentence in a federal maximum security prison.

Robert Davis (Crip)

Robert Davis was born in Cleveland, Ohio. In 1968, at the age of eight, he moved with both his parents to Los Angeles, where his family had relatives. As a child he lived in poverty. He, unlike many gang members, was raised in a two parent household. In 1974 he joined the Crips at age 15. Living in East Los Angeles, he and other gang youth viewed youth living on the west side as more affluent. West side black youth were targeted because they were viewed as being better off. Robert and members of his gang would rob west side black youth by taking their coveted leather jackets.[65]

Davis, painfully aware of his poverty, was embarrassed by his poor clothing. His sense of inequality set the context for his involvement in crime and the Crips. He felt inadequate due to his family's poverty,[66] though being poor was not the only thing that made him feel unequal. As a black youth, he experienced police harassment at a young age and became convinced that whatever he did had little to do with white acceptance.[67] The racism, prejudice, and oppression that drove inequality also fueled his involvement in the Crips.[68]

G-Rock (Crip)

G-Rock, which is an alias, is a Crip and longtime police informer.[69] He is outwardly a heavily committed OG with the Crips, but he shares information with law enforcement personnel on gang-related crimes.

A black man, he is married with children and lives in the suburbs. He grew up in a single parent household with siblings who were not involved with gangs. He was determined to gangbang but also found a career in law enforcement attractive. He took the path leading to gangs and joined the Rollin 60s Crips at the age of 14, at which point he had to be courted in by fighting an older member of the gang. Later, he shared that those wanting to join in 2008 had to commit serious crimes that in effect limited their ability to go back (leave the gang).

As a Rollin 60s, he was involved in robberies, thefts, selling drugs, drive-by shootings, and car thefts. He noted in an interview that everyone has to hustle to make money. The gang he leads is located in the area of South Central Los Angeles controlled by the Rollin 60s Crips. He reported the ages of his gang members to be between 19 and 26 years. He also shared that hanging out, drinking, and doing drugs were gang-involved activities. Following an interview in 2008 with a journalist, he continued to operate as a paid informant but also as an active Rollin 60s Crip.

Big Phil (Crip)

Big Phil started banging when he was 10 years old, in 1971.[70] He was raised by a single mother, whom he characterized as a strong woman. He grew up around Black Guerilla Family members, whom he viewed as a positive influence and good role models. He joined the Crips after seeing his brother jumped by a group of Brim (Blood) gang members. The Brims were a Bloods gang and he did not want to be like them, so he joined a Crips set. He admitted that he could have easily joined the Bloods had it been Crips who jumped his brother.

Big Phil was viewed in his neighborhood as a leader and over his years of involvement with the Crips, he recruited for, formed, and reorganized different Crip sets. One set he claims to have started is the Rollin 40s, but he later joined the Rollin 30s Crips. Later, as an established OG, he established the Harlems. Big Phil was viewed by many, including law enforcement personnel, as an important player in the gang scene. He believes that because of his success he was targeted by police and was often set up for crimes he did not commit. Consequently, he noted that he was in and out of jail and prison for crimes he knew nothing about. Eventually Big Phil would become active in gang truce efforts in the 1990s and be an advocate for peace among rival gangs. He came to the realization that believing in a supreme higher being was very important and served as a community organizer for black youth.

Concluding Observations

Crip and Blood members share a number of common characteristics, for example, most are male, black, and poor; have difficulty in school; and lack fathers and positive male role models. They tend to have histories of family dysfunction, use illegal drugs, and have been harassed by law enforcement; are unemployed; and have criminal or delinquent histories independent of the gang. Most join when they are adolescents and have friends or older siblings also involved with gangs. In a sense they are very similar to others who join non-Crip or Blood gangs. The push factors of dysfunctional families, poverty, and school and pull factors of the gang make the Crip and Blood gangster lifestyle attractive for some marginalized black youth.[71] The gangs fill a gap for youth and young adults who need others in similar circumstances to understand and accept them.

Individuals join gangs for many reasons, including masculine empowerment, identity, need for acceptance, need for structure, status, power, a sense of belonging, companionship (bonding), protection, tradition, a way to make money, and the lack of alternative economic and employment opportunities. There are also subcultural factors that make belonging to a gang attractive, such as the music, clothing, romance, and appeal to the opposite sex. In these respects, again we are left with the conclusion that their motives are very similar to other gang members. Then what separates them from others? The answer is the subculture of what it means to be a Crip or a Blood, which will be partially addressed in the next chapter.

Notes

1. Stacey Peralta, *Crips and Bloods Made in America* (Docuramafilms, 2009).
2. Christopher Adamson, "Defensive Localism in White and Black: A Comparative History of European-American and African-American Youth Gangs." *Ethnic & Racial Studies* 23 (2000), 272–298.

3. Gregg Etter, "Gang Investigation." In Michael L. Birzer and Cliff Robertson (Eds.), *Introduction to Criminal Investigation* (Boca Raton, FL: CRC Press, 2012), 323.

4. Seth Mydans, "Life in a Girls' Gang: Colors and Bloody Noses." *New York Times* (January 29, 1990), 12.

5. Washington/Baltimore High Density Drug Trafficking Area, "Crips," accessed on January 3, 2014 at: http://www.hidtagangs.org/GangLibrary.aspx.

6. Bill Valentine, *Gang Intelligence Manual* (Boulder, CO: Paladin, 1995), 62; Karine Descormiers and Carlo Morselli, "Alliances, Conflicts, and Contradictions in Montreal's Street Gang Landscape." *International Criminal Justice Review* 21 (2011), 297–314.

7. James Diego Vigil, *Barrio Gangs: Street Life and Identity in Southern California* (Austin: University of Texas Press, 1988).

8. Peter L. Patton, "The Gangstas among Our Midst." *Urban Review* 30, no. 1 (1998), 62.

9. Léon Bing, *Do or Die: America's Most Notorious Gangs Speak for Themselves* (New York: HarperCollins, 1991), 29–30.

10. Ibid., 13.

11. Donovan Simmons and Terry Moses, *Bloods and Crips: The Genesis of a Genocide* (Bloomington, IN: Authorhouse, 2009).

12. Valentine, Op. cit., 46.

13. Stanley S. Taylor, "How Street Gangs Recruit and Socialize Members." *Journal of Gang Research* 17 (2009), 1–27.

14. Bureau of Organized Crime and Criminal Intelligence, *Crips and Bloods Street Gangs* (Sacramento, CA: Bureau of Organized Crime and Criminal Intelligence, n.d.), 4.

15. Descormiers, Op. cit., 302.

16. Operation Safe Streets, "L.A. Style: A Street Gang Manual of the Los Angeles County Sheriff's Department." In Malcolm W. Klein, Cheryl L. Maxson, and Jody Miller (Eds.), *The Modern Gang Reader* (Los Angeles: Roxbury, 1995).

17. Stanley S. Taylor, "Why American Boys Join Street Gangs." *African Journal of Law and Criminology* 2, no. 1 (2012), 62.

18. Valentine, Op. cit., 46.

19. Yusuf Jah and Sister Shah'Keyah, *Uprising: Crips and Bloods Tell the Story of America's Youth in the Crossfire* (New York: Touchstone, 1995), 71.

20. Bing, Op. cit., 218.

21. Arlen Egley Jr., *Youth Gang Survey Trends from 1996 to 2000* (Washington, DC: U.S. Department of Justice and Delinquency Prevention, 2001).

22. Jody Miller, "Gender and Victimization Risk among Young Women in Gangs." *Journal of Research in Crime and Delinquency* 35, no. 4 (1998): 429–453.

23. See Chapter 4 in Robert J. Franzese, Herbert C. Covey, and Scott Menard, *Youth Gangs* (Springfield, IL: Charles C. Thomas, 2006) for a summary discussion of the research.

24. National Gang Intelligence Center, *2013 National Gang Report* (Washington, DC: Federal Bureau of Investigation, 2013), 41.

25. Ross Kemp, *Ross Kemp on Gangs Los Angeles* (British Sky Broadcasting, 2008).

26. Stanley Tookie Williams, *Blue Rage, Black Redemption: A Memoir* (New York: Simon and Schuster, 2007).

27. Gangland, "One Blood" (September 14, 2008) History Channel, originally aired May 28, 2008.

28. For a representative study of background risk factors, see Rachel Gordon, Benjamin Lahey, Eriko Kawai, Rolf Loeber, Magda Stouthamer-Loeber, and David Farington, "Antisocial Behavior and Youth Gang Membership: Selection and Socialization." *Criminology* 42 (2004), 55–87.

29. Jah, Op. cit., 126.

30. For example, see Benjamin B. Lahey, Rachel A. Gordon, Rolf Loeber, Magda Stouthamer-Loeber, and David P. Farington, "Boys Who Join Gangs: A Prospective Study of Predictors of First Gang Entry." *Journal of Abnormal Child Psychology* 27, no. 4 (1999), 261–276.

31. See Patton, Op. cit.

32. David Allender, "Gangs in Middle America." *FBI Law Enforcement Bulletin* 70, no. 12 (2001), 4.

33. Dashaun Jiwi Morris, *War of the Bloods in My Veins: A Street Soldier's March toward Redemption* (New York: Scribner, 2008), 69.

34. Taylor, Op. cit., 64.

35. Eugene L. Weems and Clarke Lowe, *America's Most Notorious Gangs: A Concise Approach to Gang Prevention and Awareness* (Dixon, CA: Universal Publishing, 2013), xi.

36. Jah, Op. cit., 152.

37. Allender, Op. cit., 4.

38. Allender, Op. cit., 4.

39. R. D. Flores, "Crips and Bloods." *Crime and Justice International* 13 (1997), 6–9.

40. See Williams, Op. cit., xvii.

41. See Jah, Op. cit., 122; Bing, Op. cit., 49.

42. Allender, Op. cit., 4.

43. Williams, Op. cit., 217.

44. Jah, Op. cit., 45.

45. Williams, Op. cit., 14.

46. Allender, Op. cit., 4.

47. See Taylor, Op. cit.

48. United Gangs, "Sylvia 'Rambo' Nunn (Gangster)," accessed on October 24, 2014 at: www.unitedgangs.com.

49. Ibid.

50. See Jah, Op. cit.

51. George Percy Barganier, III, *Fanon's Children: The Black Panther Party and the Rise of the Crips and Bloods in Los Angeles* (Ph.D. dissertation, University of California Berkeley, 2011), 63.
52. Ibid., 63.
53. Ibid., 63.
54. Nate B. Hendley, *American Gangsters, Then and Now: An Encyclopedia* (Santa Barbara, CA: ABC-CLIO eBook Collection, 2009).
55. See Barganier, Op. cit.
56. National Public Radio, "Tookie Williams and the History of the Crips" (December 7, 2005).
57. Barganier, Op. cit., 63.
58. Barganier, Op. cit., 82.
59. Williams, Op. cit., 64.
60. See Williams, Op. cit.
61. Sanyika Shakur, *Monster: The Autobiography of an L.A. Gang Member* (New York: Penguin, 1993), 13.
62. Wayne Caffey, *Crips and Bloods* (Los Angeles: Los Angeles County Sheriff's Office, 2006), 6.
63. Bing, Op. cit.
64. Bing, Op. cit., 237.
65. Barganier, Op. cit., 70.
66. Ibid., 70.
67. Ibid., 70.
68. Ibid., 70.
69. Guy Lawson, "The Inside Man." *GQ* 78 (January 2008), 84–87, 141–143.
70. Jah, Op. cit., 25–42.
71. Walter C. Reckless, "A New Theory of Delinquency and Crime." *Federal Probation* 24 (1961), 42–46.

CHAPTER FIVE

Crip and Blood
Subcultures

To be a Crip, you have to put your blue rag on your head and
wear all blue and go in a Blood neighborhood.[1]

—Unknown, Crip

Of all the gangs, the Crips and Bloods likely have had more influence
on mainstream culture in the United States and the world than any
other gang. They have been influential through their subculture in
spite of having few formal guidelines, regulations, laws, or norms.
Their ideas have helped shape culture well beyond the world of gangs.
Their subculture has influenced music, literature, film, language, television, social media, and other components of mass culture.

While Crip and Blood gang culture is unique, many traditions can
be traced back to earlier Latino and black gangs in Southern California.
Many aspects of both gangs were simply embraced from pre-existing
gang culture. The style of clothing (with the exception of reliance on
the red and blue colors), emphasizing the importance of the neighborhood and gang loyalty, pre-dates the establishment of both gangs.[2]

Crip and Blood members learn about Blood and Crip subcultures
locally through communicating with other set members and also from
the mass media. So much of what members know they learned

through face-to-face interaction with other gang members and through direct observation. But members also pay attention to how they are portrayed in the larger society and corresponding media. Current and ex-gang members have also written extensively about their experiences of belonging in both gangs. Crip and Blood members, current and past, have helped produce rap music and consulted on movies and videos. They have also become active players on the Internet and in social media. All of this contributes to a sizable watershed of subcultural ideas related to what it means to be a Blood or Crip.

Gang subculture applies to argot (language), clothing, activities, greetings, rules of interaction, and other aspects of the gang life. The subculture of the Blood and Crip gangs has grown in complexity since their inception. Early members had little to learn about membership, but over the years this grew in scope. Now members have elaborate codes of behavior, symbolism, gangsta rap, literature, websites, legends, and considerable folklore related to what it means to be a member.

Crip and Blood gang subcultures have a very high profile and can be attractive to impoverished children and youth of color in areas where both gangs have a presence. If you are part of it, you immediately get attention and a sense of respect in your community. Street gangs, whether Blood or Crip, carry a bit of romance to the outside world.[3] As outlaws they are attractive to outsiders as they resist authority and the mainstream. America and other societies around the world have been influenced by gang cultures.[4] Crip and Blood subcultures have had a major influence on gangs and the broader society. Whether it is dress, music, lifestyle, language, or art, Crip and Blood subcultures have extended well beyond their boundaries. In addition to the United States, there are copycat Crip and Blood gangs in a number of countries such as South Africa and England, for example, English gangs and crews are known to claim affiliation with the Crips and Bloods. One author noted that this claiming represents a move from a local orientation of gangs to key cultural reference points being global.[5]

The Importance of Blood and Crip Subcultures

There are multiple reasons that Crip and Blood subcultures are important to both gangs. It is through their distinctive subcultures that both gangs are able to differentiate their gangs from other street gangs. In this vein, it is very important for these gangs to be able to determine who is a member in the gang. Determining gang membership is important to ensure that those claiming to be in the gang are real members. With any community there are individuals who pretend they are members (they are sometimes called claimers or posers). These non-gang individuals can harm the gang's public image and reputation. If they have not been initiated into the gang or have not been proven to have the right stuff, there is the risk of losing respect and status in the community. Weak members or imposters diminish a gang's effectiveness in the hood. Thus members always have insider subcultural information and behaviors that help them tell who is in and who is out.

A gang's subculture, whether it relates to language, values, norms, clothing, tattoos, mannerisms, or other areas is the tool by which membership is identified. This can be critical when encountering strangers. Being able to identify gang membership and whose side a person is on can be the difference between being accepted, seriously harmed, or even killed. This identification needs to occur within a few seconds on the streets.[6]

Gang subculture helps identify external threats such as the police and rival gang members. It also helps solidify the gang with a common sense of belonging. Sharing insider subcultural information and behaviors solidifies social bonds within the gang. In addition, Crip and Blood subcultures provide a sense of tradition for members that is not always available through mainstream society.

Subcultural Characteristics of Crip and Blood Gangs

Subcultures have unique values, norms, beliefs, and behaviors. Those of the Crips and Bloods are no exception. Blood and Crip members typically share common values that have sometimes been associated with the code of the streets. It is important to acknowledge from the beginning that Crip and Blood antagonism permeates every aspect of their subcultures.[7] Their graffiti, writing, attire, argot, and mannerisms are generally directed toward disrespecting each other. Even with this antagonism, some Crips and Bloods cooperate and socialize in harmony. Some gang members even move from being Crips to Bloods and vice versa depending on circumstances.[8]

Respect

Bloods and Crips have values that they adhere to as part of their gang subcultures. An important value within Crip and Blood subcultures is the importance of respect. In a society where socially acceptable avenues for marginalized black youth, men, and women are very limited, street respect is of great importance. Gang members look for this respect because they view mainstream opportunities for respect as non-existent or limited to a few. They are, in reality, excluded from or limited in gaining respect from the larger society. Thus any hint of disrespect to a Crip or Blood solicits a reaction, which at times can be violent. Whether in a gang or not, being respected is important on the street. Respect is so important to these gangs that they will take drastic actions to protect their gang's reputation. This is because a gang that is not respected on the street does not last very long and has no power. Individuals and their gangs value being respected on the street, although much of this respect is driven by fear. Individuals earn respect in their gangs by being tough and a good fighter, having courage, and not backing down under any circumstance. Respect within the gang has to be earned by individuals. Monster Cody described how respect played out in prison, saying, "Respect is not negotiable." He added, "You get and you give, but you don't get respect unless you give it."[9] The same can be said for respect on the streets (outs). Kenny Valentine, a former gang member and now a gang intervention worker, summed up the situation:

> When you are young, whichever neighborhood you're brought up in, you're poor, there's no field trips, no jobs. That's why they love their neighborhoods so much. If they're disrespected by someone scratching their name on a wall, or someone comes in to mess with a female, that's disrespect. It's totally about respect.[10]

The importance of respect to these gangs cannot be overstated. Everyone generally wants respect, especially the Crips and Bloods.

Both demand personal respect but also respect for their hood, gang, family, gang symbols, and gang way of life.[11]

The opposite of respect on the street is to be disrespected or "dissed." Disrespect can take many forms, some of which seem minor to outsiders but to gang members are very important. One example of disrespect is to maintain eye contact too long or to stare. It could be accidently bumping into a gang member or flashing a hand sign. Disrespect could be verbally insulting one's gang, family, or hood; passing through a rival gang's turf; touching a gang member; writing over a set's graffiti; hitting on a set member's girl or guy; or otherwise insulting a gang member or their gang. Both gangs cross out the names of rival gangs or gang member names on existing graffiti as a sign of disrespect. Once disrespected, a gang member or gang must regain that respect. Gang members and friends will often encourage the disrespected individual to earn the respect back.[12]

Loyalty

Loyalty to the gang and its members is another characteristic of both gangs. Crip and Blood members' loyalty to their gangs is fierce and unquestioned. Gang loyalty supersedes family, friendship, or any other loyalties.[13] This loyalty is often tested by members over the span of a member's involvement. Gang members carry this loyalty with them as they move from community to community and across the country. Gang membership can be transferred from one neighborhood to another. Members do not typically change their affiliation and loyalty as they move from neighborhood to neighborhood. Allegiance to their hood and gang is firm and unwavering. One female Blood explained what it meant to be true to her gang and have their backs:

> Like, uh, if you say you are a Blood, you be a Blood. You wear your rag even when you're by yourself. You know, don't let anybody intimidate you and be like, "Take that rag off." You know, "you better get with our set." Or something like that.[14]

Members express gang loyalty in a number of ways. Members use tattoos, graffiti, clothing, and brands to symbolically display their loyalty to their gang. Tattoos and brands reflect a lasting and permanent commitment to the Crips or Bloods. Both are visible and public statements of loyalty. Gang members also practice a code of silence if communication negatively impacts their gang or hood. They generally do not disagree among themselves in public and present a unified front to outsiders.

No Snitching and the Code of Silence

A common and related gang value is to never snitch on others or the gang. Set members are expected to maintain a code of silence about gang members when talking to others. Sharing any information with authorities on one's set, its members, or rival sets is taboo. This is because there is little to no trust of law enforcement agencies and other authorities. Consequently, helping them in any way is prohibited. Anyone caught snitching, whether Blood or Crip, is robbed, stabbed, or killed.[15] A great example is that of Stanley Tookie Williams, co-founder of the Crips, who refused to share any information about his gang with authorities even though he had written extensively on the downside of gang membership. He went to his execution in 2005 unwilling to snitch on his gang or its members. Another gang member shared his view of this value:

> We are trained to keep our society a secret, never snitch, and protect your brother. Codes and conducts taught from an early age are embedded in us.[16]

Brotherly Love

Many gang members come from homes in which they were mistreated and impoverished; thus when their gang cares for them, they become very loyal. Many Blood and Crip members consider their set their family. Gangs become their street families. One black gang member said it this way: "My gang is my family. My homies are my blood."[17] Similar to other gangs, members will characterize their sets as being their families. Crip co-founder Stanley Williams shared this view of his set: "Bonded by our commonality—low economic status, the Crips became my family."[18]

Both gangs indicate that they value brotherly and sisterly love. They love each other as members of a common cause, the gang. In this vein, they will describe their homeboys or homegirls as their family. Brotherly love is expressed in a number of ways such as the *B* in the name Blood. They will describe beating a set member as an act of love. Having another homeboy's back or being willing to die for them is viewed as an expression of love.

Other Values

Crip and Blood values are expressed in their subcultures. Both gangs have other values that are written out, such as maintaining security, that is, watching over others in the set and protecting them from becoming victims. Ex-Crip gang member Colton Simpson expressed this value in his autobiography.[19] Other values might include never showing weakness to each other or to outsiders, especially rivals, never victimizing other members, responding to threats to the gang, and showing respect to OGs and leaders of the gang. Members value those who put in work for their sets. Another gang value is to remember the dead by avenging the death of a fellow gang member or remembering them in a gang-related fashion, for example, the gang may memorialize past members. They value getting revenge after rivals have victimized one of their homeboys as well as courage in the name of the gang when members are willing to risk their lives and futures for the good of the gang.

These values of the Crip and Blood subcultures are expressed in a variety of ways, including colors, language, clothing, mannerisms, music, public image, photographs, and writings. Many of these are expressed in the mass media.[20] Any description of how Blood and Crip subcultures are displayed must begin with the role colors have played in both gangs.

The Role of Colors in Blood and Crip Subcultures

Much of the history and tradition surrounding both gangs is their allegiance to the colors red or blue. In the beginning colors were not important, and both Crip and Blood gang members simply wore the same colors. But over time both gangs embraced the colors red or blue as part of their gang subcultures.

There is considerable lore as to why these two colors came to symbolize the two gangs. So how did colors become so important to these gangs? Some have traced the color blue to Washington High School in Los Angeles, where the Crips originated.[21] Blue was one of the school colors and was the obvious choice for Crips. The high school explanation also has been applied to the Pirus (Bloods). It is thought by some that red was adopted by the Compton Pirus because many lived near Centennial High School, where red was the school color.[22]

Other sources trace the wearing of blue by Crips and red by Bloods to the California Youth Authority (CYA) and its issuance of blue handkerchiefs to incarcerated youth in the 1970s.[23] One story is that gang youth who were sent to the Youth Training School in California were handed handkerchiefs when they entered the facility. The Crips adopted the bandanna (handkerchief) as a symbol for the Crips. Crips started wearing the blue and Bloods the red handkerchiefs as bandanas. This practice was modeled after Latino Cholo gangs in the area that had a tradition of wearing railroad bandanas. Over time each gang became strongly associated with its respective color.

Colors other than red and blue, such as green (in it for the money) and purple, have been adopted in some metropolitan areas, for example, the Grape Street Crips in Watts and some Crips in New Jersey wear purple, the Spooktown Crips wear brown, and the Asian Boy Crips wear yellow. Bloods also wear black, gray, silver, green, purple, and sometimes brown or tan. The use of multiple colors may be linked to the evolution of hybrid gangs that do not stress the traditional Crip and Blood colors.[24]

The importance of colors goes well beyond fashion. To gang members it is important to represent well their gang color in society. Color represents honor and presence in the community. As one Blood put it, "If they represent the same color than our gang, well they better represent it well." He added, "If they don't do things right, we will have to sort them out."[25]

In recent years some of the Crip and Blood gangs have limited their wearing of colors because of police crackdowns. Some gang members have avoided wearing red or blue in public altogether or do so only under specific conditions, such as special occasions. This is because law enforcement databases, heavier criminal sanctions, and other law enforcement measures make people wearing colors easy targets. Thus gang members tend to wear their colors on YouTube videos, in Internet photos, and on other forms of media when they can disguise their personal identity by covering their faces with clothing such as bandanas or scarves. In addition, when Crip or Blood members become serious about drug sales or want to quit drawing unwanted attention to themselves from law enforcement, they will either abandon their colors or deemphasize them. They do so to avoid calling attention to themselves as a matter of business and strategy. They remain Crips or Bloods but change their outward appearance based on colors or attire.

Language

In addition to values, both gangs use street slang and nonverbal gestures (hand signs) to communicate with and identify each other. Both gangs have developed their own vocabularies and codes that have special meanings to members. Many of these vocabularies and codes can be found on the numerous gang- and law enforcement–sponsored websites. Websites and especially blogs linked to both gangs have multiple examples of how gang members or those posing as gang members write with unique letters, words, and argot. The Internet has several gang-related websites and blogs through which Crips and Bloods communicate using gangster argot. To an outsider, these messages are difficult to interpret and understand. This is done to keep outsiders out of the dialogue. It is important to note that these change on a regular basis to maintain a degree of secrecy and privilege. Examples of Crip and Blood blogging that uses codes and numbers, avoids letters, and has other Crip or Blood symbols and words include:

> Whaz Craccin Cuhz? Aha we Bke killin dem sloBKz.
> > Yo that wuz cracc,en homi.
> Watz BraCKin Blood niggaz kno wat iz down here in oklahoma
> > itz Piru Blood Gang CK HK NK747.
> I B THAT YG BL61DY BANGGA, BANGIN THAT 61HARVARDPARKRENEGADE B.R.I.M. BL61D GANG . . . W61P-W61P.
> THEM TWINZ IS MY NIGGAS!, THEY GREW UP WITH US WEST L.A. TRAYS, BUT TURNED SHO-LINE CRIP

WHEN THEY GOT OLDER AND GREW UP, STILL MY NIGGAS THO!!

This unique use of words or argot is how Bloods and Crips use language (argot) to reinforce their gang identities. For example, Crips greet each other with "cuzz" (cousin) and use the initials *BK* to mean "Blood killer" as a greeting. Another greeting they use is "What it C like." They will intentionally avoid using the letter *B* in writing and spoken language. Thus words with *B*'s are spelled and pronounced with *C*'s, for example, *back* is spelled "cacc," *being* is "ceing," *bat* is spelled "cat," and *batch* is "catch." A way that Crip set members establish or confirm affiliation with other youth is to greet them with questions such as "What you be about?" or "Who you clamin?"[26] Crips have a popular mantra: "Crips don't die, they multiply."[27]

Bloods use the term *Blood* (once a sort of generic greeting between African Americans, possibly derived from the term *blood brother* or suggesting "blood" kinship, that is, a common heritage or racial background) as a greeting and the initials *CK* to mean "Crip killer" or "killa." Other salutations include "Yo Blood," "Blood," and "Wuz uo Blood." A Blood may greet another Blood by saying, "What it B like." They will avoid using the letter *C* in writing or talking in a similar fashion to Crips not using the letter *B*. Thus *Compton* becomes *Bompton*. Bloods also refer to themselves as MOBs for member of Bloods, dawgs, and ballers, which refers to selling drugs. Bloods use a common phrase "Five popping, six dropping," which means Bloods ruling and Crips losing. They also have problems with the Folk Nation (whom they consider "donuts"), which has an alliance with the Crips. Bloods on the East Coast sometimes greet each other with their signature call, "Brrrat." When making this call, they roll the *r*'s and state that when this greeting is made, everyone knows Bloods are present. As one Blood described it, "We go brrrat. It's like our signature call to each other."[28]

Hand Signs

Crips and Bloods, similar to other street gangs, use hand signals to communicate. Hand signs have been linked to black gangs of Los Angeles that have been operating since the mid-1950s.[29] Typically hands are shaped to represent letters in the set's name or gang affiliation. Often photos of sets will include members flashing or throwing hand signals. The intent of hand signals or signs often depends on the context in which they are displayed. Depending on context, hand signals can be used a variety of ways such as to greet, identify, confirm affiliation, disrespect rivals, conduct business, and bond members together. For example, Crips form *C*'s with their hands to represent the Crips. Bloods have a more challenging hand sign that spells out blood using both hands.

Each set has a unique sign language, called flashing, which serves to reinforce gang identity. Many of these hand signs can be found on the Internet and in photographs. For example, some Bloods use both hands to spell out the word blood for their gang. Pirus (Bloods) will form an upside down *P* to represent with one hand. Some hand signs are specific to local sets, such as the Rollin Harlem 30s Crips, a large Los Angeles–based gang, that points both thumbs up to represent the *H* in *Harlem*.[30]

Incarcerated Crips and Bloods are known to use hand signals to communicate. For example, East Coast Bloods developed a system of codes and hand signals they called stacks to communicate with each other while locked up. These codes and hand signals were a way for

This member of the Grape Street Crips poses with his purple bandana and flashes the double letter C with his hands. It is common when photos are taken of gang members to wear sunglass and cover their faces with their rags. (Axel Koester/Corbis)

Bloods to communicate without prison officials understanding what they were communicating. On the street these stacks were used to keep enemies from understanding Blood communications.

In addition to hand signs other physical mannerisms indicate gang membership, for example, Bloods have a particular way of walking and dancing that they label Blood-walk; Crips have a similar Crip-walk. These moves have been adopted outside of both gangs by the larger culture.

Clothing

Crips and Bloods wear distinctive clothing to identify gang membership and attract attention.[31] Heavy gold chains, national sports team shirts, jackets, hats, and brand name jogging suits are common clothing for both gangs.[32] Much of the clothing is loose fitting. Sagging, sports caps worn sideways and at different angles, jeans, bandanas, sometimes turned up baseball cap bills, team jackets, and hip-hop clothing is also popular. Hats, handkerchiefs, shoelaces, colored belts, belt buckles, and jewelry are all used to symbolize membership. The way hats or caps are worn communicates to which gang the wearer belongs.[33]

Members from both gangs have worn red or blue shoestrings to denote gang membership. "Flying the flag" refers to wearing a handkerchief of the opposing gang color in the back pants pocket. Some gang members believe that wearing the wrong color can result in physical harm or even death; it is not the color but what the color may represent that matters. It may be that one's neighborhood matters more than choice of color. One gang member commented:

> People actually think that they will kill because one wears red, and one wears blue, but we all know there is more to it than that. That's another myth I want to clear up, that Black men are not just killing each other over colors. It doesn't make any difference what you wear as long as you stay in this neighborhood, everybody knows that you stay over here, and everybody knows who you are affiliated with.[34]

Some set members disguise or hide their affiliation so as to not draw attention to their set.[35] On the West Coast, many of Crips no longer openly display their gang affiliation.

Crip Clothing Style

Tookie Williams explained why blue was selected for the Crips' color. He mentioned in his book that an original member of the gang named Buddha commonly wore blue Levi jeans, shirts, and suspenders. Buddha died on February 23, 1973, from gunshot wounds. Out of respect and to honor him, Crip gang members wore blue handkerchiefs. According to some, this wearing of the color blue would stay with and become associated with the Crips.[36] Williams wrote:

> Buddha was also the first of us Crips to style a blue bandanna. Although there have been numerous false accounts written about the origin of the blue bandanna association with the Crips, it initially became part of Buddha's color-coordinated ensemble of blue Levi's, blue shirt and dark blue suspenders. Often times, Buddha's blue bandanna hung loosely outside of his left back pants pocket— or wrapped around his head pirate style, or used to wipe his brow. (Later we would wear the blue bandanna in memorandum of Buddha's demise as a tribute to him, which eventually morphed into the allegoric color of blue for Crips.)[37]

Crips have been known to favor Dickies brand cotton work pants, athletic clothing of certain teams, and British Knights sneakers. University of North Carolina (UNC) athletic apparel has been popular for some Crips, especially for the Neighborhood Crips because both share the same initials and use the light blue color.[38] Also appealing to the Neighborhood Crips is the university's mascot, the ram, which symbolizes power and strength. In the past, Crips have used canes and worn acey-deucy hats.[39] The Crip style of dress favors the right side; thus they will dress to accent clothing on that side of the body, for example, rolling the right pant leg up, tilting their hats to the right side, wearing blue-colored laces on the right shoe, or wearing a flag to the right. However, some Crips, such as those in Minnesota, represent to the left. Crip member OG Red spoke of identity and clothing:

> If you were a Crip, you had to say you were a Crip. The clothes kind of identified you, and having your left ear pierced identified

you as being a Crip, and if you were going somewhere, no matter where you were going, you had better be dressed as a Crip.[40]

Some Crips wear clothing that conveys messages about their gang membership or is disrespectful of rival gangs. For example, to a Crip, Adidas represents "all day I disrespect all slobs" (Bloods), British Knights means "Blood killer," Burger King symbolizes "Blood killer," and Converse All Stars represents "all slobs turn and run." Sporting apparel from the Dallas Cowboys football team means "Crips out west bangin on you slobs," Colorado Rockies stands for "Crips rule," the New Orleans Saints stands for "slobs ain't shit," the Chicago White Sox means "X out slobs" or "slobs on execution," and North Carolina College stands for "Neighborhood Crips." In addition, the Georgetown Hoyas represent "Hoovers on your ass slob." Crips have also worn K-Swiss sports apparel such as shoes because to them it means "kill slobs when I see slobs."

Blood Clothing Style

Bloods, like the Crips, have their own distinctive style of clothing. Bloods often dress with certain apparel worn to the left side of the body when wearing a red bandana or flag. For example, they might wear it in their left pocket or around the ankle or wrist. They wear mostly red clothing; if they wear blue, they will put a bandage strip or a safety pin on the left side of the blue clothing to disrespect Crips.

Blood gang members, similar to Crips, like wearing their favorite sports teams' clothing. Favorite Blood teams are the San Francisco 49ers, Philadelphia Phillies, and Chicago Bulls. The Washington Nationals baseball team is also popular because of the *W*, which represents "Westside to Bloods." These teams are popular because shades of the color red are incorporated in their apparel. Blood gang members sometimes craft their own personal necklaces made from red beads. When Bloods have gatherings of members decked out in red apparel, they refer to the event as being "flamed out," "flared up," or "flamed up." A Brim (Blood) described what he and other Brims wore for identification on the street:

Our identification was one cuff up, one cuff down, and a rabbit's foot. If you were stopped by some Brims, and they said, "What set are you from?" And you said, "I'm a Brim." Well, where's your rabbit's foot?[41]

Bloods sometimes wear clothing that disrespects Crips. For example, to Bloods the CK on Calvin Klein clothing means "Crip killer," and Nike means "niggas insane and killin e-rickets."

Hair

Hairstyles among Blood and Crip members are not different from those worn by other blacks. Among the more popular styles are dreadlocks, cornrows, blade cuts with initials or designs incorporated, and plain curls. The Jheri, Jerri, Jeri, or Jerry curl is a permanent named after the hairdresser Jheri Redding, who developed the hair treatment. The Jheri curl gives the individual a glossy and loosely curled look, and it is relatively easy to maintain. Dreadlocks, dreads, dreds, or locks are worn throughout Asia, northern Africa, and the Caribbean. Dreadlocks are matted coils of hair individually styled. Typically dreadlocks are long and become twisted and matted as they grow. They are associated with the Rastafarian movement and the Caribbean, but people from many groups throughout the world have worn them. Some gang members like wearing dreadlocks.

Symbolism

Opposition to rival gangs is a central theme in gang youth's cultural imagery and symbolism. Often confrontations with rivals are a consequence of these displays, particularly in conjunction with the defense of neighborhood boundaries. For instance, Crystal explained, "If a Blood come on our set and we Crips, as long as they come on our set saying, 'What's up Blood,' they . . . just gonna start a fight. 'Cause they dis [disrespect] us by coming on our set and saying 'What's up Blood.' There ain't nobody no Blood over there."[42] A Blood named Vashelle agreed:

> A dude come over, he know what kind of hood it is to begin with. Any dude that come over there from a gang and know that's a Blood hood, you try to come over there Cripped out. You know you gonna eventually have it some way.[43]

Several Blood and Crip sets identify with specific numbers. Sometimes the numbers selected by the set correspond with the location of the housing projects they consider their turf or street blocks. There are also figures and images that have symbolic meanings for both Crips and Bloods. Examples of these include dog-faced figures in drawings and graffiti that mean down (strongly committed) to the set (gang). Gang members sometimes refer to each other as dogs.[44] One symbol shared by both gangs is hanging shoes over phone or power lines in the neighborhood. When a gang member is killed on the streets, his set members will take a pair of his or her shoes, tie them together, and throw them over a line. This means their souls are forever on the streets and always with their set. This is a form of recognition of their sacrifice for their hood and set.

Even the alphabet takes on special symbolic meanings to Crips and Bloods.[45] For example, an *S* is drawn as an upside-down *5,* and a *0* has two diagonal lines running through it. Crips also draw *K*'s backward. Bloods use a different alphabet such as a *Z* with a small star above it for the letter *I,* an upside-down *V* for *V,* and *0* with a small horizontal slash at the bottom for *P.*

Crips have their own unique group of symbols with meanings that are incorporated into their words, language, graffiti, tattoos, music, and subculture. There are too many symbols used by Crips to list here, and these are likely to change. Crip and Blood symbols are constantly changing for the benefit of the gangs and to keep ahead of the curve. Examples of symbols and meanings include Slob Killa which means "Crip who kills Bloods"; a castle, a skull, a bunny wearing a fedora (hat), a bunny head smoking, and CCN (Consolidated Crip Nation), which all mean "Crips"; and a pitchfork, heart with wings, six-pointed star, and the number 6, which all acknowledge the Crips' affiliation with the Folk Nation. C's Up! means "Crip dominance over the Bloods." East Coast Crips have a tendency to blend in a wider variety of designs into their symbols, such as adding pitchforks to their six-pointed stars.[46]

Similar to Crip symbols, there are a wide variety of Blood symbols that also change over time. To East Coast Bloods, each letter in the gang name Blood symbolizes "brotherly love overriding oppression and destruction of society."[47] References to brotherly love among Bloods are common and are frequently expressed by members from coast to coast. Bloods are represented by a five-pointed star, which stands for love, truth, peace, freedom, and justice. The five-pointed star also symbolizes Bloods' association with the People Nation of gangs. The points of the star mean body, unity, love, lust, and soul. Bloods also are represented by the name Piru, which is a Los Angeles street name and the title of a precursor gang to the Bloods; Damu, which is Swahili for "Blood"; and CK, which stands for "Crip killer." The bull and bulldog are both symbols of United Blood Nation gangs. To some Bloods, the word *dog* means "doing only gangster shit." The number 031 to an East Coast Blood means "I have love for you, Blood."[48] Thirty-six (36) and 036 mean "bitch" to East Coast Bloods. BULLS means "bloods united live longer and stronger." A black man wearing sunglasses indicates a West Coast Blood.

Bloods use a common phrase, "Five popping, six dropping," which means Bloods ruling, and the reference to six in this expression is a reference to the Crips' love of the number six.[49] Bloods also have problems with folks (whom they consider "donuts"), who have an alliance with the Crips. East Coast Blood identifiers may include graffiti such as 031, which means "I have love for you Blood." The letter *S* may be crossed out because it represents slobs (an offensive expression for Bloods). The letters *MPR* mean "money, power, and respect" to gang members.

Tattoos and Brands

Tattoos are a popular way for Crips and Bloods to communicate and are a form of gang identification. They are a mechanism by which both gangs send symbolic messages. Sometimes they are for body decoration, but mostly they tell stories. Street gangs often use tattoos and brands to indicate membership histories and roles. Tattoos and brands signify not only membership but also inside information to other gang members and opposing gangs.[50] Tattoos and brands are a permanent way to demonstrate commitment to one's set. Gangs use tattoos to distinguish who is and who is not a member, for example, some Bloods spell out the word *Bloods* across their knuckles.[51] Some Blood and Crip gang members have tattoos that include the name of the gang or set; their street name; images of weapons; other gang members' street names, deceased or alive; and other symbols of their membership. The member's life and significant events may also be represented. Some tattoos serve as historical accounts of important events that have occurred in the gang member's life such as the loss of a family member, a prison term, a fallen gang member, or girlfriends.

Representative Crip tattoos include a six-pointed star; three- or six-pointed crowns; BNC for "bad news Crip"; 211 for *B*, the second letter in the alphabet, and *K*, the eleventh letter of the alphabet to symbolize "Blood killer"; a pitchfork facing up; the number 6 in any fashion; and Crip LOB meaning "lords of brotherhood."

Bloods, such as the United Blood Nation, may have a dog paw mark (represented by three dots) on their right shoulder that is burned in by a cigarette or the red-hot barrel of a gun.[52] Tattoos are often a dog, usually the bulldog of the Mack Truck logo, that may be a burn scar or tattoo. Tattoos with the initials *MOB*, which can mean "member of Blood" or "money over bitches," are common.

Tattoos can be important to Crip and Blood gangs. Gang members sometimes use tattoos to tell their life stories, claim their set, and symbolically represent important aspects of their values and lives. Sometimes members also memorialize fallen gang members. Here a Pueblo Bishop, a Blood gang in Los Angeles, displays a stylized P and B tattoo representing his set. (Mark Peterson/Corbis)

While some gang members want to openly display their allegiance to their gang or set through tattoos, others do not want to be tagged because such symbols of gang membership may have law enforcement and legal consequences.[53] They may also identify the individual to rival gangs or sets and consequently make wearers victims. When an individual wants to leave the set, brands and tattoos can be a hindrance.

Crip and Blood Graffiti

Graffiti is one of the most important forms of gang communication. Much of the current Blood and Crip graffiti is modeled upon the original Latino gang graffiti in Southern California. Usually gang graffiti, similar to tattoos, is read from left to right and top to bottom. Sometimes both are written over or cluttered, making it difficult to read or identify. African American gangs, including the Crips and Bloods, tend to use more symbolism in graffiti to indicate gang supremacy, identity, and territory in what they call hit-ups.[54]

According to Alex Alonso, African American gang graffiti, including that of the Crips and Bloods, is less stylized than that of Latino gangs.[55] Alonso observed that Latino gangs' graffiti relies on big block letters and basic lettering. Crip and Blood graffiti has large cursive and stylized letters that flow together. Some graffiti has letters that are puffed up and can look three dimensional. Threats against other gang members and the police are common features of the graffiti. It is frequently boastful, making claims of supremacy, threatening other gangs, and making territorial claims. Blood graffiti is often in red and Crip in blue. Alonso observed:

> Bloods and Crips use a lot of symbolism and codes in their graffiti. The pit bull in the African-American gang culture of Los Angeles is always associated with the various Blood gangs and the West Blvd Crips have made use of the Warner Brothers logo as a representation of their identity. Also depictions of a chicken and a slice of bread are symbols of disrespect that have been used as challenges against rival gangs.[56]

The word *Cuzz*, or *Cuz*, is a popular salutation written in Crip graffiti.[57] Crips will replace *S*'s with *C*'s to emphasize being Crips.

Drawings of hands shaped as *C*'s, *P*'s, or other gang identification symbols may be incorporated in the graffiti. Crip symbols may include six-pointed stars, six- and three-pointed crowns, and the number six. Back-to-back *C*'s have been used by some Crip sets but may be viewed as disrespectful by some.

Graffiti numbers can be replaced with words. For example, 33 could read "trey trey," 101st Street could be written as "10 Ace Street," and 2nd Street could be "Duce Street." Gang locations are often included in the graffiti. Both gangs use arrows to identify their territories and may incorporate area codes (such as 313, 213, and 562) to identify the gang's geographical region. Dollar signs used in graffiti mean clocking dollars or making money. Messages are often coded into the graffiti, for example, the letters *MWGB* mean "murdered while gangbanging."

Tom Morgenthau provided an example of gang graffiti found on one Los Angeles wall in the late 1980s: "Big Hawk 1987 BSVG c 187." Big Hawk is the name of the gang member; *BSVG* stands for "Blood Stone Villains gang"; the *c* is crossed out, which means that the writer kills Crips and is a Blood; and *187* is the California Code offense number for murder.[58] Law enforcement agencies sometimes find that reading these codes helps them know what is going on in gang areas, and gang units typically place some importance on interpreting gang graffiti.

Gang graffiti serves multiple functions for Crip and Blood sets, as it does for other sets,[59] for example, it is a way for the gang to tell the outside world who they are and what they are about. Graffiti announces to the community that the set or gang is present and active. It communicates that a particular set is in the neighborhood and must be acknowledged and dealt with. In a sense, graffiti is a street-level advertisement for a set used to build their reputation in the hood. Sets use it as a symbol of their power and influence in the hood. Sets employ graffiti to intimidate others in the community and create a sense of fear and control. In this vein, Conquergood suggests that graffiti serves a larger purpose for sets. It symbolizes the struggle between marginalized gang members and mainstream society. Years of alienation and the lack of full opportunity, discrimination, and prejudice that are summed up in the word *marginalization* result in gangs declaring their anger against a society that excludes them.[60]

Bloods and Crips use graffiti for a variety of reasons. Often graffiti is used to mark a gang's (set's) territory. This is an example of a stylized Crip post-up in Los Angeles. (Nathan Griffith/Corbis)

A second purpose of graffiti is to mark territory/turf, which may be its most important purpose. The gangs mark their territories with graffiti, which often has coded and violent messages to rivals. For example, one gang member said the following regarding the use of X's in gang graffiti: "We put our enemies up on the wall. If there is a certain person, we 'X' that out and know who to kill."[61] Sets use graffiti to mark their boundaries and regulate neighborhoods. Gangs also use graffiti to challenge or insult rival gangs.

A further use of graffiti is listing existing members and identifying fallen members. Listing members by names or nicknames (street names) is sometimes called a roll call. Gangs use graffiti to identify members of subsets (cliques) within the gang. If a gang member is deceased, an X is often drawn through their name in the roll call. Crip and Blood sets use graffiti to honor or commemorate fallen set members. They use graffiti to memorialize gang members who have died or sacrificed for the set. These memorials to fallen set members often have more stylized lettering, are highly artistic, and are crafted to show respect.[62] These memorials sometimes reflect the status of the members when they were in the set.

Sets may use graffiti to conduct business and post news of events and activities in their territory. Past and future set activities may be posted in graffiti. Some graffiti makes statements or communicates the values of the gang to members but also to others in the hood, for example, some members may rely on graffiti to declare their allegiance to their set.

Crip and Blood gangs routinely disrespect or challenge rival gangs through graffiti. This can be a way to level threats or disrespect for rival gangs. Crip and Blood sets often embed symbols of disrespect toward each other in their graffiti. When Bloods and Crips want to disrespect each other, they write over or deface the other gang's graffiti or cross it out.[63] When gang graffiti is written over or marked up, it is generally a challenge and a sign of disrespect.

There are other ways that disrespect is demonstrated in graffiti. Bloods write names or words upside down, a clear act of gang supremacy. *B*'s or *C*'s are crossed out or defaced as a sign of disrespect by rival Crip and Blood gangs, respectively. Bloods strike through, do not use, or substitute for the letter *C* in their graffiti. Likewise, Crips do not use the letter *B* in their graffiti. Some graffiti will have *TOS* written through the name of a rival gang or member, which means "terminate on sight."[64] For some, graffiti is a safe way to inflict violence on a rival set without actual physical conflict.[65]

Nicknames

It is very common in Crip and Blood subcultures for members to have street names, or nicknames. The names used by both gangs are similar, with spellings of names avoiding *B*'s or *C*'s depending on the gang. Typically nicknames are based on some unique characteristic of the homeboy or homegirl, for example, Sexy Wayne, Tuck, Lil Loc, Big Cat, Rambo, Loc, OG, Monster, and Peanut. One of the reasons sets use nicknames is to strengthen the sense of bonding among members. The suggestion has also been made that "The real motive is to be reborn as someone, to carve out a recognition and respect that society denies."[66]

Photography

Tough guy posters and photographs of sets and gangs are very much part of the Crip and Blood subcultures. These images of gangs and sets are important in defining identities and subcultures.[67] Set members emphasize posing for photographs, as witnessed by the multitude of posed Crip and Blood images on the Internet. Photographic images of Bloods and Crips almost always emphasize unity, power, weapons, toughness, brotherhood, identity, and the threat of violence. Symbols of membership are also always present. These photographs reinforce many of the external public's stereotypes of gangs and sets.[68]

Closing Observations

There is something about gang culture that attracts youth to join. It may be the oppositional culture that gangs promote. Culturally, gangs are largely a response to a society that often rejects the youth most at risk of joining. Even so, it is important to note that even in the worst neighborhoods, most youth do not join gangs in spite of pressure to do so.

Some youth and young adults have found the Blood and Crip subcultures appealing enough to embrace and become committed members. The Bloods and Crips have been more successful than other gangs in promoting their subcultures and passing them on to mainstream society. These subcultures are fluid and constantly changing; thus they remain vibrant and not stagnant in the eyes of at-risk youth and adults. Portions of what is written today may be outdated in the near future. While some elements of these subcultures have been institutionalized and thus are permanent, others seem fleeting and evasive.

The importance of Crip and Blood subcultures to members cannot be overstated. As one author remarked:

> It is difficult to reduce gangs to organizational units alone, since there is a mercurial subculture of posses, cliques, crews, taggers, and other factions, all blending into the larger worlds of gangsta rap and hip-hop.[69]

Blood and Crip subcultures make both gangs more than simple organizational entities. Without these subcultures, there would be very little to distinguish a Crip or Blood from any other street gang. The subcultures encompass exactly what it means to be a Crip or Blood. Much of the subcultures become mythologized, that is, gang members memorize, embellish, and make them larger than life.[70]

Notes

1. Scott H. Decker, "Collective and Normative Features of Gang Violence." *Justice Quarterly* 13, no. 2 (1996), 243–264.
2. Malcolm W. Klein, "Hoover Crips: When Cripin' Becomes a Way of Life." *Contemporary Sociology: A Journal of Reviews* 37 (2008), 588.
3. Richard Swift, *Gangs* (Toronto: Groundwork, 2011), 20.
4. Herbert C. Covey, *Street Gangs throughout the World* (Springfield, IL: Charles Thomas, 2009).
5. John Pitts, "Reluctant Criminologists: Criminology, Ideology and the Violent Youth Gang." *Youth & Policy* 109 (2012), 27–45.
6. Gregor Halff, "Trusting 'Gangbangers' in War and Peace." Case Collection, accessed on August 15, 2014 at: http://ink.library.smu.edu.sg/cases_coll_all/33.
7. Juan Francisco Esteva Martínez, "Bloods." In Louis Kontos and David C. Brotherton (Eds.), *Encyclopedia of Gangs* (Westport, CT: Greenwood, 2008), 14.
8. David Starbuck, James C. Howell, and Donna J. Lindquist, "Hybrid and Other Modern Gangs." *Juvenile Justice Bulletin, December 2001* (Washington, DC: Office of Juvenile Justice and Delinquency Prevention, 2001).
9. Léon Bing, *Do or Die: America's Most Notorious Gangs Speak for Themselves* (New York: HarperCollins, 1991), 242.
10. Beth Barrett, "Gangster Menace." *Los Angeles Daily News* (September 30, 2004), accessed on May 15, 2014 at: http://lang.dailynews.com/social/gangs/articles/dnp5_main.asp.
11. Loren W. Christensen, *Gangbangers: Understanding the Deadly Minds of America's Street Gangs* (Boulder, CO: Paladin, 1999), 15.
12. Colton Simpson and Ann Pearlman, *Inside the Crips: Life Inside L.A.'s Most Notorious Gang* (New York: St. Martin's Griffin, 2005), 236.
13. Gregg W. Etter, "Gang Investigation." In Michael Birzer and Cliff Robertson (Eds.), *Introduction to Criminal Investigation* (Boca Raton, FL: CRC Press, 2012), 317.
14. Jody Miller, "Gender and Victimization Risk among Young Women in Gangs." *Journal of Research in Crime and Delinquency* 35, no. 4 (1998), 429–453.
15. Simpson, Op. cit., 98.
16. Dashaun Morris, *War of the Bloods in My Veins* (New York: Scribner, 2008), 126.
17. Ibid., 18.
18. Stanley Tookie Williams, *Blue Rage, Black Redemption: A Memoir* (New York: Simon and Schuster, 2007), 106.
19. Simpson, Op. cit.
20. See Chapter 7 for additional examples of how Crip and Blood subcultures are expressed to the broader society.
21. Etter, Op. cit., 324.
22. Bureau of Organized Crime and Criminal Intelligence, *Crips and Bloods Street Gangs* (Sacramento, CA: Author, n.d.), 3.

23. Nate B. Hendley, *American Gangsters: Then and Now; An Encyclopedia* (Santa Barbara, CA: ABC-CLIO eBook Collection, 2009).

24. Starbuck, Op. cit.

25. Karine Descormiers and Carlo Morselli, "Alliances, Conflicts, and Contradictions in Montreal's Street Gang Landscape." *International Criminal Justice Review* 21 (2011), 307.

26. Dwight Conquergood, "Street Literacy." In James Flood, Shirley Brice Heath, and Diane Lape (Eds.), *Handbook of Research on Teaching Literacy through the Communicative and Visual Arts* (New York: Simon and Schuster, 1997), 27.

27. James Diego Vigil, *A Rainbow of Gangs* (Austin: University of Texas Press, 2002), 77.

28. Gangland, "One Blood" (September 14, 2008), History Channel, originally aired May 28, 2008.

29. Shawn Booth, "Symbols." In Louis Kontos and David C. Brotherton (Eds.), *Encyclopedia of Gangs* (Westport, CT: Greenwood, 2008), 76.

30. Federal Bureau of Investigation, *Dozens of Members of Violent Street Gang Charged with Narcotics and Weapons Violation following Joint Investigation Known as Operation Thumbs Down* (Los Angeles: Federal Bureau of Investigation, Los Angeles, August 29, 2013).

31. Edward F. Dolan and Shan Finney, *Youth Gangs* (New York: Simon and Schuster, 1984).

32. Bureau of Organized Crime and Criminal Intelligence, Op. cit., 4.

33. Peter L. Patton, "The Gangstas in Our Midst." *Urban Review* 30 (1998), 49–76.

34. Yusuf Jah and Sister Shah'Keyah. *Uprising: Crips and Bloods Tell the Story of America's Youth in the Crossfire* (New York: Touchstone, 1995), 69.

35. R. Garot and J. Katz, "Provocative Looks: Gang Appearance and Dress Codes in an Inner-City Alternative School." *Ethnography* 4 (2003), 421–454.

36. Williams, Op. cit.

37. Ibid., 136.

38. Etter, Op. cit.

39. Jah, Op. cit., 124.

40. Ibid., 45.

41. Ibid., 124.

42. Jody Miller and Scott H. Decker, "Young Women and Gang Violence: Gender, Street Offending, and Violent Victimization in Gangs." *Justice Quarterly* 18 (2001), 126.

43. Ibid., 126.

44. Bill Valentine, *Gang Intelligence Manual* (Boulder, CO: Paladin, 1995), 11.

45. Patton, Op. cit., 58.

46. PoliceOne, "Gangs: East Coast Crips" (April 8, 2014), accessed on September 12, 2014 at: http://blutube.policeone.com/gang-videos/3222043850001-gangs-east-coast-crips/.

47. Gangland, "One Blood," History Channel, originally aired May 28, 2008.

48. Lou Savelli, *Gangs across America and Their Symbols* (Flushing, NY: Looseleaf, 2009), 25.
49. Gangland, "One Blood," Op. cit.
50. Valentine, Op. cit., 7.
51. Booth, Op. cit., 74.
52. Etter, Op. cit., 324.
53. Booth, Op. cit., 75.
54. Alex Alonso, *Territoriality among African American Street Gangs in Los Angeles* (Masters Thesis, University of Southern California, 1999).
55. Ibid.
56. Ibid., 18.
57. Randall R. Shelden, Sharon K. Tracy, and William B. Brown, *Youth Gangs in American Society, Second Edition* (Belmont, CA: Wadsworth, 2001), 99.
58. Tom Morgenthau, "The Drug Gangs." *Newsweek* (March 28, 1988), 20–27.
59. Jeff Ferrell, "Gang and Non-Gang Graffiti." In Louis Kontos and David C. Brotherton (Eds.), *Encyclopedia of Gangs* (Westport, CT: Greenwood, 2008), 58.
60. Conquergood, Op. cit.
61. Scott H. Decker, "Collective and Normative Features of Gang Violence." *Justice Quarterly* 13, no. 2 (1996), 258.
62. Savelli, Op. cit., 11.
63. Patton, Op. cit., 58.
64. Savelli, Op. cit., 12.
65. Ibid., 58.
66. Tom Hayden, *Street Wars: Gangs and the Future of Violence* (New York: New Press, 2004), 5.
67. Donna Decesare, "Gang Photography." In Louis Kontos and David C. Brotherton (Eds.), *Encyclopedia of Gangs* (Westport, CT: Greenwood, 2008), 70–71.
68. Ibid.
69. Hayden, Op. cit., 3.
70. See John M. Hagedorn, *A World of Gangs: Armed Young Men and Gangsta Culture* (Minneapolis: University of Minnesota Press, 2008), 11, for a discussion of how mythology is a characteristic of established gangs throughout the world.

CHAPTER SIX

Crip and Blood Involvement with Crime and Violence

It was a mind blower to hear how extreme, twisted, and powerful the hate has gotten. It's sickening. I had to ask him why? And you know what? He couldn't tell me why. All he said was "I just hate Lincoln." He didn't know why he hated them or how the war began. He was involved and hated anyone representing the green flag (Green is the Lincoln color).[1]

—Poohbie, Piru Blood

Yeah! Ain't no fun just sittin' there. Anybody can just sit around, just drink, smoke a little Thai. But that ain't fun like shootin guns and stabbin' people. That's fun.[2]

—Sidewinder, Crip

Society emphasizes Blood and Crip involvement with crime and violence. Those outside of both gangs define them through their involvement in crime, although they are mostly social entities. Many of the activities, beliefs, and attitudes of the Crips and Bloods, and for that matter other gangs, parallel ordinary youth and young adult culture. The desire to belong, bond with others of similar backgrounds, be aggressive, attach meanings to distinctive symbols, and rebel against authority are all commonly associated with youth and young adult subcultures. Viewing Crips and Bloods as primarily criminal groups separates them from these fairly normal adolescent and young adult activities.

Most members spend their time socializing, not committing crimes. Nevertheless, their involvement in crime influences most of our perceptions about them and their reactions to society. This perception reduces these gangs to criminal enterprises and diminishes their subcultural and social aspects. This is not to suggest that they are free of crime, only that we should not overemphasize their criminal involvement to the neglect of other aspects of both gangs.[3] Finally, by definition of being gangs, they and their members do have more of a criminal orientation than those individuals not belonging to gangs.[4] We know that in general gang involvement results in members committing more crimes than they would otherwise.[5] Gang membership, whether it is Blood, Crip, or some other street gang, almost always implies the individual will commit more crime, and not only do they commit more crimes, but these crimes tend to be more serious.

According to Ira Reiner, three realities of gang subculture drive crime rates: fighting, unemployment, and partying.[6] Reiner's rationale is that partying requires alcohol and drugs and that some gang members, such as Crips and Bloods, commit crimes to obtain both. Drug and alcohol use reduces inhibitions toward committing crimes. Because many gang members are out of work, crime becomes a part-time occupation to support the Blood and Crip gangster lifestyles. Drug dealing and robbery become an easy way to make quick money for unemployed gang members wanting to party.

Gang involvement in fighting also promotes criminal behavior. Blood and Crip members are at risk of increased involvement in criminal behaviors as offenders but also as victims. For example, a Crip may be shot at during a drive-by, and the code of the gang sparks feelings related to disrespect, honor, manhood, and loyalty to the gang that require a violent response. Consequently, the victimized Crip is obligated at a personal and set level to commit a violent crime in retaliation. Members of both gangs get increasingly drawn into violent behaviors because of their membership in the gang.

In addition to directly committing crimes, gang members can also be indirectly involved with collecting fees or "taxes" from non-gang members who sell drugs, are prostitutes, or commit other crimes. They extort others involved in crimes in their territories through threats and acts of violence. They also offer protection from other gangs and criminals to those in the hood. One non-Crip or Blood gang member linked his involvement in drug sales to the need for protection:

> It's mainly protection. If I'm gonna sell some dope then I got somebody to protect me. Like if a Blood or Crip try to fight me then I have some protection so we won't get no interference. If the police come I get away quicker while they be fighting.[7]

It should be noted that individuals who join gangs typically have had prior involvement with crime. By joining a gang, whatever level of involvement an individual had with criminal behavior almost always increases. In addition, research has found that gang members are more likely than those not involved with gangs to engage in violent behaviors and drug trafficking.[8] This is partially because they are now associating with others in the gang who are more committed to criminal activities. They simply have more opportunities to commit crime through their association with other gang members. They commit a disproportionate amount of crime compared to non-gang individuals. They are also more likely to be victimized than if they had never joined a set. Through their membership, they become targets.

It is essential to note that crimes committed by both gangs are typically committed by individuals or small groups of the set, not by the entire set. These individuals and small groups may or may not have the gang's objectives in mind when they commit crimes, but because they are members, the crime is often identified as being gang related. The reality may be that the gang does not condone or encourage criminal behaviors by these smaller and somewhat independent groups that often do not share their criminal profits.[9]

We know that the Crips' early crimes centered on extracting money and items from blacks in their local neighborhoods through burglary and assault.[10] Robbing perceived better-off black youth of their leather jackets would become an activity for which first-generation Crips would become notorious.[11] Reacting to being victims of Crip crimes helped fuel the evolution of the Bloods.[12]

Types of Crimes

Since their inception, Blood and Crip sets have been involved in a variety of crimes such as auto theft, burglary, assault, theft, armed robbery, homicide, and drug sales. They are best known for their involvement in drug sales, robberies, and violent crimes. The mid-1980s witnessed increased involvement by both gangs in illegal drug sales and distribution. The sale of crack cocaine would become an important criminal activity for some gangs and individual members. Their involvement in these crimes continues to present times but, similar to the overall crime rate for the nation, has been declining since roughly 1992. Recently gang-related crime has been decreasing in Blood- and Crip-dominated areas of Los Angeles. Some of this can be attributed to members of the community becoming involved in anti-crime efforts and changes in law enforcement practices. Stronger racketeering laws that hand out longer prison sentences have also made a dent in gang-related crime. The fact that many black males convicted of crimes are already incarcerated may also contribute to declining crime rates.

While assault, robbery, theft, homicide, armed robbery, and illegal drug sales continue to be the most common crimes committed by Crips and Bloods, recently some sets have expanded into non-traditional gang crimes, for example, some have delved into identity theft, human trafficking for sex, counterfeit goods, and other crimes. As one example, according to a 2012 FBI report, members of the Baby Insane Crips stole Social Security numbers and other personal identification information, falsified tax returns, and funneled refunds through family members. They used the money to purchase guns, cars, and electronics.[13] In September 2012 the leader of the Underground Gangster Crips was sentenced to prison for operating a juvenile prostitution and sex trafficking enterprise in Virginia.[14] A similar case of juvenile sex trafficking involving the Rollin 60s Crips occurred in southern California in 2012.[15] Law enforcement agencies have made connections between both gangs and the distribution of counterfeit goods such as clothes, shoes, jewelry, DVDs, medicine, and other consumer items.[16] There is some evidence that specific gangs specialize in certain crimes. Jacqueline Schneider found in Columbus, Ohio, that gangs committed certain crimes more than others and that they find their niches. She noted that a Crips gang was primarily involved in violent offenses, whereas a gang named the Freeze Crew focused on property crimes.[17]

Blood and Crip Involvement in Violent Crime

Crip and Blood involvement in violent offenses has attracted much of the public's attention. The extent of this violence is difficult to assess. This is because much of it depends on who is doing the measuring or research. One gets the impression that either there is an excessive amount of activity or it has been greatly exaggerated by the media, law enforcement personnel, and gang members. It appears that in recent years Crip and Blood violence has been declining, at least in the greater Los Angeles area and other cities.[18]

Scott Decker and G. David Curry studied gang, some of which were Crips and Bloods, and non-gang violence in St. Louis. They reported that all 100 homicide suspects were African American; only 91 percent of suspects in non-gang murders were African American.[19] Of 394 homicides not related to gangs, 82 victims were white; there was just one white victim in 77 gang homicides. Decker and Curry found the mean age of victims of homicides not related to gangs to be 31.9 years compared to 22.7 years for gang-related homicide victims, which parallels Maxson's findings.[20] Additionally, the authors reported that over half (56.7 percent) of non-gang homicide victims had an intimate relationship with gang members; 58.6 percent of gang-related homicide victims had such a relationship. More than half of the homicide victims in each category were killed on the streets, and gang members were far more likely to be killed than were people who were not in gangs. Members of gangs who were killed were most often murdered by members of their own gangs.[21]

Nationally, law enforcement statistics show that gang-related homicides declined from 2,020 in 2010 to 1,824 in 2011.[22] However, the homicide rate declined only slightly in urban areas. Evidence suggests that Crip- or Blood-related homicides do not differ from this overall pattern. Los Angeles, a stronghold of Crip and Blood sets, has seen this same pattern of decline. Gang-related homicides are reported to have decreased by almost 68 percent over an eight-year span.[23] Although not categorized by gang, Blood and Crip homicides were included in these data.

Being Street Warriors

Crip and Blood gangs have embraced the street warrior culture to facilitate their image and actions in their hoods. Gang members value being street tough and being seen as fearless warriors for their gangs. Warrior culture involves assuming the role of street or race warrior and is almost always used to promote gang objectives,[24] and acting as fearless warriors projects a tough image on the streets instills fear in the community; feared gangs and their individual members are respected and powerful in their neighborhoods. For example, by appearing and acting hard and ready to kill or do serious harm solidifies the gang's power in the community. To some, instilling fear becomes like a game.[25] The ability to stare outsiders and rivals down is part of the game. Most outsiders look away or avoid eye contact, which is interpreted as a sign of weakness and an acknowledgment of superiority on the streets. Some Crips and Bloods are better than others at staring outsiders down to submission.

The image of street warrior can be seen in books, gangster rap, and other forms of media and includes acts of intimidation, threats, and control of turf. Display of weapons, threats or acts of revenge, and actual violence serves several purposes. The warrior image can be seen on covers of books about gangs, such as Shakur's *Monster* and Léon Bing's *Do or Die,* both of which show Monster Cody as a very muscular man holding an automatic weapon. The warrior image also helps gangs exercise some level of control over their communities' underground economy. Even gang member names can reflect the street warrior image.[26] Gang members and gang names are often selected to enhance their violent image. The street warrior image is a way to control others and gain status in the community. It is a powerful influence and a way to achieve the individual's and/or gang's goals.

Attitudes toward Violence

To some observers and gang members, some neighborhoods and streets are war zones due to the pervasiveness of gang violence. In these war zones, Crip and Blood violence is an every day feature of life. Some homeboys consider themselves soldiers in gangland wars. General Robert Lee, a Blood, commented:

> Like I was telling my brother, I never considered myself a gang member, I called myself a soldier in the Brim Army. The other Brims would say, "Brim gang," I would say "Brim Army," because I felt I was a solider for the hood. The police department is the biggest gang to me.[27]

Another Blood named Bruno stated, "The hood meant life or death. It was that deep. If you said, 'F Six-Deuce,' I'd try to kill you. It was that deep."[28] Ronald Preston, an ex-gang member, summed up his view:

> We face violence every day. We hear gunshots and ambulances every day. This is not arbitrary violence; there is a logic.[29]

The logic he is referring to is the purposeful violence of the streets. Colton Simpson shared his attitude toward violence when he was a teenage Crip and the price paid when a gang member was caught in a rival gang's territory, which is referred to as slippin:

> In my 'hood, those who perfect robbing, selling drugs, and killing rise to celebrity status and have supreme power that keeps them from becoming victim to someone else's violence. We believe this so wholeheartedly, when a friend is killed, we figure it's a fluke— he's in the wrong place at the wrong time. Or we blame him—he was caught "slippin."[30]

To Simpson, violence was something that happened to others because they messed up or were unlucky. He attributed some of his beliefs to the distortion that comes from heavy drug use. Regardless, violence is assumed to be a natural and expected aspect of life in the hood.

It is difficult to find a homeboy who has not lost at least one friend or family member to gang violence. Many homeboys are fatalistic and do not expect to have long lives or any future. Some do not expect to live much beyond their mid-twenties. They believe that the American dream is not out there for them, and the only options are death or prison; hence with nothing to lose they are willing to take risks that others would not. They view death as at their doorstep, certain, and a reality of life. The constant violence results in stress that weighs heavy on some, as they must constantly be looking over their shoulders. Skip Townsend, a Rollin 20 Blood from West Adams in Los Angeles summed up his day-to-day life in the hood:

> I mean I couldn't even pump gas. I couldn't go to the grocery store. I couldn't do anything without interacting with someone who would want to hurt me or I'd have to hurt them.[31]

Many homeboys have scars from violence encountered due to membership in their sets. To these homeboys, the scars are similar to badges of honor that they proudly display. For some members to die for the gang at the hands of rivals is to die with honor. They assume that if they die for their set, they will become legends. Members are obligated to stand up and fight for their sets, and those who choose not to can face negative consequences. A Blood stated:

> If you can't stand up for yourself in my hood, if you can't bang, you are considered dry, weak, a punk. You are looked down upon, laughed at, beat up, and humiliated.[32]

Public image is important to both Bloods and Crips. As OG Red, a Crip, stated:

> The thing I want to say to the younger homiez is that we all try to portray an image that we don't have any feelings, and that we're so hard, when the whole thing that's generating that is fear. Fear to really let somebody know what's in your heart.[33]

Crip and Blood members often view violence as the only way they can get what they want in life. In the hood violence is an effective way to exercise power, have control, and accomplish what you want. Homeboys know that status in the hood is gained by the use of violence and antisocial behavior.[34] Individually and collectively, homeboys often do not have non-violent tools for resolving disputes; thus they resort to violence. Put simply, it works well for them. As one female Crip shared in a 1996 video on gang violence, pointing a gun at someone is a rush because they will do whatever you want,[35] it is exciting and powerful.

Given the pervasiveness of violence, survival depends on deciding within seconds whether to trust or attack others.[36] Some have noted that Crips and Bloods today are quicker to turn to violence and use weapons than other gangs, perhaps because of the perceived necessity of deciding quickly to attack or become a rival's victim. Santaya Shakur suggested that getting the drop on a rival can be the difference between life and death. He shared with journalist Léon Bing:

> At any time you can be on either side of the gun. It's as simple as carrying one. And drawing first. . . . Speed, agility, experience determine who is going to be the victim and who will be the assailant. And of course, luck enters into it.[37]

Violence can help unite groups, including street gangs.[38] External threats to any group, whether it be the United States following 9/11, Israel during the Six Day War, or Londoners under German bombardment, serve to unite people. Having a common foe, such as a rival gang or law enforcement agencies, can help a gang, including the Crips and Bloods, coalesce into a tighter unit.[39] However, violence may also break down some gangs. Scott Decker and Janet Lauritsen found evidence that some members leave their gangs to avoid violence.[40] They get tired of seeing people die or be hurt and worry about their own safety.

Culture of the Gun

Today guns in the possession of gang members translate into power and status on the street. To use guns in drive-bys or other shootings is a way to gain a reputation on the streets. For example, gang member

Moses shared that among gang members, "Just to have a gun was cool." He added, "The power of having a .22 or .25 in my waistband was exhilarating."[41] A Blood shared his habit of brandishing his gun: "As I rap in chorus, I wave my gun around in the air."[42]

Some gang members are not enamored with guns. In the beginning, the founders of the Crips and Bloods preferred fists over the use of weapons. However, when they did use weapons, rocks, clubs, bats, and knives were selected over guns. Fistfights were viewed as the more manly way to establish neighborhood power and control. Crip co-founders Raymond Washington and Stanley "Tookie" Williams both wrote and spoke about their dislike for weapons, especially guns. They viewed the use of guns and other weapons as a sign of weakness. In their opinion real men fought it out without weapons. In his memoir Williams wrote about hating the use of guns: "The horrors of gunplay disturbed me so much that for a long time, I had to distance myself from possessing one."[43] However, he was eventually came to use guns out of necessity.

Guns are a major part of Crip and Blood gangs. This photograph shows guns confiscated by law enforcement personnel during a June 17, 2014, raid on the Broadway Gangster Crips in Los Angeles. The display shows a wide variety of weapons, many automatic, that were found during the raid. Guns are relatively easy to acquire on the streets. (Jonathan Alcorn/Corbis)

Over time weapons came to be seen as a necessary component of any gang conflict. In the late 1960s the violence escalated to the point that handguns became increasingly prevalent and were used during confrontations.[44] Some Blood and Crip members say guns were introduced into their scene in the mid-1970s; others say it was in the 1980s.[45] Regardless, both gangs started to use guns and showed little remorse for their victims.

The increasing availability of guns on the streets is often linked to the large amount of gang violence. Easy access to powerful automatic weapons has affected the balance of power on the streets. The violent and risky nature of the drug trade coupled with easy access to weapons has made conditions ripe for gun-associated violence. The weapon of choice is now a handgun or an automatic weapon. When Bloods and Crips have a gun, it is most often a handgun.[46] According to law enforcement agencies the Bloods and Crips ranked numbers one and two, respectively, for firearm recoveries in 2013.[47] The proliferation of semiautomatic weapons, automatic weapons, and sawed off shotguns on the streets as well as the profitability of the drug trade fuel much weapon-related violence. Over the years automatic weapons such as Mac-10s, Mac-9s, Uzis, and AK-47s became more common. Images of Bloods and Crips more frequently incorporated guns. In photographs set members hold or display weapons. A good example of this is the cover photo of Monster Kody (Shakur Sanyika) on Léon Bing's book *Do or Die*.

In Los Angeles law enforcement data indicate that 80 to 82 percent of all gang-related homicides involved guns. It is well documented that gang members, including Bloods and Crips, are more likely to carry and use guns than are people who do not belong to gangs. However, it is important to note that research has also found that many gang members used guns before joining gangs.[48] When gang members drop out of gangs, their involvement with guns typically decreases.[49] Whether gun-involved youth are attracted to the Crips and Bloods or whether the gangs are inclined to recruit these youth is unclear.

Gang Rivalry and Violence

Gang banging, or banging, is a common expression in both gangs and is often incorporated into their dialogue. Conflicts among gangs or sets may occur for a variety of reasons, including turf battles, interpersonal disagreements, and retaliation.[50] Some Crip and Blood members view violence as a way to become a hero, if they are killed in the service of the gang. It is important to note that inter-gang violence is not always present. In some cities Crip and Blood homeboys and homegirls interact across set lines as friends, lovers, and business associates.[51] There is no strict rule in this regard, but violence between the two gangs and within the gangs is widely acknowledged as the more dominant pattern.

In his research on drive-by shootings in San Diego, William Sanders made an important point about the rivalry between the Bloods and Crips.[52] In San Diego both gangs had no reason to hate each other, but the lore of both being violent enemies with a deep-rooted distain for each other in Los Angeles carried over to the gangs in San Diego. This same pattern has been carried into other cities. Ironically, although they appear to hate each other due to neighborhood affiliation, Bloods and Crips generally come from the same racial and socioeconomic backgrounds,[53] that is, they have low incomes, are black, come from the same neighborhoods, are unemployed, and are not formally educated. In response to racism, oppression, and inadequate education, one homeboy noted, "We started blaming each other, and taking it out on one another."[54] Although many of them share common backgrounds, they nevertheless treat the other as the enemy.

Viewing other street gangs of different ethnicities as enemies (at least outside of prison walls) occurs but not to the same extent as between Crips and Bloods or Crips and Crips. On Crip and Blood rivalry with Latinos, rapper Ice T wrote an observation in 1995:

> The Blacks and the Latinos never had any beef with each other in L.A. If you go to prison, everybody sides up because that's prison, prison is another whole game. But on the streets of L.A. there has never been Black vs. Latino warfare.[55]

This pattern may be changing, as MS 13, Nutreno, and Sureno gangs are beginning to push into traditionally black neighborhoods in Los Angeles.

Crip and Blood gang members can be quick to react to threats, disrespect, or anything that they view as interfering with gang values.

Ice T likened the willingness of gang members to gang bang with being in love. He wrote:

> What gang-banging really is, is male love pushed to the limits. It's like surrogate families and brothers bonding together to the death, because it's not about selling drugs or all about banging, it's about kickin' it with the homiez and backing the homiez. It's love. . . . To the layman it will look like it's a world based on hate, but it's not, it's based on love. It's a love for the hood.[56]

An example of Crip and Blood rivalry that resulted in significant violence was the 2005 South Central Los Angeles shooting of Branden Bullard. Bullard, the leader of the Grape Street Crips, was shot in the face on Christmas morning. This resulted in a gang war between the Crips and the Bloods involving more than 20 shootings and 8 deaths. The following Crip statement captures how quickly the Crip versus Blood violent rivalry can be expressed:

> Somebody who is fighting over colors. Somebody approach me and say, "What's up Blood," and I'm going to say killer. They down on my set, they know I'm a Crip. If they come here and say "What's up Blood," I'm going to say killer. That mean I'm a killer. Then we will probably fight or shoot or whatever. Whatever happen it happen.[57]

Crip and Blood gangs are portrayed as having a violent and bitter rivalry. Getting revenge seems to be a common motivation for gang violence. Nikko, a Crip, explained how set rivalries played out on the street, saying, "Whatever they do, you counterattack."[58] One Blood homeboy stated, "We must fight the Crips at a moment's notice. We attack by drive-bys or doing walk ups."[59] Another Blood describing the relationship between Bloods and Crips characterized it as "Negative, because they are Blue." He added, "Everything that's Blue, we clean up."[60] One account by a Brim (Blood) described how gang rivalry played out in the early 1970s when a Blood was buried:

> His coffin was in a Crip neighborhood at the funeral place, and the Crips went in there and turned his casket over and wrote crazy

things in the sign-in book, and then wrote up his casket. That's when the war started. After that we made a bond that every year on his birthday, and on the day he got killed, we had to go out and kill some of them.[61]

Gang rivalries and other conflicts can quickly get out of hand and seem crazy to participants, for example, Sanyika Shakur described what it was like to be caught up in a gang war:

By now, with the wars raging out of control and my paranoia peaking, I had ceased to recognize people—that is to say, gang members—by name. Gang members became recognizable as streets or sets. Further recognition fell into "enemy" or "friend" categories, which of course meant kill or let live. I forgot individual names, but I never failed to link a face with a set.[62]

The Crips are also known for their intra-gang rivalries and violence. Original fights were over hangout spots, parties, or high school but this changed. When the Crips were a relatively small set confined to a few neighborhoods, Crip on Crip violence was likely rare. As the Crips grew in number and split into numerous independent sets, the chances of violence between these splintered sets increased, and they began to battle each other. By the 1980s, Crips had developed rivalries with other Crips.[63] Intra-gang warfare, especially between Crip sets, has been a major source of violence. One Crip shared, "You see, most Crip gangs' worst enemies are other Crips." He added, "This produces a lot of Crip-on-Crip violence, especially in the modules."[64] Modules refers to pods of cells in a correctional facility. In the Los Angeles area Crip gangs such as the South Side Village Gangster Crips from Pomona declared war on all Crip gangs with names ending with a zero, such as the Rollin 40s and Rollin 50s.[65] It has often been noted that more Crips kill other Crips than kill Bloods. Wes McBride, a deputy sheriff and anti-gang detail member reported that Crips kill other Crips at three times the rate that they do Bloods.[66] Because there are more Crips than Bloods, this makes sense. When Bloods fight with Crips, it is important for as many Bloods to be involved as possible because overall there are fewer Bloods.[67]

Fights between Crip factions were said to be responsible for up to half of all inter-gang fights in the Los Angeles area in 1988.[68] One study conducted in Saint Louis found that homicides involving Crips killing other Crips accounted for 61.5 percent of all gang-related homicides.[69] In the same vein, a multiyear study of Chicago gangs found that most of the gang homicides were intraracial and occurred within the gangs, not between them.[70]

One of the bloodiest conflicts occurred from 1979 to 1980 between two Crip sets, the Eight Trays and the Rolling 60s.[71] The rivalry started in South Central Los Angeles when OG Raymond Washington of the Eastside Crips was killed by the Hoover Crips. Following his murder, Crip members from all over began to pick sides, which resulted in several shootings and the deaths of two dozen individuals.[72]

The Los Angeles County Sheriff's Department has concluded that Bloods fight Crips and Crips fight Crips, but Bloods do not typically fight other Blood gangs.[73] But not everyone agrees. Blood gang member Dashaun Morris stated, "Unlike what most people believe, on the East Coast there is more Blood-on-Blood killings than Blood vs. Crip."[74] An example of Bloods having conflicts with other Bloods can be seen with the Bounty Hunter Bloods of the Nickerson Gardens housing project in South Central Los Angeles.[75] This ongoing conflict started when younger Bounty Hunters challenged older members who had returned from prison as to who should control the gang. The confrontation resulted in shootings and multiple homicides.

In recent years violence between Latino gangs and the Crips and Bloods has been occurring in some areas of Los Angeles such as Compton.[76] As Latinos moved into traditional black neighborhoods and housing projects in Los Angeles, they began to come into conflict with blacks. Initially the conflicts were over control of illicit drug distribution. Regarding the inter-gang violence in Compton, one gang member commented, "It's all about the money."[77] At times these drug wars have taken on racist overtones.

Finally, a recent study found that most Crip and Blood violence targeted non-gang members, calling into question the hypothesis that most gang-related violence is directed toward rival gang members.[78] Whether this pattern is common or emerging will require more study.

Drive-By Shootings

Blood and Crip gangs participate in drive-by shootings and have done so since they adopted the use of guns. According to the Los Angeles Police Department:

> The "drive-by" shooting is the most frequent violent crime committed by gangs. Members from one gang will seek out the homes, vehicles or hang-outs of a rival gang and, using an assortment of weapons, will drive by and shoot at members of that gang. Usually, the gang member will yell out the gang name or a slogan so the attacked gang will know who was responsible.[79]

Drive-by shootings are viewed as a way to extend the gang's reputation as being violent and tough, a way to control territory, a way to exact revenge against rivals, and as an initiation ceremony for new gang members; the most prevalent purposes are payback to resolve ongoing issues between gangs and revenge killings. They are often the result of long-term inter-gang feuds and revenge cycles that take on lives of their own.

Some gang members mention the adrenaline rush (high) and excitement they get from a drive-by shooting; they feel that to shoot at an unsuspecting group of rivals and get away with it is exciting. Diwi Morris, a Blood, described a typical drive-by:

> Once we get to Dodd Town, we ride around looking for the prey before spotting a group of guys huddled around a car. I tell Tiffany to circle the block, and pull alongside them so we can blast them. It's five of them and two females in the car from what I can see. Dodd Town is known for Crip activity, so anything in blue is an immediate target. As we drive past these guys, they seem to all be dressed down in blue, or so I think. The mission is to eliminate anything breathing, Operation paint the town Red.[80] ... Boom! Boom! I fire again as the remaining targets run in all directions, desperately trying to avoid slugs meant to erase them.[81]

A Crip described how a drive-by worked in his set. He shared that a car with four homeboys and one OG would play gangsta rap music loud, drink alcohol, and smoke marijuana in the car. They would then drive to a location where rival Bloods were known to hang out. One younger homeboy would be given a gun and told to shoot at the rivals. If there was only one rival, the option was for the shooter to get out of the car and shoot at the intended victim and meet the car around the corner. The alcohol, rap music, marijuana, and peer pressure energized the youth to shoot.[82]

The mechanization of violence through guns and especially rapid-fire guns, has shortened the duration of violent encounters between rival gangs. Drive-by shootings between Crips and Bloods occur within seconds and have nothing in common with the gang rumbles and street fights of earlier decades. Violent gang conflicts became short-term armed forays into a rival gang's neighborhood. The drive-by can happen almost anywhere at any time. Thus the element of surprise is a critical element of the drive-by. The best drive-bys are those that are done quickly on unsuspecting victims. Drive-bys are and will continue to be a source of power for all gangs, including the Crips and Bloods, into the foreseeable future.

Because Bloods and Crips often are under the influence of drugs and/or alcohol while partying or just hanging out, they make excellent targets for drive-by shooters. William Sanders provides examples of drive-bys that occurred in San Diego, California, involving Crips and Bloods:

> Members of the Eastside Piru were hanging out in front of a liquor store when a car drove by. Some Crips in the car said "What's up, Blood?" The Pirus ignored them and walked away. After a Piru member refused to come over to their car, the Crips began firing, hitting the victim three times. Then the Crips drove away.
>
> A member of the Neighborhood Crips was sitting on a wall when he heard a car drive up. He turned to look at the car and then turned back. At this point he was shot in the head. The victim ran into a friend's house, noting only that the shooter was wearing red.[83]

Innocent Bystanders

At times, it seems like the media pays relatively little attention to gang-related homicides, other violence, and other crimes. Occasionally violent encounters between Bloods and Crips have been documented and have led to public concern. This is especially true when innocent bystanders get caught up in episodes of gang violence. On a societal level, it seems there is little concern over gang-related deaths if it is simply one gangster killing another. However, when innocent victims are caught up in gang violence, the stakes are raised, and there is often public outcry for something to be done. In their book on gang violence, Simmons and Moses describe a drive-by shooting during which a brother-in-law is shot to death:

> "Look out," somebody screamed as a car drove by and just started shooting at anyone that was out and about. When the gunfire ceased, my brother-in-law Sherman Dobbins was shot, laid out, shot by a drive-by shooter. The Nickerson Garden Projects was where this took place at. Sherman was a married man in his forties that had nothing to do with gangs.[84]

There are notable examples of innocent people being victims of gang warfare. Tennis stars Venus and Serena Williams lost an older sister to gang violence while she was sitting in an SUV in Compton. The 1988 accidental shooting of Karen Toshima in Hollywood is another example. Other incidents of innocent bystanders being injured or killed by Bloods and Crips have occurred.[85]

Concluding Observations

There is little question that with membership in the Bloods or Crips comes increased involvement in crime and violence. As is documented in the literature, both gangs are involved in serious crime and violence. Both gangs commit property crimes such as theft, carjacking, and robbery for economic gain. Violent crimes tend to be associated with pride, reputation, and territory, and they can be expressive, such as over respect, or instrumental, such as over control of drug distribution. Gang-related homicide and assault may be increasing due to heightened competition for limited territory. No one questions that Crip and Blood violence can be extremely brutal. For some gang members this violence is linked to making money. For others it is only part of what they do as members of a set and is not a focus.

The reliance on using weapons has increased over the history of both gangs. Initially the gang founders did not rely on weapons, as they were viewed as a sign of weakness. With the increased availability of guns, and generations of younger gang members more than willing to use them, there has been an escalation of Crip and Blood violence. In recent years, however, in some areas of the country this violence has seemed to be waning.

Both gangs nurture criminal and violent public images. Members of both gangs promote their image as street warriors. The more criminal and violent an individual is on the streets, the more respect they garner in the neighborhood. This theme is expressed in the autobiographies of current and ex-gang members.[86] Certainly violence and homicide rates are higher for gang members than those not belonging to gangs. But it is important to note that when gang members are alone, they often report how uncomfortable they are with the violence, and they want it to stop.[87] In other words, the tough gangster and warrior image is for social consumption, not the way they feel on the inside.

Notes

1. Donovan Simmons and Terry Moses, *Bloods and Crips: The Genesis of a Genocide* (Bloomington, IN: Authorhouse, 2009), 62.
2. Léon Bing, *Do or Die: America's Most Notorious Gangs Speak for Themselves* (New York: HarperCollins, 1991), 49.
3. Mark Fleisher, "Inside the Fremont Hustlers." In Jody Miller, Cheryl L. Maxson, and Malcolm W. Klein (Eds.), *The Modern Gang Reader, Second Edition* (Los Angeles: Roxbury, 2001), 100.
4. G. David Curry and Scott H. Decker, "What's in a Name? A Gang by Any Other Name Isn't Quite the Same." *Valparaiso University Law Review* 31 (1997), 501–514. See also G. David Curry and Scott H. Decker, *Confronting Gangs: Crime and Community, Second Edition* (Los Angeles: Roxbury, 2003).
5. Numerous studies have documented the increase in crime and delinquent behavior resulting from gang membership, for example, see Finn-Aage Esbensen and David Huizinga, "Gangs, Drugs, and Delinquency in a Survey of Urban Youth." *Criminology* 31 (1993), 565–589; Sara Battin, Karl Hill, Robert Abbott, Richard Catalono, and J. David Hawkins, "The Contribution of Gang Membership to Delinquency Beyond Delinquent Friends." *Criminology* 36 (1980), 105–106;

Terence Thornberry, Marvin Krohn, Alan Lizotte, and Deborah Chard-Wierschem. "The Role of Juvenile Gangs in Facilitating Delinquent Behavior." *Journal of Research in Crime and Delinquency* 30 (1993), 55–87.

6. Ira Reiner, *Gangs, Crime and Violence in Los Angeles: Findings and Proposals from the District Attorney's Office* (Arlington, VA: National Youth Gang Information Center, 1992), 55.

7. Ibid., 506.

8. James C. Howell and Scott H. Decker, "The Youth Gangs, Drugs, and Violence Connection." *Juvenile Justice Bulletin* (Washington, DC: OJJDP, January 1999).

9. Randall G. Shelden, Sharon K. Tracy, and William B. Brown, *Youth Gangs in American Society, Second Edition* (Belmont, CA: Wadsworth, 2001), 108.

10. United Gangs of America, "Crips," accessed on August 14, 2014 at: UnitedGangs.com.

11. See George Percy Barganier, III, *Fanon's Children: The Black Panther Party and the Rise of the Crips and Bloods in Los Angeles* (Ph.D. dissertation, University of California, Berkeley, 2011), 68; Yusuf Jah and Sister Shah'Keyah, *Uprising: Crips and Bloods Tell the Story of America's Youth in the Crossfire* (New York: Touchstone, 1995), 152.

12. See Chapter 2 for a detailed account of why this was the case.

13. National Gang Intelligence Center, *2013 National Gang Report* (Washington, DC: Federal Bureau of Investigation, 2014), 26.

14. Ibid., 44.

15. Ibid., 45.

16. Ibid., 27.

17. Jacqueline Schneider, "Niche Crime: The Columbus Gangs Study." *American Journal of Criminal Justice* 26 (2001), 93–107.

18. For example, see Centers for Disease Control and Prevention, "Gang Homicides: Five U.S. Cities, 2003–2008." *Morbidity and Mortality Weekly Report* 61, no. 3 (January 27, 2012), 46–51.

19. Scott H. Decker and G. David Curry, "Gangs, Gang Homicides and Gang Loyalty: Organized Crimes or Disorganized Criminals?" *Journal of Criminal Justice* 30 (2002), 343-352.

20. Cheryl L. Maxson, "Gang Homicide: A Review and Extension of the Literature." In M. Dwayne Smith and Margaret A. Zahn (Eds.), *Homicide: A Sourcebook of Social Research* (Thousand Oaks, CA: Sage, 1999).

21. Decker and Curry, Op. cit., 350.

22. Office of Juvenile Justice and Delinquency Prevention, *Highlights of the 2011 National Youth Gang Survey* (Washington DC: Author, 2013), 1.

23. KPCC Wire Services, "Crime in Los Angeles Drops in First Quarter of 2013" (April 5, 2013).

24. Gregg W. Etter, "Gang Investigation." In Michael Birzer and Cliff Robertson (Eds.), *Introduction to Criminal Investigation* (Boca Raton, FL: CRC Press, 2012).

25. Bing, Op. cit., 40–41.

26. See Etter, Op. cit.

27. Jah, Op. cit., 121.

28. Jah, Op. cit., 174.

29. Beth Barrett, "Gangster Menace." *Los Angeles Daily News* (September 30, 2004), accessed on July 14, 2014 at: http://lang.dailynews.com/social/gangs/articles/dnp5_main.asp.

30. Colton Simpson and Ann Pearlman, *Inside the Crips: Life Inside L.A.'s Most Notorious Gang* (New York: St. Martin's Griffin, 2005), 151–152.

31. Frank Stoltze, "Forget the LA Riots: Historic 1992 Watts Gang Truce Was the Big News," accessed on September 12, 2014 at: http://www.scpr.org/news/2012/04/28/32221/forget-la-riots-1992-gang-truce-was-big-news/.

32. Dashaun Morris, *War of the Bloods in My Veins: A Street Soldier's March toward Redemption* (New York: Scribner, 2008), 69.

33. Yusuf Jah and Sister Shah'Keyah, *Uprising: Crips and Bloods Tell the Story of America's Youth in the Crossfire* (New York: Touchstone, 1995), 61.

34. Etter, Op. cit., 314.

35. A & E Home Video, 20th Century with Mike Wallace, *Gang Violence in America* (New York: A & E Home Video, 1996).

36. Gregor Halff, "Trusting 'Gangbangers' in War and Peace," accessed on August 15, 2014 at: http://ink.library.smu.edu.sg/cases_coll_all/33.

37. Léon Bing, Op. cit., 245.

38. Malcolm W. Klein, *Street Gangs and Street Workers* (Englewood Cliffs, NJ: Prentice Hall, 1971).

39. See Ibid.; Malcolm W. Klein, *The American Street Gang* (New York: Oxford University Press, 1995).

40. Scott H. Decker and Janet L. Lauritsen, "Leaving the Gang." In C. Ronald Huff (Ed.), *Gangs in America III* (Thousand Oaks, CA: Sage, 2002), 51–67.

41. Simmons, Op. cit., 2.

42. Morris, Op. cit., 115.

43. Williams, Op. cit., 81.

44. Wayne Caffey, *Crips and Bloods* (Los Angeles: Los Angeles County Sheriff's Office, 2006), 2.

45. Jah, Op. cit., 50, 70.

46. National Gang Intelligence Center, *2013 National Gang Report* (Washington, DC: Federal Bureau of Investigation, 2013), 35.

47. Ibid., 36.

48. Beth Bjerregaard and Alan J. Lizotte, "Gun Ownership and Gang Membership." In Jody Miller, Cheryl L. Maxson, and Malcolm W. Klein (Eds.), *The Modern Gang Reader, Second Edition* (Los Angeles: Roxbury, 2001), 224.

49. Ibid., 224.

50. Scott H. Decker and David C. Pyrooz, "Gang Violence Worldwide: Context, Culture, and Country." In Eric G. Berman, Keith Krause, Emile LeBrun, and

Glenn McDonald (Eds.), *Small Arms Survey 2010: Gangs, Groups and Guns* (New York: Cambridge University Press, 2010).

51. Mark S. Fleisher, *Beggars and Thieves* (Madison: University of Wisconsin Press, 1995).

52. William B. Sanders, "Drive-Bys." In Jody Miller, Cheryl L. Maxson, and Malcolm W. Klein (Eds.), *The Modern Gang Reader, Second Edition* (Los Angeles: Roxbury, 2001), 200.

53. It is interesting to note that East Coast Bloods sometimes refer to their victims of violence as "food." Possibly this is a Blood reference to having an appetite for violence.

54. Jah, Op. cit., 69.

55. Ice T, "Foreword." In Yusuf Jah and Sister Shah'Keyah, *Uprising: Crips and Bloods Tell the Story of America's Youth in the Crossfire* (New York: Touchstone, 1995), 15.

56. Ibid., 23.

57. G. David Curry and Scott H. Decker, "What's in a Name? A Gang by Any Other Name Isn't Quite the Same." *Valparaiso University Law Review* 31 (1997), 506.

58. Stacy Peralta, *Crips and Bloods Made in America* (Docuramafilms, 2009), 37, 50.

59. Morris, Op. cit., 116.

60. Karine Descormiers and Carlo Morselli, "Alliances, Conflicts, and Contradictions in Montreal's Street Gang Landscape." *International Criminal Justice Review* 21 (2011), 306.

61. Jah, Op. cit., 123.

62. Sanyika Shakur, *Monster: The Autobiography of an L.A. Gang Member* (New York: Penguin, 1993), 77.

63. See the Crip on Crip violence discussion in Bill Valentine, *Gang Intelligence Manual: Identifying and Understanding Modern Gangs in the United States* (Boulder, CO: Paladin, 1995); John C. Quicker and Akil Batani-Khalfani, "From Boozies to Bloods: Early Gangs in Los Angeles." *Journal of Gang Research* 5 (1998), 15–21.

64. Simmons, Op. cit., 92.

65. Valentine, Op. cit., 50.

66. National Public Radio, "Tookie Williams and the History of the Crips" (December 7, 2005).

67. Valentine, Op. cit., 49.

68. Bob Baker, "Homeboys: Players in a Deadly Drama." *Los Angeles Times* (June 26, 1988).

69. Decker and Curry, Op. cit., 350.

70. Andrew V. Papachristos, "Murder by Structure: Dominance Relations and the Social Structure of Gang Homicide." *American Journal of Sociology* 115 (2009), 74–128.

71. Juan Francisco Esteva Martínez and Marcos Antonio Ramos, "Crips." In Louis Kontos Louis and David C. Brotherton (Eds.), *Encyclopedia of Gangs* (Westport, CT: Greenwood, 2008), 44; Randall G. Shelden, Sharon K. Tracy, and William B. Brown, *Youth Gangs in American Society, Second Edition* (Belmont, CA: Wadsworth, 2001), 117.

72. Bob Baker, Op. cit.

73. Los Angeles County Sheriff's Department, *L.A. Style: A Street Gang Manual of the Los Angeles County Sheriff's Department*. Los Angeles, Los Angeles Sheriff's Department, 1992.

74. Morris, Op. cit., 166.

75. Wayne Caffey, *Crips and Bloods* (Los Angeles: Los Angeles County Sheriff's Office, 2006), 6.

76. Ross Kemp, *Ross Kemp on Gangs: Los Angeles* (British Sky Broadcasting, 2008).

77. Ibid.

78. Jasmin B. Randle, *Los Angeles County's Criminal Street Gangs: Does Violence Roll Downhill?* (Electronic Theses, Projects, and Dissertations. Paper 10, 2014)

79. Los Angeles Police Department, "What Gangs Do," accessed on February 15, 2014 at: http://www.lapdonline.org/get_informed/content_basic_view/23469.

80. Morris, Op. cit., 110.

81. Ibid., 117.

82. Stanley S. Taylor, "Why American Boys Join Gangs." *African Journal of Law and Criminology* 2, no. 1 (2012), 56–68.

83. Sanders, Op. cit., 200.

84. Simmons, Op. cit., 9.

85. Karen Umemoto, *The Truce: Lessons from an L.A. Gang War* (Ithaca, NY: Cornell University Press, 2006), 2.

86. For example, see Sanyika Shakur, *Monster: The Autobiography of an L.A. Gang Member* (New York: Penguin, 1993); Colton Simpson and Ann Pearlman, *Inside the Crips: Life Inside L.A.'s Most Notorious Gang* (New York: St. Martin's Griffin, 2005).

87. For example, see comments in Daniel Duane, "Straight Outta Boston." *Mother Jones* (January 1, 2006), accessed on September 1, 2014 at: http://www.mother jones.com/print/15100.

Blood and Crip Involvement with Alcohol and Illegal Drugs

In our neighborhoods, the number one thing affecting the black male is the alcohol. Everybody wants to drink.[1]

—Angelo, Blood

They don't smoke rock, but they smoke Primos, smoke weed, and drink Michelob.[2]

—Unknown Name, St. Louis 6th Street Hoover Crip

Alcohol and Illegal Drug Use by Gang Members

Similar to other gangs, it is well established that Crips and Bloods use alcohol and illicit drugs. Given the social nature of gangs, this should come as no surprise. The observation is often forwarded that gang involvement leads to more use of alcohol and illicit drugs. Studies have shown that use of marijuana, phencyclidine (PCP), heroin, crack, and cocaine is higher among gang members than among those not affiliated with a gang.[3] However, other studies suggest that it depends on the type of illicit drug and gang. For example, Scott H. Decker found that while drug use is high among gang members, it may be even higher among non-gang members. Specifically, in many of the gangs he studied, marijuana use was acceptable, but use of more serious drugs was not.[4] One Blood from Saint Louis said, "Naw, just smoke weed, that's all."[5] Researchers mentioned that gang members often mentioned alcohol and illegal drugs. A Crip reflecting on his life on the street shared:

> I realize I was under the influence of PCP practically all of my life. I was walking in an intoxicated haze and believe me when I say at times it feel like I still am.[6]

Crip and Blood Involvement in Illegal Drug Sales

One of the more controversial topics regarding the Crips and Bloods is the nature of their involvement in drug trafficking. Many would agree that the expansion of Crip and Blood gangs across the United States is due to their involvement with the drug trade.[7] In the mid-1980s they were involved with distributing drugs such as marijuana, amphetamine, LSD, and PCP. It is generally thought that Crip and Blood gangs expanded considerably in the 1980s due to their participation in the crack cocaine trade. Drug distribution and sales proved to be profitable to both, and controlling territories for the distribution of drugs became important. Driven by profits from the distribution of crack cocaine, the number of Bloods grew, inducing some "entrepreneurial" homeboys to move to urban areas outside of Los Angeles to establish new illegal drug markets. In addition to crack, PCP dominated the streets and provided a way for gang members to make money. One gang member recalled PCP:

> Some smoked it to become the greatest gangbanging killers of all time. While others like myself wanted to get rich from the deadly poison. This manmade drug brought power, money, and madness to the Crip and Blood gangs.[8]

Before the 1980s crack, crystal meth, and PCP were relatively unknown in black communities, and neither gang had much involvement in illegal drug sales or distribution. By the 1980s these illegal drugs fueled gangs' underground economy. The combination of high unemployment, poverty, lack of opportunity, discrimination, and the relative accessibility of illegal drugs created ideal conditions for the gangs to move into drug trafficking. For some drug trafficking became a way of life that was supported by their sets. For some homeboys illegal drug sales remain a way to make fast and good money.

The importance and nature of gangs' involvement in the drug trade has been subject to much debate. Research and opinions differ on just how involved both gangs are in trafficking. This section explains some of the research on their level of use and involvement in trafficking. Several gang researchers have reported that some gangs are very much involved in drug trafficking.[9] These researchers characterize gangs involved in drug trafficking as being highly organized with hierarchal businesslike structures devoted to profiting from illegal drug sales. These researchers see these gangs as violent when it comes to controlling their drug distribution territories.[10] Law enforcement agencies have also found a strong connection between drug trafficking and gang violence, especially homicide.

Members of the Dodge City Crips/Second Street Mob operating in San Pedro, California, in 1987 show their earnings from selling crack cocaine. Several Crip and Blood gangs discovered in the mid-1980s that selling crack was highly profitable. (Axel Koester/Corbis)

The connection between gang violence and illegal drug sales has been documented by several scholars and journalists. Business competition over the trafficking of crack cocaine has been identified as a cause of violence between Crips and Bloods. Gang involvement in drug trafficking has resulted in extensive brutality throughout cities where the demand for drugs is strong and gangs compete for control of distribution networks and territories; for example, when Los Angeles gangs attempted to take over in San Diego, local Bloods and Crips fought together to keep the Los Angeles–based gangs out.[11]

However, some studies show limited gang involvement in drug tracking and the corresponding violence.[12] Cheryl Maxson studied the connection between street gangs, illicit drug sales, and violence and found that street gangs are far less likely to be involved in the illegal drug trade and the associated violence than the law enforcement literature suggests. She discovered in the mid-1990s that only a few gangs seemed to specialize in drug sales.[13] Others have also found that gangs were less involved in the distribution of crack cocaine than were individual gang members.[14] They and other researchers have concluded that individual gang members sometimes act as independent drug dealers within their gangs.[15] They point out that although some gang members do traffic drugs, they do so as independent operators within but not as formal operatives of the gang. These homeboys would be involved with drug trafficking whether they were in the gang or not. Referring to the Crips and Bloods, gang expert Anne Campbell wrote:

> These rival groups, identifiable by their preference for blue and red attire respectively, were heralded by the *New York Times* as, "the main distributors of crack throughout the Western United States." But, researchers who have worked for many years with Los Angeles gangs maintain that they are not, and have never been, drug dealing organizations. Selling drugs has been a staple economic means of survival for some gang members, but it is an individual activity, not a product of an orchestrated group enterprise.[16]

From this perspective street gangs such as the Bloods and Crips lack the organizational capacity to be involved in drug distribution. While few would dispute that both gangs sell and use cocaine, some suggest that they are not as involved, organized, and sophisticated as we are led to believe by law enforcement personnel and the media.[17] Malcolm Klein and colleagues have concluded that too much has been made of both gangs' involvement in the drug trade and what is more likely occurring is individual gang members selling drugs on their own behalf.[18]

However, there is other evidence that at least some sets are well organized in the drug trade. For example, Jerome Skolnick and colleagues noted Blood and Crip gang migration into new territories to expand illicit drug markets.[19] There is some evidence that both gangs, especially the Crips, are organized into multistate drug distribution networks, and the two have been known to cooperate in trafficking drugs.[20] In some jurisdictions law enforcement agencies have identified links between Crips, Bloods, and drug cartels such as Los Zetas, the Gulf Cartel, and La Familia Michoacán,[21] which indicates a high level of organization that has not historically characterized Crip and Blood gangs. It could be the case that while initially the gangs lacked the organizational capability necessary to operate major drug operations, over time some sets became more sophisticated and organized.

It is likely that gang involvement in drug trafficking is widespread, but the degree of involvement differs greatly from set to set and location to location. A number of high-profile drug cases involving Crips and Bloods across the nation underscore the involvement of these gangs as organized illicit drug dealers. There are several FBI reports of Crips and Bloods being arrested in major cases for trafficking illegal/illicit drugs. In February 2014, for example, 28 members of Patterson, New Jersey, Blood gangs were arrested for distributing heroin, crack cocaine, and powdered cocaine in addition to firearms offenses.[22]

There have been other major drug cases involving Bloods and Crips; for example, the Fruit Town Brims and Sex Money Murder operated in New Jersey in a collaborative and coordinated manner. Specifically, it was reported that OGs from several Blood gangs met to resolve issues among their rank and file soldiers. In Los Angeles 35 members or associates of the Rollin 30s Harlem Crips were arrested on illicit drug and firearm charges.[23] The gang was involved in the distribution of crack and powdered cocaine. In North Carolina four members of the United Blood Nation were convicted of distributing controlled substances and conspiring to commit murder.[24] The Bloods in prison used smuggled cell phones to communicate with members outside of prison and conduct high-level management meetings. Others have identified direct connections between the gangs and major drug importers that use Southern California as a base for cocaine and crack distribution.[25]

Other evidence suggests that, at least in some cases, Blood and Crip sets may have well-organized drug trafficking operations. There is evidence that Bloods and Crips have been buying up legitimate businesses such as motels, nightclubs, and auto body shops to launder money earned through drug trafficking.[26] They are also known to register their vehicles under the name of someone not in the gang to avoid seizure by law enforcement.[27]

Another example of gang involvement in the drug trade occurred in Oakwood, California, in 1993 and 1994 over a 10-month period when a gang war between three sets, including the Venice Shoreline Crips, left 17 dead and 50 injured.[28] The initial issue was control over the local drug trade, but the conflict evolved to include issues of honor, reputation, and race. Racial targeting in this multicultural community was a key factor in the gang violence. A Centers for Disease Control and Prevention study of gang homicides in five cities found that the percentage of gang-related homicides linked to drug trafficking ranged from 0 to 25 percent. The same study concluded that these gang-related homicides were likely due to ongoing conflicts among gangs and to occur in public settings with firearms.[29] Most observers have concluded that both gangs rely heavily on violence when carrying out drug trafficking operations.

Concluding Observations

Crip and Blood involvement with illegal drugs and alcohol is well established. More is known about drug trafficking by both gangs than the extent of their drug use. As a general rule, substance abuse increases with gang participation. But during the 1980s and 1990s, there was debate about the nature of their involvement in trafficking. Now, in the second decade of the twenty-first century, it is clear to most observers that both gangs have members who are actively involved in drug use and distribution. The nature of this involvement ranges from individuals within sets making a little money by selling drugs on the side to what appear to be major coordinated efforts by multiple sets. Some of these latter efforts cross state lines. Regardless, most of the literature reports that Crip and Blood members are more likely than non-gang members to be engaged in illegal drug use and distribution. It is also very probable that their involvement will continue and expand in the future.

Notes

1. Yusuf Jah and Sister Shah'Keyah, *Uprising: Crips and Bloods Tell the Story of America's Youth in the Crossfire* (New York: Touchstone, 1995), 73.
2. Scott H. Decker, "Legitimating Drug Use: A Note on the Impact of Gang Membership and Drug Sales on the Use of Illicit Drugs." *Justice Quarterly* 17, no. 2 (2000), 404.
3. For example, see Finn Aage Esbensen and David Huizinga, "Gangs, Drugs, and Delinquency in a Survey of Urban Youth." *Criminology* 31 (1993), 565–590; Jeffery Fagan, "The Social Organization of Drug Use and Drug Dealing among Urban Gangs." *Criminology* 27 (1989), 633–670.
4. See Decker, Op. cit.
5. Ibid., 404.
6. Donovan Simmons and Terry Moses, *Bloods and Crips: The Genesis of a Genocide* (Bloomington, IN: Authorhouse, 2009), 90.
7. Gregg Etter, "Gang Investigation." In Michael L Birzer and Cliff Robertson (Eds.), *Introduction to Criminal Investigation* (Boca Raton, FL: CRC Press, 2012), 324.
8. Simmons, Op. cit., 86.
9. For example, see Felix Padilla "The Working Gang." In Scott Cummings and Daniel J. Monti (Eds.), *Gangs* (New York: New York University Press, 1993).
10. Scott H. Decker, "Youth Gangs and Violent Behavior and Aggression." In Daniel J. Flannery, Alexander T. Vazsongi, and Irwin D. Waldman (Eds.), *The Cambridge Handbook of Violent Behavior and Aggression* (Cambridge, MA: Cambridge University Press, 2007); Carolyn R. Block and Richard Block. "Street Crime in Chicago." In *Research in Brief* (Washington, DC: United States Department of Justice, 1993); Brenda C. Coughlin and Sudhir Alladi Venkatesh, "The Urban Street Gang After 1970." *Annual Review of Sociology* 29 (2003), 41–64.
11. William B. Sanders, "Drive-bys." In Jody Miller, Cheryl L. Maxson, and Malcolm W. Klein (Eds.), *The Modern Gang Reader, Second Edition* (Los Angeles: Roxbury, 2001), 211.
12. Ibid.

13. Cheryl L. Maxson, "Street Gangs and Drug Sales in Two Suburban Cities." In *Research in Brief* (Washington, DC: National Institutes of Justice Research, 1995).

14. Malcolm W. Klein, Cheryl L. Maxson, and Lea C. Cunningham, " 'Crack,' Street Gangs, and Violence." *Criminology* 29 (1991), 623–650.

15. See Steven D. Levitt and Sudhir Alladi Venkatesh, "An Economic Analysis of a Drug-Selling Gang's Finances." *Quarterly Journal of Economics* 115, no. 3 (2000), 755–789.

16. Anne Campbell, *The Girls in the Gang, Second Edition* (Cambridge, MA: Basil Blackwell, 1991), 274.

17. See Malcolm W. Klein, Cheryl L. Maxson, and Lea C. Cunningham, " 'Crack,' Street Gangs, and Violence." *Criminology* 29 (1991), 623–650; Malcolm W. Klein and Cheryl L. Maxson, *Street Gangs and Drug Sales* (Los Angeles: University of Southern California, Center for Research on Crime and Social Control, 1990).

18. Malcolm W. Klein, *The American Street Gang* (New York: Oxford University Press, 1995).

19. Jerome Skolnick, R. Bluthenthal, and Theodore Correl, "Gang Organization and Migration." In Scott Cummings and Daniel J. Monti (Eds.), *Gangs: The Origins and Impact of Contemporary Youth Gangs in the United States* (Albany: State University of New York Press, 1993).

20. A. G. Thornburgh, *Blood and Crips Street Gangs: Briefing Book* (Washington, DC: Office of Justice Programs, 1988).

21. National Gang Intelligence Center, *2013 National Gang Report* (Washington, DC: Federal Bureau of Investigation, 2013), 22–23.

22. Federal Bureau of Investigation, *Twenty-Eight Members and Associates of Patterson Bloods Street Gang Charged in Manhattan Federal Court with Distributing Heroin, Crack Cocaine, and Powder Cocaine and with Firearms Offenses* (Newark, NJ: Federal Bureau of Investigation, U.S. Attorney's Office, February 24, 2014).

23. Federal Bureau of Investigation, *Dozens of Members of Violent Street Gang Charged with Narcotics and Weapons Violation Following Joint Investigation Known as Operation Thumbs Down* (Los Angeles: Federal Bureau of Investigation, Los Angeles, August 29, 2013).

24. Federal Bureau of Investigation, *Four United Blood Nation Members Convicted of Racketeering Charges Following a Six-Day Trial* (Federal Bureau of Investigation, U.S. Attorney's Office, May 9, 2013).

25. Lisa Porché-Burke and Christopher Fulton, "The Impact of Gang Violence." In Richard C. Cervantes (Ed.), *Substance Abuse and Gang Violence* (Newbury, CA: Sage, 1992).

26. Bureau of Organized Crime and Criminal Intelligence, *Crips and Bloods Street Gangs* (Sacramento, CA: Author, n.d.), 9.

27. Ibid., 5.

28. Karen Umemoto, *The Truce: Lessons from an L.A. Gang War* (Ithaca, NY: Cornell University Press, 2006), 2.

29. Dawn McDaniel, Arlen Egley Jr., and J. Logan, "Gang Homicides: Five U.S. Cities, 2003–2008." *Morbidity and Mortality Weekly Report* 61 (January 27, 2012), 46–51.

CHAPTER EIGHT

Crips and Bloods in the Media

They [black youth] don't learn a lesson or learn any moral values from watching a movie. There are no positive messages in the movies.[1]

—Angelo, Blood

Crip and Blood subcultures are two of the most recognized in the United States and for that matter, much of the world.[2] This is largely because information about the subcultures associated with these gangs has been widely disseminated by gang members through the mass media and the entertainment industry. There is evidence that the gangs also transfer some aspects of their subcultures as members migrate from city to city.[3] Throughout the world, youth and young adults have easy access to these subcultures through the Internet, communications, television, music, mass media, social media, film, video games, clothing, and the retail industry. Gang authority Malcolm Klein has stressed in much of his writing the important role these gang subcultures play in shaping the actions of youth and young adults.[4] Building on Klein's point, gang expert Cheryl Maxson noted that youth do not always depend on direct contact with gang members to learn about gang subcultures. They can get it through more public and mass media.[5] Some gang-involved youth imitate both gangs based on what they believe to be Blood or Crip subcultures.

In addition, the media and law enforcement personnel at times, overly exaggerate subcultural differences and rivalries between Crips and Bloods by stressing inter-gang tensions.[6] The rivalry as depicted by the media and law enforcement personnel at times has reached legendary proportions.[7] Youth and young adults assume that these rivalries and gang tensions are integral aspects of being a Crip or Blood. While there is little question such rivalries exist, there are also examples of Crips and Bloods getting along reasonably well. The media generally stresses differences between Blood and Crip coalitions, though relationships within these alliances are more symbolic than real. Decker and Van Winkle wrote about how popular culture fueled preexisting antagonisms among gangs:

> The powerful images of Los Angeles gangs, conveyed through the movies, clothes, and music, provided a symbolic reference point for these antagonisms. In this way, popular culture provided the symbols and rhetoric of gang affiliation and activities that galvanized neighborhood rivalries.[8]

The media has fed the rivalry between the two, as it favors drama over the sublime. Promoting divisiveness in the community makes for a better story. The homeboys of both gangs also enjoy feeding into the media's story.

Most Americans, including Crips and Bloods, derive their knowledge about the two gangs from the mass media. Most of the general public has little to no contact with either gang outside of the mass media. Few have read academic studies or law enforcement reports on either gang. Lacking alternative information, the public—and Crips and Bloods—is influenced by what the media chooses to report. Unlike the general public, however, Crips and Bloods have access to internal folklore and traditions by virtue of being gang members, much of which is in the form of oral tradition passed on from member to member. Increasingly, the Internet is shaping perceptions about both gangs, and gang-supported websites and blogs offer information.

Major media attention toward the Crips may have started with an incident in November 1971 in Los Angeles when a 13-year-old black

Los Angeles gang members flashing hand signs symbolizing that they are
Bloods. They are forming the letter B with their hands. Their red attire also
signals they are Bloods. (Steve Starr/Corbis)

boy died while in police custody. The police concluded and reported to
the press that the boy committed suicide by hanging himself. Following this announcement, black youth took to the streets in protest.
Later a white youth was shot by a sniper, and fights between white
and black youth ensued. White residents and school officials blamed
the violence on the presence of outside agitators, specifically the Crips,
even though there was no evidence that the Crips were in any way
involved with these events. Crips were also blamed by the press for
the death of a military veteran on February 28, 1972. The *Los Angeles
Times* ran a story blaming the Crips that it later retracted for a lack
of evidence.[9] Though the media blamed the Crips for the incident,
no link between them and the victim was ever established. The Crips
had become the scapegoat for the violence occurring on the streets.

   News stories about gangs are sometimes sensationalized for their
entertainment value rather than addressing the root social conditions
leading to the formation of gangs. The media during the 1980s and
1990s helped create myths and misperceptions about the true nature
of gangs, including the Crips and Bloods.[10] The media, and in particular Hollywood, has glamorized the gangster lifestyle.[11] This has led

some youth and young adults to romanticize the gangster lifestyle and base their perceptions on media stereotypes rather than the facts. Rather than revealing the true conditions research has documented, the media abounds with stereotypes about Bloods and Crips.

Most of the public perception and discourse regarding the Crips and Bloods relates to criminal activity or negativity. In 2008 Kontos and Brotherton wrote about the public's growing fascination with gangs.[12] They pointed out that the media exploits this fascination by embellishing and creating scary images and perpetuating stereotypes of gangs. The result is an explosion of misinformation and a sizable industry that aims to address how to cope with gangs and gang members. Even academics have jumped on the bandwagon, with scores of publications about gangs being produced each year. Gang members have taken advantage of media attention. One black street gang member summed up what some must feel when he said, "I like to get media coverage because everyone will know who we are. The more people know who you are, the less they will mess with you."[13]

Examples of Myths and Stereotypes of Blood and Crip Gangs

Stereotypes and myths about Bloods and Crips abound, and the media has helped create many misconceptions.[14] One stereotype is that these gangs are organized solely around committing crimes. The media and law enforcement personnel consistently promote the view that everything gangs do is somehow linked to crime. While it is undeniable that they do commit more than their share of crimes, and many of these are serious, a small fraction of their time is taken up with crime. Most of their time is spent hanging around, drinking, partying, and otherwise socializing within and outside of the gang.[15] Gangs and gang membership have been glamorized by the mass media. The notion of Crip and Blood gangs being romantic and adventurous has been played out in the media since the beginning of both gangs.

It is true that Crip and Blood gangs are involved in criminal activity, but their involvement may be exaggerated in the media and by law enforcement personnel and thus sensationalized;[16] for example, there is some research that questions the media and law enforcement personnel's perception that gang involvement in drug trafficking leads to increased violence and reliance on guns.[17] This perception may be driven more by how local law enforcement agencies define gang involvement or link crime to a gang.[18]

Another myth is that belonging to a gang is very profitable and that members reap large financial rewards. For disenfranchised individuals lacking opportunities, gangs do represent a way to make money, such as in drug trafficking. However, research has not consistently supported mass media claims of great financial gains being made by gangs involved in trafficking drugs.[19] A few members of some sets appear to make good money from gang-related criminal activities, but most homeboys do not.

Some of the myths and stereotypes about Crips and Bloods are fueled by the gangs themselves. According to Marcus Felson, gangs such as the Bloods and Crips create myths about themselves that he calls the big gang theory.[20] Gangs, by exaggerating their toughness and nastiness, gain some level of protection from others because they appear to be dangerous and better organized than they actually are. The hope is that rival gangs will fear of retaliation and thus not target them.[21] A gang's reputation often exceeds its ability to carry out its threats, but there are exceptions. The murders of rap stars such as Tupac Shakur and Suge Knight serve as testimony that some of these gangs can carry out their objectives.

Autobiographies

Unlike other gangs, the Crips and Bloods have taken advantage of media outlets and have been actively involved in creating and shaping public perceptions about gangs, the gangster lifestyle, and what it means to belong. One venue homeboys have used is the autobiography. Most of these autobiographies were written by former members of the Crips. A number of former and current Crips and Bloods have written autobiographies and compiled testimonials from other gang members of what their lives were like when they were actively involved with gangs. These books tell about ex-Crip and ex-Blood members' negative experiences and personal losses caused by belonging to the gangs. The books contain personal testimonials of the tragedies these individuals and their associates experienced due to being involved with their gangs. These tell-all books, sometimes written from prison, speak to the reality of the gangster lifestyle. They almost always are directed toward youth and potential gang members considering the gangster lifestyle; they aim to dissuade individuals from joining either the Crips or the Bloods. It is generally hoped that the reader will learn from the mistakes of those who went before them.

The following are some representative books written to discourage people from becoming involved with gangs, specifically the Crips and the Bloods. The authors are anti-gang activists who typically describe life in and outside of their respective gangs.

Bloods and Crips: The Genesis of a Genocide (2009) was mostly written by a former Crip and a former Blood who are serving life sentences, Donovan Simmons and Terry Moses. This book describes what the authors believe is the insanity of black men killing other black men on the sole basis of gang affiliation. It contains the testimonials of other gang members to the senselessness of gang violence and drug use. The co-authors express regret for what they did as gang members to their victims.

War of the Bloods in My Veins: A Street Soldier's March toward Redemption (2008) was written by Dashaun Morris, a member of the Bloods. It describes how he moves across the country, and regardless of where he lives, he finds it difficult to avoid gangs and racism.

Monster: The Autobiography of an L.A. Gang Member (1993) was written by a major Crip leader named Sanyika Shakur. It is one of the most popular autobiographies related to Crip and Blood violence as well as the gangster lifestyle. Shakur, also known by the name Monster Kody Scott, depicts the extreme violence engendered by the rival warfare between the two gangs. The book also addresses his increased awareness of and withdrawal from the gangster lifestyle. Shakur was a member of the Eight-Tray (83) Crips. The autobiography provides an insider's view of how and why street gangs operate. Some have suggested that his book romanticizes the gangster lifestyle and blame this book for the creation and promotion of new street gangs.[22]

Life in Prison (1998) is an autobiography by Stanley "Tookie" Williams, a co-founder of the Crips. It addresses his life in prison.[23] Williams was on death row from 1981 until he was executed on December 13, 2005. His writings over time, often in the form of children's books, were dedicated to helping youth avoid joining gangs. His autobiography focused on the horrors of prison life that await youth who remain in gangs. In his later and better known book *Blue Rage, Black Redemption: A Memoir* (2007), Williams shared his thoughts about the downside of his violent gang involvement and how he reformed his gangster lifestyle, realizing that it was a dead end that would result only in harming the community and others.

Do or Die: America's Most Notorious Gangs Speak for Themselves is a 1991 book written by Léon Bing who although she was not a gang member, was trusted by both gangs. She spent four years with the Bloods and Crips in Los Angeles to better understand them as people. Her book provides an early account of the desperation, lack of hope, and violence experienced by gang members in Los Angeles. It also provides an early firsthand impression of gangs in Los Angeles and within the California Youth Authority system.

Inside the Crips: Life inside L.A.'s Most Notorious Gang (2005) is the autobiography of Colton Simpson written with the help of Ann Pearlman. This volume describes how Simpson became involved with the Crips at an early age. It depicts his escalating commitment to the Crips and his many incarcerations within the California youth and adult correctional systems. The book provides many stories of gang violence within both systems. It also tells of his transition out of the Crips.

Films

Colors (1988) was one of the first films dedicated to the romance and excitement of gang membership. Some observers have noted that the movie was a hyped-up disappointment to Crips and Bloods because it emphasized Latino gangs rather than their gangs.[24] The movie is thought to have generated some violence among gang members; for example, two members of a Blood gang encountered some Crips after seeing the movie, and a shootout occurred, leaving two dead. Such media attention via movies, television, literature, newspapers, music, and other forms of expression gives gang members a sense of importance and status unavailable through other means.

The film *Menace II Society* (1993) focuses on the gangster and hoodlum lifestyle in South Central Los Angeles. The dramatic film plays on the extreme violence experienced by those living in Watts.

The main character, Caine Lawson, and his best friend Kevin Anderson (O-Dog) rob a local store and kill the owner and his wife. This film flashes back to Caine's father committing similar crimes. Parallels between his life of crime and his father's serve as a subplot. Caine and his cousin are later victims of a car jacking, and the cousin is murdered. He then gets revenge against these individuals. Caine begins selling cocaine and continues to engage in a life of crime and violence. The film has multiple violent exchanges, with the main characters being either offenders or victims. Eventually Caine dies in a violent exchange, and the ending message is that everything you do in the gang catches up with you.

Other films such as *Redemption* (2004), *Boyz in the Hood* (1991), *C-Walk,* and *Ricochet* helped introduce perspectives on the Crips and Bloods across the United States and other countries. The television movie *Redemption: The Stan Tookie Williams Story* starred Jamie Foxx as Williams. The film's theme was that Williams had changed his life and had become a major anti-gang activist, but it was not enough to save his life. The movie won several awards and other honors but failed to deter Williams's execution in 2005.

Documentary Films

Crips and Bloods Made in America (2009), directed by Stacy Peralta, is a documentary about the historical development of the Crips and Bloods. The central theme of this film is that both gangs are the product of racist discriminatory policies of government, law enforcement agencies, and mainstream society, which is why the title includes the words *Made in America*. According to the film, the Crips and Bloods also evolved in response to declining prosperity and the resultant poverty in the 1960s and 1970s. The central theme of the film is that the two gangs evolved in response to racism, unemployment, drugs, police brutality, discrimination, increasing poverty, and exclusion from white mainstream society.

The film relies on case histories of Crip and Blood members who describe their childhoods and how they turned to the gangs. One of the main speakers in the film is Kumasi, who points out that "part of the mechanics of oppressing people is to pervert them to the extent that they become their own oppressors." This point of view is easily understood from a gang member's perspective given law enforcement harassment and societal marginalization. The emotions related to the experience of living in the repressive conditions of Los Angeles led some to take out their frustrations on those living under the same negative conditions.

The *Bloods and Crips Shooting* (2008) video, which is against gang violence, shows members of both gangs lined up over an open grave with the member in the front being shot and falling into the grave. This continues until a young member says, "Stop ... Why are we doing this?"

Bastards of the Party (2005) is directed by Cle "Bone" Shaheed Sloan, a Blood. The film sets out to explain the cycle of violence among gang members. The film begins in the antebellum era of slavery and then traces the racism and discrimination faced by blacks migrating to the north and west during World War II. The poverty and racial segregation faced by these black migrants seeking a better life, violent police repression of blacks, and white racist gangs, especially in Los Angeles, set the stage for gangs in the late twentieth century.

With the destruction of the Black Panthers and similar black power groups, black street gangs stepped in to fill the void. The gangs became the radicals of the black power groups. The gangs were less about black power than the power groups and more about meeting individual objectives; in other words, the "we" became "me."

The History channel's series titled *Gangland* (2007–2010) has multiple episodes that cover Crip and Blood sets.[25] These one-hour episodes typically cover the creation and operations of both gangs and representative sets. The episodes focus on subcultural aspects of the gangs and major leaders. The series focuses on the criminal and violent activities of the gangs.

Numerous videos on subcultural aspects of both gangs can be found on the Internet; for example, the Crip Walk, or C Walk, consists of dance moves that can be seen in several video examples on YouTube and other websites. The rapper CJ Mac released a documentary titled, *Cwalk: It's a Way of Livin* (2003) that focuses on the beginnings of the Crip Walk and its rise in popularity. The video features rappers such as Snoop Dogg, WC, and Ice T with members of the Crips.

There are many other examples that can be found by searching the Internet.

Gangster Rap and Hip-Hop Music

A key cultural reference point for gangs is music. Music, and more specifically rap and hip-hop, are important dimensions of Crip and Blood gang subcultures. Gangster rap is a worldwide phenomenon.[26] Before the emergence of rap and hip-hop, funk and p-funk were the preferred music of some of the initial Crip and Blood members. Groups such as the Ohio Players, Bootsy Collins, Rick James, Bar-Kays, and Parliament were popular. Later, gangsta rap would do much to spread Blood and Crip gang subcultures to the outside world.

Rap music has been part of black street culture since the 1970s. Since its inception it has been viewed as a pathway for disenfranchised black youth to speak to the world about their lives, values, experiences, and views of the world. Rap music started on the East Coast and was quickly embraced on the West Coast. Initially rap music focused on the individual and his concerns, but over time it started to reflect the gangster lifestyle. Former and current gang members viewed rap as a way to make quick money and express the frustrations they faced as black men marginalized from mainstream society. Rap became a medium for telling their story of struggles to a larger audience.

The origin of rap and related hip-hop music can be attributed to three disc jockeys (DJs) from the Bronx, Kool Herc, Grandmaster Flash, and Afrika Bambaataa.[27] Of the three, Kool Herc is credited with originating rap. Kool Herc, whose real name is Clive Campbell, moved from Jamaica at age 12 brought island sounds to the New York street music scene.[28] By the mid-1980s a form of rap emerged that was labeled gangsta rap. Todd Shaw, also known as Too $hort, was the first person to be called a gangsta rapper.[29] His first commercial production was in 1985 with the rap group NWA (Niggers with Attitude), which was credited with officially beginning gangsta rap music.[30] NWA's most successful production was *Straight outta Compton*, which was produced in 1988.

In alternative accounts Ice T and Ice Cube are credited with creating gangsta rap. Ice T began recording singles in the early 1980s, but they did not initially achieve commercial success.[31] Eventually both would become highly successful rap artists. Both Ice T and Ice Cube are also known because they achieved commercial success in other areas, such as community service and acting. Ice T would become very visible as a community leader, film star, and celebrity.

Later artists such as Tupac Shakur, Shorty B., Pee Wee, Snoop Doggy Dogg, Suge Knight, Dr. Dre, Biggie Smalls, and Sean Combs (Puff Daddy) would further develop and produce gangsta rap promoting gang subcultures. Gangsta rap increasingly became more ingrained in mainstream popular culture. Concurrent with the success of these and other related artists was a gang-involved feud between West Coast and East Coast rappers that resulted in the very public assassinations of Tupac Shakur in 1996 and Biggie Smalls (Notorious B.I.G.) in 1997.[32]

Initially gang involvement with rap music was limited due to technology and the cost of production. With the development of cheap recording technology and low-cost production, along with the explosion of social media, more Crip and Blood gang members became involved in the rap music industry. There are many links between this type of music and the Crips and Bloods. Some gang members, ex-members, and affiliates have been very successful in the music industry. Black gang members have adopted hip-hop and/or rap as their musical style of expression. Gangsta rap and hip-hop are found throughout television, music, radio, movies, videos, the street, and the Internet. The cable station Black Entertainment Television (BET) created programs highlighting hard-core rap videos.[33]

Several current or former gang members are players in the music industry. Suge Knight, the former chief executive officer (CEO) of Death Row Records, was affiliated with the Compton Pirus (Bompton Pirus). Death Row, and the competing Bad Boy Entertainment, were successful at the global level. Their music, which often focuses on violence, hatred, alienation from mainstream society, rejection of authority, sex, and street wars, sparks some of the compassion expressed by gang members. Gangsta rap and hip-hop, two similar music genres, clearly glorify the gangster lifestyle. Gangster rap artists such as Snoop Dogg (Rollin 20s Crips), Lil Wayne, DJ Quick (Treetop Piru Bloods), and Tupac Shakur were and continue to be idolized by youth who want to be like them. Tupac Shakur was gunned down in a drive-by shooting in Los Angeles, and Snoop was charged as an accessory to his murder. Both did little to disassociate themselves from the gang culture they came from and developed their public and marketing images around their gang identities.

Gangsta rap artists associated with the Crips include Goldie Loc, Warren G, Coolio, Tone Loc, CJ Mac, Eazy E, Swoop G, Tha Comradz, NC-Bo, Scareface, Young Jeezy, Richie Rich, AWOL, BK, Big Freeze, Blue Rag, Broncoe, C-Note, Cixx Pac, Do or Die, Sin Loc, G-Bone, Koollay, and Twin Loc. Nipsey Hussle is a rapper associated with the Rollin 60s, and he created the gangster rap trilogy titled *Bullets Ain't Got No Names*, which contained the successful song *Hussle in the House*. Rappers CJ Mac and Kurupt also have ties with the Rollin 60s. Artists associated with the Bloods include D.J. Quik, Top Dogg, B-Real, G.P., Lil Wayne, Birdman, Jay Rock, Nuttz, CK, KP, Batman, Big Y, Bloody Mary, Peanut II, Lil' 8, Redrum, Lil' Hawk, Lil' Stretch, Green Eyez, B-Brazy and G Spider, Tip-Toe, G-Len, June Dawg, Baby Maniak, and Big Mad-Eyez.

Music magazines that feature gangster rap articles refer to gangs or the gangster lifestyle. Compact disc (CD) jackets portray gang signs, symbols, and other subcultural symbolism. As gangster rap continues to grow in popularity, some segments of society are embracing it. Various gangster rap songs mention selling and using drugs, violence, reforming drug laws, abolishing the "three strikes" laws, prohibiting trying and sentencing juveniles as adults, and other gang goals. Much, but not all, gangster rap promotes gang life, gang symbols, gang subcultures, and gang values, that is, that money equals power, and power equals respect.[34]

The Internet and Social Media

The Internet, or cyberspace, has evolved over the years so that it is now a tool the Bloods and Crips use to exert great influence. Without too much effort, one can find several gang and set websites that promote the values of and send messages about the gangster lifestyle and subcultural practices. David Décary-Hétu and Carlo Morselli conducted a keyword search on a set of criminal organization names on MySpace, Facebook, and Twitter.[35] They found that gang presence on social networking sites is linked primarily to the promotion of a general gang or street culture. In most cases the sites were designed and managed by members and associates who emphasized their allegiance to well-known groups such as the Crips, Bloods, or Latin Kings. These gangs were prominent on the social networking sites the researchers studied.[36]

Research by Décary-Hétu and Morselli also found that gangs are dramatically increasing their use of social media to project images of the gangster lifestyle and their specific gangs. They found that from 2010 to 2011 Crip and Blood involvement on social media sites dramatically increased. They also found that the Bloods are one of the most popular gangs on Facebook.[37] The Crips and Bloods have Facebook fans throughout the world. Their investigation found that gang Facebook pages may include rap videos praising the gangster lifestyle, reports of arrests of gang members, news reports of gang exploits, profiles of gang members, group images, and photos of guns, wealth, and attractive women. A conscious effort is made on these sites to protect the individual identities of gang members. Inflammatory comments about other gangs are sometimes made on Facebook to disrespect and fuel rivalries. The gangs also use Twitter to communicate.

It has been speculated that gangs use the Internet to recruit new members. Studies have found that gangs use some of their websites to brag about their exploits. Décary-Hétu and Morselli and found that websites are not directly used for recruitment but may, by virtue of promoting gang culture, be appealing to youth at risk of joining gangs such as the Bloods or Crips.[38] The main intent of these websites is to bolster a gang's reputation and promote the public image of local gangs.

Concluding Observations

The Crips and Bloods, more than any other American-based gangs, have had a major presence in the mass media. Unlike other gangs, both have helped shape their public image through the mass media and by marketing their subculture and its items such as music and clothing. They have not been complacent but have capitalized on their notoriety and stereotypes advanced by the media. They have consciously shaped their image in society through writing, acting, rap music, and filmmaking, all of which have influenced all of American culture, whether or not they are involved with gangs.

They will continue to influence American culture for the foreseeable future and will continue to expand their presence on the Internet. Hundreds of blogs, websites, videos, and other information about the Bloods and Crips are readily available to those who have an interest, for example, GangStyle.com has postings from ex-members that tell of their regrets and sorrows resulting from their involvement with gangs, including the Bloods and Crips. For a very few Crips and Bloods, involvement in the media has led to commercial success. Most Bloods and Crips do not financially gain from media involvement. The media has certainly contributed to the notoriety of both gangs, which has resulted in tours of their neighborhoods in Los Angeles. LA Gang Tours is a business that provides escorted tours into gang-controlled neighborhoods such as those of the Crips and Bloods.[39]

Notes

1. Yusuf Jah and Sister Shah'Keyah, *Uprising: Crips and Bloods Tell the Story of America's Youth in the Crossfire* (New York: Touchstone, 1995), 71.
2. Herbert C. Covey, *Street Gangs throughout the World* (Springfield, IL: Charles Thomas, 2007).
3. Cheryl L. Maxson, "Gang Members on the Move." *Juvenile Justice Bulletin* (Washington, DC: Office of Juvenile Justice and Delinquency Prevention, 1998).
4. Malcolm W. Klein, *The American Street Gang* (New York: Oxford University Press, 1995).
5. See Maxson, Op. cit.
6. Karine Descormiers and Carlo Morselli, "Alliances, Conflicts, and Contradictions in Montreal's Street Gang Landscape." *International Criminal Justice Review* 21 (2011), 298.
7. Ibid.
8. Scott H. Decker and Bill Van Winkle, *Life in the Gang* (New York: Cambridge University Press, 1996).
9. George Percy Barganier, III. *Fanon's Children: The Black Panther Party and the Rise of the Crips and Bloods in Los Angeles* (Ph.D. dissertation, University of California, Berkeley, 2011), 78.
10. Randall G. Shelden, Sharon K. Tracy, and William B. Brown, *Youth Gangs in American Society, Second Edition* (Belmont, CA: Wadsworth, 2001), 5.

11. Eugene Weems and Clarke Lowe, *America's Most Notorious Gangs: A Concise Approach to Gang Prevention and Awareness* (Dixon, CA: Universal Publishing, 2013), x.

12. Louis Kontos and David C. Brotherton (Eds.), *Encyclopedia of Gangs* (Westport, CT: Greenwood, 2008), viii.

13. Loren W. Christensen, *Gangbangers: Understanding the Deadly Minds of America's Street Gangs* (Boulder, CO: Paladin, 1999), 37.

14. Klein, Op. cit.

15. See Chapter 3 for a more detailed discussion of this point.

16. There are clear examples of Crip and Blood crime that indicate a strong gang-related criminal orientation that are identified in Chapter 6 and elsewhere in the literature.

17. See Chapter 7 for a detailed discussion of this subject.

18. Cheryl L. Maxson, *Street Gangs and Drug Sales in Two Suburban Cities: Research in Brief* (Washington, DC: Department of Justice, Office of Justice Programs, National Institute of Justice, 1995).

19. Jeffery Fagan, "The Social Organization of Drug Use and Drug Selling among Urban Gangs." *Criminology* 27 (1989), 622–667.

20. Marcus K. Felson, *Crime and Nature* (Thousand Oaks, CA: Sage, 2006).

21. Ibid.

22. Wayne Caffey, *Crips and Bloods* (Los Angeles, Los Angeles County Sheriff's Office, 2006), 6.

23. Stanley Williams and Barbara Cottman Becnel, *Life in Prison* (San Francisco: Chronicle, 1998).

24. Donovan Simmons and Terry Moses, *Bloods and Crips: The Genesis of a Genocide* (Bloomington, IN: Authorhouse, 2009), 111.

25. For example, for coverage of the East Coast United Bloods Nation, see Gangland, "One Blood" (September 14, 2008), History Channel, originally aired May 28, 2008.

26. John M. Hagedorn, *A World of Gangs: Armed Young Men and Gangsta Culture* (Minneapolis: University of Minnesota Press, 2008), 106.

27. Darby E. Southgate, "Rap." In Louis Kontos and David C. Brotherton, (Eds.), *Encyclopedia of Gangs* (Westport, CT: Greenwood, 2008), 201–208.

28. Jeff Chang, *Can't Stop Won't Stop* (New York: St. Martin's, 2005).

29. Ibid., 202.

30. Ibid.

31. Ibid.

32. Ibid., 205.

33. Caffey, Op. cit., 5.

34. Andrew M. Grasciak, "Gangster Rap: The Real Words behind the Songs." *Journal of Gang Research* 11 (2003), 55–63.

35. David Décary-Hétu and Carlo Morselli, "Gang Presence in Social Network Sites." *International Journal of Cyber Criminology* 5 (2011), 876–890.

36. Ibid.

37. Ibid., 884.

38. Ibid.; Carlo Morselli and David Décary-Hétu, "Crime Facilitation Purposes of Social Networking Sites: A review and Analysis of the 'Cyberbanging' Phenomenon." *Small Wars and Insurgencies* 23, no. 5 (2013), 152–170.

39. LA Gang Tours, "LA Gang Tours," accessed on August 15, 2014, at: www .lagangtours.com.

CHAPTER NINE

Crip and Blood Snapshots: Examples of Crip and Blood Gangs

I stayed doin' it movin', thumped up, red rag freshly creased flashin', hangin' out my back pocket, flamed up from head to toe, represtin' this Damu dynasty to the fullest.[1]

—Monroe Jones, Blood

Descriptions and examples of Crip and Blood sets are numerous on the Internet. However, these descriptions are often brief and inconsistent. In spite of their national notoriety, factual descriptions of Crip and Blood sets are surprisingly limited. Very few members post detailed information about their sets, how they are organized, and how they operate. Given their involvement in illegal activities and apprehension regarding law enforcement personnel, this makes good sense. When ex-gang members write about their involvement in their sets, they make little effort to describe their sets and focus more on their experiences as members. In contrast, law enforcement and government websites focus on gang identification and criminal activities, to the exclusion of many other details. To obtain descriptions about Blood and Crip sets, one must combine law enforcement reports, brief references by homeboys, a handful of research articles, gang manuals, and Internet summaries. By looking at multiple sources, it is possible to find points of agreement that can serve as the foundation of case examples. Put differently, when multiple sources seem to agree about a characteristic of a specific set, a rough description can be developed. The difficulty is that pieces of these descriptions such as gang size and type of leadership may be absent. The following are some Crip and Blood set descriptions that either are the product of a case study or were pulled together from multiple sources.[2] Caution must be exercised because each of these sources is biased or incomplete.

Venice Shoreline Crips

The Venice Shoreline Crips are located in the Oakwood area near Venice Beach, California. The set was founded by Abbot Kinney and was comprised of mostly black and mixed race members. The set is reported to have several hundred members, but its numbers may have declined due to redevelopment and gentrification of their traditional territory. The set has been around for decades in the Venice area. It is thought to be the largest black gang in Venice. It became involved in the sale of cocaine in the 1980s, as did other Crip and Blood sets. Members were mostly adolescent and young males that came from lower-income neighborhoods where their families resided in public housing. Being territorial, the set protected its boundaries from rival sets such as Culver City 13 and Santa Monica 13. The Shoreline Crips were involved in the drug trade and other criminal activities, including shootings. The set was characterized by a high degree of racial tension, and it consequently targeted people of different racial heritages. Its predominant rivals were Latinos and their sets.[3]

Flow Boyz and The Cash Money

These two Blood sets operate in New York City. They are comprised of several sets that carry the same Blood affiliation but operate more like cliques. They avoid wearing red flags and prefer to wear "crates," which are bracelets made of red and black beads that they wear so that people can easily see them. These sets have links to and communicate with inmates at Rikers Island in New York. Historically both have been involved in cycles of retaliation that involve shooting rivals.

Rollin 60s Crips

The Rollin 60s (also called Rich Rollin 60s or Rollin 60s Neighborhood Crips) is one of the largest Crip sets in Los Angeles. One estimate places its membership in the range of 6,000 to 8,000 homeboys. If this range is accurate, the 60s would be the largest black gang in the Los Angeles area. The set's large membership permits it to dominate other areas of the city simply due to numbers. Its primary locus of control is the Hyde Park area of South Central. The set was founded in the mid-1970s and is a splinter gang of the West Side Crips. It is credited with being the first gang to incorporate *Rollin* into its name.

The subculture of the Rollin 60s is akin to other Crip gangs, and members wear clothing similar to that of other Crips. Rollin 60s have adopted sports apparel associated with the Seattle Mariners baseball team because of the *S*, which to members symbolizes 60 (60s Crip). Organizationally, the Rollin 60s have cliques, or subsets, with names such as the Avenues and Overhills.

Members of the Rollin 60s have a bitter and violent rivalry with the Eight Tray Gangster Crips that has resulted in over 60 deaths. The two sets started out as allies, but over time disputes led to one of the most bitter and violent rivalries among either Crip or Blood gangs. This rivalry is thought by outsiders to be the first case of Crip versus Crip conflict. This rivalry peaked from 1980 to 1995 and remains today, though it has diminished in importance. Shakur's 1993 autobiography *Monster* describes how violent encounters between the two Crip sets could be when the sets fought. The Rollin 60s have other rivalries with the 83 Hoovers, School Yard Crips, Van Ness Gangsters Bloods, and other gangs such as the Inglewood Family Bloods.

One of the most notorious Rollin 60s Crips was Tiequon Aundray Cox. Cox, also known as Lil Fee, was involved with murdering a family of four, was sentenced to death, and was incarcerated at San Quentin. While on death row in 1988, he stabbed Tookie Williams, the famous leader of the Eight Tray Gangster Crips. Also in 1988 another Rollin 60s Crip, Durrell Dewitt Collins, accidently shot Karen Toshima, who was waiting in line outside a Hollywood movie theatre.[4] Collins was sentenced to 27 years to life and remains in prison.

Bounty Hunter Bloods

The Bounty Hunter Bloods were started in 1969 and became well established in 1972 in the Watts section of Los Angeles. The Bounty Hunters control one of the biggest areas of Los Angeles and are believed to be one of the largest, if not the largest, Blood sets in the United States. The original name of the set was the Green Jackets. Gary Barker and Bobby Jack are generally thought to have founded the set. Its main rival was the Grape Street Watts Crips, but a truce was established in 1992 that seems to be holding for the most part. The set's main territory is the Nickerson Gardens projects. The Bounty Hunter Bloods are thought to have a presence in areas outside of Watts such as Norfolk, Virginia, and Trenton, New Jersey.

52 Hoover Gangster Crips

The 52 Hoover Gangster Crips (also known as the 5-Deuce Hoover Gangster Crips) are a Los Angeles West Side Crips set. The set has an estimated 1,000 members. It is aligned with other sets such as the Hoovers Criminal Gang, 51-Deuce, and Trouble Gangster Crips. It also is a rival of the Rollin 40s Crips and Fruit Town Brims.

The set has been involved in various crimes, including drug trafficking in the South Central area of Los Angeles. The set is believed to have other drug operations in Houston, Washington DC, New Jersey, and New York. The colors of the 52 Hoover Gangster Crips are blue and orange, with the blue associating them with the Crips and the orange linking them to Hoover Criminals. The set shares characteristics with other Crip gangs.

Fremont Hustlers–Kansas City (Crips)

Mark Fleisher's study of the Fremont Hustlers in Kansas City, Missouri, provides a rare academic glimpse into a Crip set.[5] Fleisher found that the mixed gender set of approximately 70 members did not refer to each other as members of a gang (set), nor did they think of themselves as having joined a gang. The concept of "belonging" to the Fremont Hustlers did not make sense to members; rather, they viewed their involvement with the group as more fluid and informal—they simply hung out with other Fremont Hustlers.

The Fremont Hustlers had no formal hierarchical structure. Consequently, there were no recognized leaders giving orders to others and no cohesive organizational structure. The set did subdivide into cliques that provided support for small groups of members. Females were more likely than males to form these cliques. Fremont had no formal rules; thus there were no sanctions for breaking the rules. New members were not required to endure initiation rituals or pass challenges to participate in Fremont. Initiation rituals found in other sets, such as beating in or being jumped in, were not present. New members were not expected to prove their worth by committing crimes for the set; rather, the pattern was for individuals to hang out with Hustlers and if accepted, slowly be assimilated into the set.

Members of Fremont shared the same social backgrounds. They grew up together and had social relationships before becoming members. They had similar experiences related to family backgrounds, schools, juvenile justice agencies, and the streets. Many of the members had been down with other street sets before assimilating into Fremont. The Fremont Hustlers were involved in crime, most commonly the sale of illicit drugs.

Fremont had its own vocabulary (argot). For example, *do shit* means "commit crimes" and *everyday* refers to members hanging out all of the time. Three terms were often used to note the nature of social ties: *niggah, dog*, and *mothafucka*. *Niggah* was used without regard to color and was sometimes a synonym for *homey* (member of the set). Fremonts use the term *dog* as a friendly greeting, such as in the commonly expressed "What's up, dog?" *Mothafucka* has several meanings, for example, "close friend," but could also be an insult in tense situations. Fleisher noted that terms such as *mothafucka, bitch, dog*, and *niggah*—if used correctly with the set—were signs of companionship.[6] Outsiders could easily view the use of such terms as offensive.

Fleisher discovered two concepts, tightness and time, that shaped relationships within the Fremont Hustlers. In this context, tightness refers to the intensity of a relationship. Youth who were considered tight spent much of their time hanging out together and were close enough to commit crimes together. Tightness was not necessarily linked to long-term relationships and varied in length of duration; rather, tightness was a matter of shared social history.

In comparison, for the Fremont Hustlers the concept of time was how much chronological time one was involved with the Fremont Hustlers. Fleisher divided members' time commitment into four categories: "here all the time," "here a lot," "come around," and "will be there if we need him."[7] Even youth that were killed and the children of female members were considered to be Fremont Hustlers. The amount of time a youth is involved with the group helped define the nature of their involvement. Few Fremont members spent all of their time being involved, and others seem to be only marginally involved, similar to being on call.

Fremont members made distinctions between the types of membership on another level. Members who were born and raised in the Fremont neighborhood were called Fremont Fremont. In contrast, people from other areas who were down with Fremont were referred to simply as Fremont.

Hanging out was a major activity of Fremont members. Much of this time was spent joking around and laughing. Members spend more energy talking about violence than committing acts of violence. Members, within unspoken boundaries, had verbal duels with each other to let off tension without becoming physically violent. According to Fleisher, these verbal duels can be described as "street theater" because of their public nature.[8] The duels served several functions, such as providing a safe way for females to show their bravery and giving participants a way to control their emotions. Females were more inclined than males to engage in verbal duels. These verbal duels involved trading insults and teasing and had parameters that were generally followed by set members. Similar exchanges with those outside of the group took on different meanings and could result in physical confrontations.

The Westside Rollin 30s Harlem Crips

The Westside Rollin 30s Harlem Crips are based in South Central Los Angeles. This Crips gang started in the early 1970s as the Original Harlem Godfathers (OHC) and eventually became a Crips gang at the end of that decade. They are rivals with the West Side Rolling 20s Neighborhood Bloods, Almighty Black P Stone Bloods, and the Rollin 40s Crips. They control one of the largest areas of all black gangs in Los Angeles, second only in size to the area controlled by the Eight Trey Gangster Crips.

The gang is also present outside of Los Angeles—in North Carolina, New Jersey, New York, and Colorado. The Westside Rollin 30s Harlem Crips started the East Side Rolling 30s Harlem Mafia Crips (HMC) in East Harlem. This offshoot is thought to be the first Los Angeles–based gang to start up in New York. The West Coast and East Coast gangs are thought to operate independently of each other.

Currently the FBI estimates that the Westside Rollin 30s Harlem Crips may have between 700 and 1,000 members. One website notes that the gang has initiation rites involving males being beaten in by three members for half a minute or so. Females have to be either sexed in for 70 minutes or beaten in for 33 seconds by three members. Females can choose their initiation. Once in, members must follow the rules of the gang, which include a number of prohibitions against snitching, stealing from each other, rape, leaving the gang, giving false information to the gang, homosexuality, killing each other, homeless members, throwing up enemy signs, using cocaine or dope, and missing meetings without notifying gang leaders. The rules also stipulate what members should do: all LOCs must help others in the set, have their boyfriends or girlfriends join, pay dues of $3 per week, help others in need regardless of the situation, stand behind each other when conflicts occur with others outside of the set, and look presentable.

Westside Rollin 30s Harlem Crips is well known for its violent crimes in the community. A number of homicides within its territory have been linked to gang activities. The Westside Rollin 30s is mostly comprised of five sets: the Avenues, Denker Park, 35th, 37th, and 39th Streets. Each of these sets claims specific territories with the area controlled by the Rollin 30s Harlem Crips. Each set also has designated shot callers that direct the set's activities.

The gang has an elaborate system of ranking positions from lowest to highest using the following general structure: baby, soldier, foot soldier, shot caller, gangsta, lil homie/lil shawty, homeboy/homegirl, big homie/big shawty, baby gangsta (BG), little baby gangsta (LBG), original little baby gangsta (OLBG), young gangsta (YG), original young gangsta (OYG), original gangsta (OG), double OOG, and triple OOOG.

The Rollin 30s Harlem Crips have been involved in drug trafficking, specifically crack and powder cocaine, and the illegal sales of firearms. Robberies, homicides, and assaults are common in the areas controlled by these Crips. They are suspected of committing "knock-knock" burglaries, that is, gang members knocking on a door and if no one answers, entering the property to commit burglary. Gang members call this floccin.

Concluding Observations

From these examples, it is evident that the range of Crip and Blood characteristics is remarkably wide. Yes, there are commonalities in name, values, rules, norms, mannerisms, and subcultures, but the essence of these sets is essentially local. Each takes on a local flavor and implements what it believes is meant by being a Crip or Blood.

Notes

1. Eugene L. Weems and Clarke Lowe, *America's Most Notorious Gangs* (Dixon, CA: Universal Publishing, 2013), 3.
2. Compiled from multiple websites, including: "Rollin 60s Neighborhood Crips in Los Angeles, California–Hyde Park Area," accessed at www.streetgangs.org; "Rollin 60s Neighborhood Crips," accessed at www.unitedgangs.org; "Bounty Hunter Bloods," accessed at: http://unitedgangs.com/2010/04/06/bounty -hunters/; "Rollin 30s Crip Knowledge," accessed at http:/thehoodup.com/ board/viewtopic.php?t=43871#.U_pkd0tPEpE; "Rollin 30s Harlem Crips," accessed at: http://www.rapdict.org/Rollin_30's_Harlem_Crips. The information presented here was also compiled from Federal Bureau of Investigation, *Dozens of Members of Violent Street Gang Charged with Narcotics and Weapons Violation Following Joint Investigation Known as Operation Thumbs Down* (Los Angeles: Federal Bureau of Investigation, Los Angeles, August 29, 2013).
3. Umemoto, Karen, *The Truce: Lessons from an L.A. Gang War* (Ithaca, NY: Cornell University Press, 2006).
4. See Chapter 6 for a more detailed discussion of this accidental shooting.
5. Mark Fleisher, "Inside the Fremont Hustlers." In Jody Miller, Cheryl L. Maxson, and Malcolm W. Klein (Eds.), *The Modern Gang Reader, Second Edition* (Los Angeles: Roxbury, 2001), 94–103.
6. Ibid., 98.
7. Ibid., 95.
8. Ibid., 99.

CHAPTER TEN

The Future of the Crips and Bloods

Is there life after the gang?

—Diwi Morris (Blood)[1]

It's not enough to say that I had transcended the mind-set of being a banger by this time. After having spent thirteen years of my young life inside what had initially seemed like an extended family but had turned into a war machine, I was tired and disgusted with its insatiable appetite for destruction. Destruction no longer fed my narcissism.[2]

—Sanyika Shakur, Crip

The Demographic Realities Faced by Gangs

The Crips and Bloods are a product of impoverished inner cities and suburbs. They exist in urban areas of high poverty, crime, racial segregation, substance abuse, and decay. As poverty has expanded to suburban areas, so have the Crips and the Bloods. The chances for the continued existence and expansion of both gangs remain high. Until there is a commitment to change the situations from which gangs arise and thrive, they will flourish in our cities and suburbs. Some factors that ensure their continuation include:

- Unemployment that is and will remain high for at-risk youth and adults who face few options. For these disenfranchised groups street gangs such as the Crips and Bloods will continue to be viewed as a financial and social option. Some will view gangs as a way to obtain wealth, respect, and status, although few will actually succeed.
- Census data that confirm a widening gap between the rich and the poor in the United States. There is no indication that this trend will reverse anytime soon, if ever. As the national economy moves to focus on the service sector and low-skill positions that seldom pay a livable wage, even those who do find work will struggle; national employment data indicate that a livable wage is not available in 6 out of the 10 most common jobs. This leaves impoverished individuals and families locked in neighborhoods where many Bloods and Crips originate and operate. The families from which both gangs draw members will continue to have few prospects to move on to better lives. Faced with the prospect of poverty and no way out, some people may see gangs as the only option.
- Historical factors such as discrimination, prejudice, racism, other long-term socioeconomic consequences of enslavement, and lack of public investment in decaying communities. These factors will continue to affect people and spawn street gangs. Blighted and segregated communities will continue to fuel the formation and continuation of Blood and Crip sets.
- Missing male role models. This lack of guidance will continue to promote the attractiveness of street gangs such as the Bloods and Crips. In his ethnographic study of black gangs conducted in the late 1990s, Peter Patton reported that 84 percent of gang members lived in single parent households.[3] There is no indication that this pattern has improved, and if anything, it has worsened. Single parent households can perpetuate poverty, which helps fuel gang membership. Single women with children they cannot afford without government assistance limit opportunities for their offspring to work their way out of poverty.

- Gang culture and lifestyle that continue to appeal to some youth and young adults. The trappings, perceived glamour, and romance of gangs such as the Crips and Bloods will continue to resonate in the minds of marginalized youth.
- The existence of Crip and Blood gangs in juvenile and adult correctional facilities that continues to support gang involvement.[4]
- Insufficient government resources to effectively prevent illegal substance use and distribution. As long as there is demand, gang members can make money selling drugs, and their gangs will provide the needed infrastructure for them to do so. When drug sales are the only game in town, gangs will participate.
- School dropout rates that continue to be high for marginalized populations from which street gangs like the Crips and Bloods draw their membership.
- Insufficient government assistance to impoverished areas of Los Angeles that have a high prevalence of street gangs. This lack of assistance along with insufficient economic and social development perpetuates a vicious cycle of violence and revenge. The amount of funding for schools and infrastructure will continue to be marginal in impoverished areas.

Expert Malcolm W. Klein, who has been studying street gangs for decades, once stated, "As long as there are gangs in our communities, it is a viable option to our kids."[5] Society must have the political and economic will to eliminate the root causes of gang formation, or gangs will continue to thrive. The situation in Los Angeles is a good example. Local, state, and federal governments have provided little help to the impoverished areas of Los Angeles that are home to many street gangs.

Following the Rodney King beating in 1992, the Crips and Bloods put together a strategic plan to revitalize the blighted areas of Los Angeles.[6] Their motto was "Give us the hammer and the nails, we will rebuild the city." The plan called for an investment of $3.728 billion in the community for items such as increased funding for schools, recreation, health care, landscaping, sanitation, law enforcement, and economic development. The goal was to provide employment and new prosocial opportunities for residents. Government officials never took this proposal seriously.[7] Whether adopting this plan or an alternative,

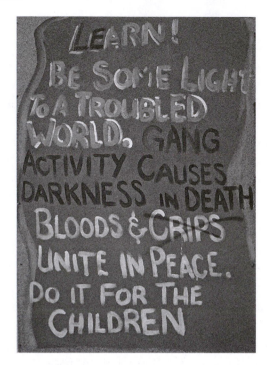

A sign in Los Angeles pleads for peace between rival gangs, the Bloods and the Crips. Crips has already been crossed out, presumably by a member of the Bloods. This signifies that some Bloods have not bought into the truce. Eventually, conflicts between the two gangs declined. (Joseph Sohm/Visions of America/Corbis)

the bottom line is that billions of dollars would be needed to significantly impact the communities that spawn gangs. The private and public sectors have not shown an interest in investing in our blighted communities.

Official Responses to Gangs

Society has taken a variety of approaches as it seeks to address gangs, ranging from prevention to intervention to suppression. In the areas where Crips and Bloods flourish, a number of gang suppression approaches have been attempted, with the aim of making gang members feel so uncomfortable they would decide being in a gang was not worth it. In 1977 a gang suppression strategy called Community Response against Street Hoodlums (CRASH) was implemented in

Los Angeles. Its approach was to use gang-like tactics to suppress gang activities. In the minds of some, CRASH units were just another form of gang that combatted gangs in the streets. With names like CRASH and SWAT (Special Weapons and Tactics), it is easy to understand why gang members would view law enforcement agencies as the enemy. Some gang members viewed law enforcement personnel as an occupying army in their hoods.

In 1988 the chief of police in Los Angeles, Daryl F. Gates, implemented Operation Hammer. The approach of this anti-gang intervention was to have large groups of police sweep through black neighborhoods on weekends and enforce every law, no matter how trivial. This and other suppression strategies typically result in the arrest and removal of gang members from the streets. They are built around an approach that has no tolerance for gang-related activities. During this intervention, thousands of black youth were arrested and held in detention over the weekend and then released on Monday. Consequently, black and other minority youth were alienated from law enforcement personnel, and the efforts helped solidify existing sets. Sets now had a common enemy and threat: the police. Police learned that after almost every arrest new youth filled vacancies in the sets. There was no shortage of disenfranchised youth willing to join.

Another problem with this approach is that it is difficult to distinguish gang members from individuals who are not involved with gangs. Consequently, the latter felt harassed by law enforcement and became oppositional and non-compliant.

Another suppression strategy was called Operation Safe Streets, which took gang members off the streets and detained them in separate Crip and Blood modules in the Los Angeles County Jail. According to some gang members, this housing situation caused some comrades to turn against each other and consequently broke down gang alliances[8]—Crips in detention had issues with other Crips, and conflicts resulted, and the same was true for Bloods in their module.

The other informal practice was to place individual Bloods in holding tanks full of Crips and let them brutalize the Bloods. Crips would have similar experiences when placed in Blood modules. The individual would get beaten within an inch of his life and then be pulled out by guards. In a sense, this was law enforcement brutality meted out by the gangs. Similar practices occurred in court holding cells.

Marshalling law enforcement efforts is one way to suppress gangs, and another involves stricter legal consequences for those convicted of gang involvement. In 2005 the Gang Deterrence and Community Protection Act of 2005 ("Gangbusters bill") was passed by the U.S. House of Representatives. The bill, if passed into law, would have enhanced the consequences of gang-related activities. It would have made several gang-related violent offenses federal crimes, imposed mandatory sentences of 10 years to life, expanded the reach of the death penalty, and allowed 16- and 17-year-old gang members to be prosecuted as adults for federal crimes. The bill was defeated in the Senate. Even as far back as 1988, with the implementation of California's STEP (Street Terrorism Enforcement and Protection) Act, legislation aimed to deter the formation of gangs and their involvement with criminal activity. With the STEP Act, prosecutors can impose greater sentence enhancements on individuals involved in criminal activity if it is found that they fit the criteria necessary to label them as gang members.

Over time, law enforcement personnel learned that people care more about how they are treated by authorities than the legal consequences of illegal behavior. Subsequently, showing respect became a component of law enforcement's response to crime, and they eventually came to show more respect to the black community through efforts such as community policing.

Even though the situation improved to a degree, many continue to view the police with distrust. Periodic instances of police brutality against people of color have not helped improve police–community relations. Many view law enforcement personnel as problematic and an intrusion in their lives. Suppression strategies also enhance gang cohesion, and there are almost always individuals willing and able to fill vacancies in gangs.

These gang suppression programs typically do not address why gangs form in the first place; rather, they encourage youth to lay down their guns and quit gangbanging without offering meaningful options or addressing the socioeconomic reasons gangs remain a viable option for some youth and young adults. No simple, straightforward solution will adequately address the problem of street gangs. As long as gangs effectively meet the needs of their members, most interventions will result in short-term fixes rather than long-term solutions. However, some progress is possible. Key components of a successful strategy would be to train ex-gang members and community leaders to intervene in the lives of youth who are at risk or are already involved with gangs, including the Bloods and Crips. Former gang members are in a good position to understand what gang members are experiencing.

In recent years a number of black political and religious organizations have come to actively influence black street gangs, including the Crips and Bloods, and their subcultures. These groups include the Black Liberation Army, United Blood Nation, 415 African Nation, Black Riders Liberation Army, All African Peoples' Revolutionary Party, and Nation of Islam.[9]

Concluding Observations

Whether we like them or do not, the Bloods and Crips will remain part of American society. If current patterns continue, we can expect the Bloods and Crips to be increasingly involved in a diverse range of crimes. Their involvement in traditional activities such as drug sales, homicide, assault, automobile theft, larceny, and prostitution will continue. They will also likely expand their efforts to include human trafficking, sex trafficking, smuggling, selling counterfeit goods, credit card fraud, and other non-traditional street crimes.[10]

According to the National Gang Intelligence Center, gangs will continue to expand in the United States.[11] They will continue to fight to control territories for criminal and financial objectives. In this regard, more partnerships between gangs will occur as both Crips and Bloods expand into non-traditional criminal activities. Gangs will continue to increase their use of technology to perpetuate crimes and promote their gangster lifestyle.

Notes

1. Dashaun Morris, *War of the Bloods in My Veins* (New York: Scribner, 2008), 143.
2. Sanyika Shakur, *Monster: The Autobiography of an L.A. Gang Member* (New York: Penguin, 1993), 355.

3. Peter Patton, "The Gangstas in Our Midst." *Urban Review* 30 (1998), 50.

4. Ibid.

5. Phillip W. Browne, "Gang Problem Needs to Be Tackled in the Schools, Home." *Los Angeles Daily News* (October 3, 2004), accessed August 1, 2014, at: http://lang.dailynews.com/social/gangs/articles/dnp8_main.asp.

6. Crips and Bloods, "Crips' and Bloods' Plan for the Reconstruction of Los Angeles," accessed on September 6, 2014, at: http://gangresearch.net/Gang Research/Policy/cripsbloodsplan.html.

7. Tom Hayden, *Street Wars: Gangs and the Future of Violence* (New York: New Press, 2004).

8. Donovan Simmons and Terry Moses, *Bloods and Crips: The Genesis of a Genocide* (Bloomington, IN: Authorhouse, 2009), 96–97.

9. Wayne Caffey, *Crips and Bloods* (Los Angeles: Los Angeles County Sheriff's Department, 2006), 6.

10. National Gang Intelligence Center, *2013 National Gang Report* (Washington, DC: Federal Bureau of Investigation, 2013).

11. Ibid.

Glossary

This is a glossary of some of the terms used by Crips and Bloods. The language of the street is an important cultural aspect of all gangs, including the Bloods and Crips. Some of the terms that follow may be out of date or no longer in use because gang culture is constantly evolving and with it gang vocabulary. Changing vocabulary is an important aspect of Crip and Blood subcultures because it helps both stay one or two steps ahead of authorities and rival gangs.

A buck fifty: East Coast Blood reference to the initiation ritual of slashing a rival or a stranger with a razor on the face. The number 150 refers to the number of stitches required to repair the cut to the face.

Against the curb: Describes an individual who is out of money or smoked out on crack.

AK: Abbreviation for an AK-47 automatic Russian-made rifle sometimes used by sets.

B: Homeboy who is like a brother; sometimes used as a derogatory term for a female, short for bitch.

Bacon: Name for police.

Baller: Blood making money on the street.

Ballin: Having more money than others.

Banga: Slang for gun.

Bangin or banging: Gang fighting, as in gang banging, or running with a set.

Beamin: Being high on crack cocaine.

Beat in: Pre-member's initiation into a gang by fighting an established member or being subjected to a beating by members of a gang.

Behind the wall: Being in jail or prison.

BG/pee wee: Baby gangster or very young member of a set.

BK: Crip abbreviation for Blood killer.

BKA: Crip abbreviation for Blood killer always.

Black Rag Gang: Set that does not claim affiliation with either Crips or Bloods.

Bling: Jewelry that sparkles and usually has gemstones and a lot of gold.

Blob/slob: Negative and disrespectful term Crips use to describe Bloods.

Blood: Member of a Blood gang. The name is possibly based on the practice of black soldiers in Vietnam greeting other black soldiers as "blood." Likely used to refer to being of the same African American heritage.

Blood drop: Unborn child or infant of a Blood; a Blood member's baby.

Blood in: To initiate into the Bloods.

Bloodlette: Female member of the Bloods.

Bo: Marijuana.

Bomb: To cross out a rival gang member's name from gang graffiti.

Boned out: Used to describe someone who ran away or chickened out, as in running away from a fight with a rival gang.

Braggin: Boasting about one's exploits.

Breakdown: Shotgun.

Brrrt: East Coast Blood greeting or an announcement that Bloods are present.

Bud: Marijuana.

Bullet: A year in jail or prison.

Bumpin titties: Fighting.

Burner: Blood term for gun.

Bussin: Shooting at someone.

Bust a cap: Shoot at someone.

Bust a heat: Shoot a gun.

Bust back: Shoot back at a rival gang.

Buster: Blood term for a fake gang member.

B-walk: Walk or dance step associated with being a Blood.

Capped: Shot, to have shot at someone or to have been shot.

Cappin: Shooting someone.

Chair: Gang member that oversees security over drug sales.

Cheddar/snaps: Money.

Chillin: Hanging out or getting together with other gang members and talking, joking around, and otherwise spending time together socializing.

Chop it up: Talk.

Chronic/bhronic: High-quality marijuana (Crip or Blood spelling, respectively).

CK: Blood abbreviation meaning Crip killer.

Claimer: Person claiming to be in a gang when he or she is not.

Clockin: Selling drugs.

Color Tripping: Crip or Blood gang that follows traditional gang subculture in name and/or that has issues with other gangs based solely on what color they claim.

Crab: Negative and disrespectful term used by Bloods in reference to a Crip.

Crab killa: Blood who kills or claims to kill Crips.

Crack house: Location, often a house, where crack cocaine is used and/or sold.

Crew: Set or gang.

Cripin or Crippin: Being a Crip and acting in the role of a Crip. For example, a gang member might say, "We be Crippin." It also means gang banging as a Crip.

Criplette: Female Crip.

Cross over: Switch membership from one gang to another.

Custer: Crip expression for a fake gang member.

Cuzz or cuz (cousin): Friendly greeting from one Crip to another.

C-walk: Dance created and popular in the 1970s; done to a musical style known as gangsta rap. Also referred to as the Crip walk.

Damu: "Blood" in Swahili.

Dawg: Title for a friend; Blood reference to another Blood; player with females.

Dead president: Money.

Dead rag: Red rag (handkerchief).

Dew rag or durag: Bandana, usually showing the gang's colors, worn on the head.

Dirty work or doing dirt: Doing things for the gang that few others will do. Sanyika Shakur gave examples such as going into someone's house when no one else would or shooting people.

Dis/diss: To disrespect another person.

Doggin: Treating someone badly.

Double-deuce: A .22 caliber handgun.

Down: Okay or in favor of something.

Down for the set: Describes a gang member who is loyal to his gang (set) and will fight to defend it.

Draped: Describes someone who is wearing a lot of flashy jewelry.

Drop a dime: Snitch on someone or inform law enforcement personnel.

Duce-five: A .25 caliber handgun.

Eating spreads: Eating jail meals.

8 ball: Malt Liquor or Old English 800, a popular alcoholic drink in the hood; an eighth of an ounce of a drug, usually cocaine.

Ends: Money.

Fade: Originally used by gang members as a code word to kill someone

Faded: To be intoxicated (drunk) or disrespectful.

5–50: Blood reference to someone who is not part of the Blood circle (set).

Five-O or 5-0: Cops, police.

Flag: Bandana worn by gang members that is the gang's color.

Flaggin, flashin, or flashing: Throwing up gang signs or hand gestures. While always used as a greeting among gang members, it is viewed as a sign of disrespect when a rival gang flashes its gang sign. Flashing is sometimes used by gang members at funerals out of respect for fallen gang members.

Flame out: Blood dressing up in red attire.

Flip: Change membership from one gang or set to another.

Food: Blood reference to a target of Blood violence.

Forty: A 40-ounce bottle of beer.

Four feet: To be waiting to fight, as in "I had four feet and then the shots occurred."

Four-five: A .45 caliber handgun.

Fresh: Describes a young gang member who does not have a police record. Gang members who are fresh are good candidates for carrying out risky assignments for the gang because if caught, they will serve lighter juvenile or criminal justice sentences.

G: Gangster, as in "What's up, G?" Used as a friendly greeting for a gangster or someone a gang member associates with.

Gage or gauge: Shotgun.

Gangbanger: Gang member who is involved in gang-related activities at the street level such as banging, selling drugs, and drive-bys.

Gangsta: Gangster or one who acts, dresses, and talks like a gang member.

Gangsta rap: Musical style that combines hip-hop and rap styles. The name gangsta first gained widespread recognition in a song titled *Gangsta* by Ice T in 1988.

Gat: Gun. The term is short for the first true rapid-fire gun (machine gun), the Gatling gun from the nineteenth century.

G checking: Testing a person claiming to be a Blood about his knowledge of the Bloods. G checking is used to separate true Bloods from imposers claiming to be Bloods.

Gee'd up: Dressed up as a gangster.

Get down: Fight.

Ghetto star: Gang leader who is well known and respected in the neighborhood.

Glock: Brand of German-made handgun popular on the streets. Glocks are sometimes made of plastic and have a large number of rounds, which makes them attractive on the street. They are also popular because of their simplicity and dependability.

Going on line: Joining a gang.

Got off: To have shot a gun.

Governor: In some highly structured gangs a high level of authority rests with members who are sometimes called governors. Governors carry out instructions from the OGs in the gang's territory.

G ride: Stolen car.

Hard: Strongly committed to one's gang, as in to be hard.

Ho: Whore.

Homeboy/Homegirl: Member of the local gang, male or female, respectively.

Homes: Gang member.

Homie: Fellow local gang member.

Hood: Short for the neighborhoods where Crip or Blood gangs operate and hang out. A hood is one's territory.

In the mix: Involved in gang activities.

Jam: Confront.

Kicking back: Relaxing or chilling.

Lace: Teach, as in teach young members about the code of the gang.

Loc/locs: Refers to Crips who are are locked into the gang; also refers to wearing dark sunglasses. Bloods spell it *lok* to disrespect Crips.

Looped up: Intoxicated.

Lovely: Marijuana mixed (sprayed) with phencyclidine (PCP).

Mad dawg/mad dogging: Staring someone up and down from head to toe as if to initiate a fight, test their courage, or see if they are intimidated.

Mark: Criminal perpetrator.

Merk: To beat someone to death; to abuse or kill someone.

Mission: To go out to commit a crime, such a theft or murder.

MOB: Money over bitches.

Mobbing: Gang members hanging out.

Nation: Preferred reference to one's gang; similar to a set but usually a more global reference to all Crips or Bloods.

Neutrals: Non-gang individuals who may claim membership in a gang. The East Coast Bloods targeted neutrals when OG Mac was released from prison.

Nine: A 9 mm handgun.

Nine hundred and ninety nine (999): To snitch to authorities.

Off brands: Rival gang members.

OG: Original, older, and/or leader of a set.

187: Refers to the California penal code for murder. This term was popularized in the film *Deep Cover*, which had a rap song by Snoop Dogg titled *1-8-7 on an Undacova Cop*.

186: To be on alert.

One time: Police.

Other side: Rival gang.

Out of pocket: Refers to being in rival gang territory.

Packing: Set member carrying a gun.

Pass: Allow a rival gang member to travel or be in a gang's territory without harming them, as in "Give him a pass."

Peter rolled: Murder.

Pipehead: Person who uses crack cocaine.

Player: Person claiming to be in a gang who is not.

Poobutt: Person claiming to be in a gang who is not.

Popo: Police.

Posse up: To meet and head out with gang members with the intent to commit a crime such as attacking another gang.

Props: Respect.

Put 'em in check: Correct or discipline a member of a gang for breaking a gang norm or rule.

Put in work: To act on behalf of the gangs, for example, committing a criminal offense or fighting a rival gang. Sometimes used to mean doing dangerous activities for the gang.

QC: Abbreviation for queen Crip or the highest ranking woman in a Crip set.

Rag: Handkerchief in the gang's color.

Regent: One who holds mid-level status in the gang; reports to the governor. Typically oversees the gang's drug sales.

Relative: How a Blood member may refer to another Blood gang member.

Rickets: Derogatory Blood term for Crip.

Road dog: Partner.

Rock: Crack cocaine.

Rollin: Drug dealing.

Ru: Shorthand for a Piru gang member.

Saggin: Wearing your pants low on your hips.

Scuzz: Disrespectful term for Crips.

Set: Members of a specific gang; often used interchangeably with the word *gang*.

Shortie: Lower-status gang member who carries out the objectives of the gang at the street level, for example, a shortie could directly sell drugs to individuals.

Shot caller: Gang leader, or OG.

Slippin: Gang member letting his or her guard down, acting carelessly, making mistakes, or getting caught in a rival gang's territory.

Slob: Crip term for a Blood.

Smoked out: To be burned out on drugs.

Smoker: Person who uses cocaine.

Snoop: Crip name for a Blood.

Spot: Where a gang hangs out, such as a corner or house; a specific location where drugs are sold, such as a corner or street block.

Stacks: System of codes and hand signals Bloods created to communicate with each other; they allow Bloods to communicate with each other in a way that hides the nature of their communications from prison officials. Codes and stacks on the street are used to keep enemies from understanding the Blood communications.

Strap: Gun.

Stripes or stars: Recognition that a gang member has done important things for the gang (put in work). Gang stripes or stars are earned and respected.

TG: Tiny (young) gangster.

Throw up your set: To gesture your gang sign.

Tray-eight: A .38 caliber gun.

UBN: United Blood Nation.

Uzi: Israeli-made automatic weapon popular on the street.

Wet: Name for PCP; used by Crips.

What it B like?: Blood greeting.

What it C like?: Crip greeting.

What set you claiming?: What is your gang?

What up, G?: Used to greet another gangster.

References

A and E Home Video. (1996). *Gang violence in America.* 20th Century with Mike Wallace. A and E Home Video.

Adamson, C. (2000). Defensive localism in white and black: A comparative history of European-American and African-American youth gangs. *Ethnic and Racial Studies* 23(2), 272–298.

Allender, D. (2001). Gangs in middle America. *FBI Law Enforcement Bulletin* 70(12), 1.

Alonso, A. (1998). Urban graffiti on the city landscape. Paper presented at Western Geography Graduate Conference, San Diego State University, February 14, 1998.

Alonso, A. (1999). *Territoriality among African Americans street gangs in Los Angeles.* Masters Thesis, University of Southern California.

Alonso, A. (2004). Radicalized identities and the formation of black gangs in Los Angeles. *Urban Geography* 25(7), 658–674.

Bailey, R. W. (2012). *Speaking American: A history of English in the United States.* New York: Oxford University Press.

Baker, B. (1988). Homeboys: Players in a deadly drama. *Los Angeles Times,* June 26.

Barganier, G. P., III. (2011). *Fanon's children: The Black Panther Party and the rise of the Crips and Bloods in Los Angeles.* Ph.D. Dissertation, University of California, Berkeley.

Barrett, B. (2004). Gangster menace. *Los Angeles Daily News,* September 30. Accessed April 1, 2014, at: http://lang.dailynews.com/socal/gangs/articles/dnp5 _main.asp.

Battin, S., Hill, K., Abbott, R., Catalono, R. & Hawkins, J. D. (1980). The contribution of gang membership to delinquency beyond delinquent friends. *Criminology* 36, 105–106.

Bing, L. (1991). *Do or die: America's most notorious gangs speak for themselves.* New York: HarperCollins.

Bjerregaard, B. (2002). Self-definitions of gang membership and involvement in delinquent activities. *Youth and Society* 34, 31–54.

Bjerregaard, B. & Lizotte, A. J. (2001). Gun ownership and gang membership. In J. Miller, C. L. Maxson, and M. W. Klein (Eds.), *The modern gang reader, second edition.* Los Angeles: Roxbury.

Block, C. R. & Block, R. (1993). Street Crime in Chicago" In *Research in Brief.* Washington, DC: U.S. Department of Justice.

Booth, S. (2008). Symbols. In L. Kontos and D. C. Brotherton (Eds.), *Encyclopedia of gangs.* Westport, CT: Greenwood.

Browne, P. W. (2004, October 3). Gang problem needs to be tackled in the schools, home. *Los Angeles Daily News.* Accessed September 7, 2013, at: http://lang .dailynews.com/socal/gangs/articles/dnp8_main.asp.

Bureau of Organized Crime and Criminal Intelligence. (n.d.). *Crips and Bloods street gangs.* Sacramento, CA: Author.

Caffey, W. (2006). *Crips and Bloods.* Los Angeles: Los Angeles County Sheriff's Office.

Campbell, A. (1991). *The girls in the gang, second edition.* Cambridge, MA: Basil Blackwell.

Campbell, A. & Muncer, S. (1989). Them and us: A comparison of the cultural context of American gangs and British subcultures. *Deviant Behavior* 10, 271–288.

Campbell, A., Muncer, S. & Galea, J. (1982). American gangs and British subcultures: A comparison. *International Journal of Offender Therapy and Comparative Criminology* 26, 76–89.

Centers for Disease Control and Prevention (CDC). (2012). Gang homicides: Five U.S. cities, 2003–2008. *Morbidity and Mortality Weekly Report* 61(3), 46–51.

Chang, Jeff. (2005). *Can't stop won't stop.* New York: St. Martin's.

Christensen, L. W. (1999). *Gangbangers: Understanding the deadly minds of America's street gangs.* Boulder, CO: Paladin.

Conquergood, D. (1997). Street literacy. In J. Flood, S. B. Heath, and D. Lape (Eds.), *Handbook of research on teaching literacy through the communicative and visual arts.* New York: Simon and Schuster.

Coughlin, B. C. & Venkatesh, S. A. (2003). The Urban Street Gang after 1970. *Annual Review of Sociology* 29, 41–64.

Covey, H. C. (2007). *Street gangs throughout the world.* Springfield, IL: Charles Thomas.

Crips and Bloods. (2014). Crips' and Bloods' plan for the reconstruction of Los Angeles. Accessed September 6, 2014 at: http://gangresearch.net/Gang Research/Policy/cripsbloodsplan.html.

Cureton, S. R. (2002). Introducing Hoover: I'll ride for you, gangsta. In C. R. Huff (Ed.), *Gangs in America, third edition.* Thousand Oaks, CA: Sage.

Cureton, S. R. (2008). *Hoover Crips: When Cripin' becomes a way of life.* Lanham, MD: University Press of America.

Cureton, S. R. (2009). Something wicked this way comes: A historical account of black gangsterism offers wisdom and warning for African American leadership. *Journal of Black Studies* 40, 347–361.

Curry, G. D. & Decker, S. H. (1997). What's in a name? A gang by any other name isn't quite the same. *Valparaiso University Law Review* 31, 501–514.

Curry, G. D. & Decker, S. H. (2003). *Confronting gangs: Crime and community, second edition.* Los Angeles: Roxbury.

Davis, M. (1992). *City of quartz.* London: First Vintage.

Décary-Hétu, D. & Morselli, C. (2011). Gang presence in social network sites. *International Journal of Cyber Criminology* 5(2), 876–890.

Decesare, D. (2008). Gang photography. In L. Kontos and D. C. Brotherton (Eds.), *Encyclopedia of gangs.* Westport, CT: Greenwood.

Decker, S. H. (1996). Collective and normative features of gang violence. *Justice Quarterly* 13(2), 243–264.

Decker, S. H. (2000). Legitimating drug use: A note on the impact of gang membership and drug sales on the use of illicit drugs. *Justice Quarterly* 17(2), 393–410.

Decker, S. H. (2007). Youth Gangs and Violent Behavior and Aggression. In D. J. Flannery, A. T. Vazsongi, and I. D. Waldman (Eds.), *The Cambridge handbook of violent behavior and aggression.* New York: Cambridge University Press.

Decker, S. H. & Curry, G. D. (2002). Gangs, gang homicides and gang loyalty: Organized crimes or disorganized criminals. *Journal of Criminal Justice* 30, 1–10.

Decker, S. H. & Lauritsen, J. L. (2002). Leaving the gang. In C. R. Huff (Ed.), *Gangs in America III*. Thousand Oaks, CA: Sage.

Decker, S. H. & Pyrooz, D. C. (2010). Gang violence worldwide: Context, culture, and country. In E. G. Berman, K. Krause, E. LeBrun, and G. McDonald (Eds.), *Small arms survey 2010: Gangs, groups and guns*. New York: Cambridge University Press.

Decker, S. H. & Van Winkle, B. (1996). *Life in the gang*. New York: Cambridge University Press.

Descormiers, K. & Morselli, C. (2011). Alliances, conflicts, and contradictions in Montreal's street gang landscape. *International Criminal Justice Review* 21, 297–314.

Dolan, E. F., Jr. & Finney, S. (1984). *Youth gangs*. New York: Simon and Schuster.

Duane, D. (2006, January 1). Straight outta Boston. *Mother Jones*. Accessed September 1, 2014, at: http://www.motherjones.com/print/15100.

Dunn, W. (2007). *The gangs of Los Angeles*. New York: iUniverse.

Egley, A., Jr. (2002). *Youth gang survey trends from 1996 to 2000*. Washington, DC: U.S. Department of Justice and Delinquency Prevention.

Esbensen, F. A. & Huizinga, D. (1993). Gangs, drugs, and delinquency in a survey of urban youth. *Criminology* 31, 565–590.

Etter, G. W. (2012). Gang investigation. In M. L. Birzer and C. Robertson (Eds.), *Introduction to criminal investigation*. Boca Raton, FL: CRC Press.

Fagan, J. (1989). The social organization of drug use and drug selling among urban gangs. *Criminology* 27, 622–667.

Federal Bureau of Investigation. (2013). *Dozens of members of violent street gang charged with narcotics and weapons violation following joint investigation known as Operation Thumbs Down*. Los Angeles: Federal Bureau of Investigation, Los Angeles.

Federal Bureau of Investigation. (2013). *Four United Blood Nation members convicted of racketeering charges following a six-day trial*. Charlotte, NC: Federal Bureau of Investigation, U.S. Attorney's Office.

Federal Bureau of Investigation. (2014). *Twenty-eight members and associates of Patterson Bloods street gang charged in Manhattan federal court with distributing heroin, crack cocaine, and powder cocaine and with firearms offenses*. Newark, NJ: Federal Bureau of Investigation, U.S. Attorney's Office.

Felson, M. (2006). *Crime and nature*. Thousand Oaks, CA: Sage.

Ferrell, J. (2008). Gang and non-gang graffiti. In L. Kontos and D. C. Brotherton (Eds.), *Encyclopedia of gangs*. Westport, CT: Greenwood.

Fleisher, M. (2001). Inside the Fremont Hustlers. In J. Miller, C. L. Maxson, and M. W. Klein (Eds.), *The modern gang reader, second edition*. Los Angeles: Roxbury.

Fleisher, M. S. (1995). *Beggars and thieves*. Madison: University of Wisconsin Press.

Fleisher, M. S. (1998). *Dead end kids: Gang girls and the boys they know*. Madison: University of Wisconsin Press.

Fleisher, M. S. (2006). Youth gang social dynamics and social network analysis: Applying centrality measures to assess the nature of gang boundaries. In J. F. Short Jr. and L. A. Hughes (Eds.), *Studying youth gangs*. Lanham, MD: AltaMira.

Fleisher, M. S. & Decker, S. H. (2001). An overview of the challenge of prison gangs. *Corrections Management Quarterly* 5, 1–9.

Flores, R. D. (1997). Crips and Bloods. *Crime and Justice International* 13(9), 6–9.

Franzese, R. J., Covey, H. C. & Menard, S. (2006). *Youth gangs*. Springfield, IL: Charles C. Thomas.

Gangland. (2008). *One Blood*. https://www.youtube.com/watch?v=WHKYiE-zjE8. History Channel, originally aired May 28, 2008.

Gangland. (2014). *Crips vs. Bloods gangs war documentary*. Accessed September 12, 2014, at: http://www.youtube.com/watch?v=CbGW6R8B_zU.

Garot, R. & Katz, J. (2003). Provocative looks: Gang appearance and dress codes in an inner-city alternative school. *Ethnography* 4, 421–454.

Gordon, R., Lahey, B., Kawai, E., Loeber, R., Stouthamer-Loeber, M. & Farington, D. (2004). Antisocial behavior and youth gang membership: Selection and socialization. *Criminology* 42, 55–87.

Grasciak, A. M. (2003). Gangster rap: The real words behind the songs. *Journal of Gang Research* 11, 55–63. Accessed June 15, 2014, at: https://www.ncjrs.gov/App/Publications/abstract.aspx?ID=203323.

Hagedorn, J. M. (2008). *A world of gangs: Armed young men and gangsta culture*. Minneapolis: University of Minnesota Press.

Halff, G. (2013). Trusting "gangbangers" in war and peace. Case Collection. Accessed August 15, 2014, at: http://ink.library.smu.edu.sg/cases_coll_all/33.

Hayden, T. (2004). *Street wars: Gangs and the future of violence*. New York: New Press.

Hayden, T. (2008). Williams, Stanley Tookie. In L. Kontos and D. C. Brotherton (Eds.), *Encyclopedia of gangs*. Westport, CT: Greenwood.

Hendley, N. B. (2009). *American gangsters, then and now: An encyclopedia.* Santa Barbara, CA: ABC-CLIO eBook Collection.

Hoodup.com. (2010). Rollin 30s Crip knowledge. Accessed April 1, 2014, at: http://thehoodup.com/board/viewtopic.php?t=43871#.U_pkd0tPEpE.

Howell, J. C. (2012). *Gangs in America's communities.* Thousand Oaks, CA: Sage.

Howell, J. C. & Decker, S. H. (1999). The youth gangs, drugs, and violence connection. In *Juvenile Justice Bulletin.* Washington, DC: Office of Juvenile Justice and Delinquency Prevention.

Hunt, G., Joe, K. & Waldorf, D. (1996). Drinking, kicking back and gang banging: Alcohol, violence and street gangs. *Free Inquiry in Creative Sociology* 24, 123–132.

Jah, Y. & Keyah, S. (1995). *Uprising: Crips and Bloods tell the story of America's youth in the crossfire.* New York: Touchstone.

Jankowski, M. S. (1991). *Islands in the street: Gangs and American urban society.* Berkeley: University of California Press.

Kemp, R. (2008). *Ross Kemp on gangs Los Angeles.* British Sky Broadcasting.

Kennedy, D. (2014). Violence and street groups: Gangs, groups and violence. In J. Hawdon, J. Ryan, and M. Lucht (Eds.), *The causes and consequences of group violence* Lanham, MD: Lexington.

Klein, M. W. (1967). *Juvenile gangs in context.* Englewood Cliffs, NJ: Prentice-Hall.

Klein, M. W. (1971). *Street gangs and street workers.* Englewood Cliffs, NJ: Prentice-Hall.

Klein, M. W. (1995). *The American street gang.* New York: Oxford University Press.

Klein, M. W. (2008). Hoover Crips: When Cripin' becomes a way of life. *Contemporary Sociology: A Journal of Reviews* 37, 587–589.

Klein, M. W. & Maxson, C. L. (1990). *Street gangs and drug sales.* Los Angeles: University of Southern California, Center for Research on Crime and Social Control.

Klein, M. W. & Maxson, C. L. (1996). *Gang structures, crime patterns, and police responses.* Unpublished final report. Los Angeles: Social Science Research Institute, University of Southern California. Report available at: www.cops.usdoj.gov/...gang_crime/../GangStructuresSummaryReport.

Klein, M. W. & Maxson, C. L. (2006). *Street gang patterns and policies.* Oxford: Oxford University Press.

Klein, M. W., Maxson, C. L. & Cunningham, L. (1991). Crack, street gangs, and violence. *Criminology* 29, 623–650.

Kontos, L. & Brotherton, D. C. (Eds.). (2008). *Encyclopedia of gangs*. Westport, CT: Greenwood.

KPCC Wire Services. (2013, April 5). Crime in Los Angeles drops in first quarter of 2013.

Krikorian, M. War and Peace in Watts. Accessed February 15, 2014, at: www.laweekly.com/2005-07-14/news/war-and-peace-in-watts/full/

Krikorian, M. (2005). War and peace in Watts. Accessed September 15, 2013, at: http:/www.laweekly.com/news/war-and-peace-in-watts-2140289.

L.A. City Attorney Gang Prosecution Section. (2001). Civil gang abatement: A community based policing tool of the Office of the Los Angeles City Attorney. In J. Miller, C. L. Maxson, and M. W. Klein (Eds.), *The modern gang reader, second edition*. Los Angeles: Roxbury.

L.A. Gang Tours. (2014). LA gang tours. Accessed August 15, 2014, at: http://www.lagangtours.com.

Lahey, B. B., Gordon, R. A., Loeber, R., Stouthamer-Lober, M. & Farington, D. P. (1999). Boys who join gangs: A prospective study of predictors of first gang entry. *Journal of Abnormal Child Psychology* 27(4), 261–276.

Lavigne, Y. (1993). *Good guy, bad guy*. Toronto: Random House.

Lawson, G. (2008, January). The inside man. *GQ*, 78, 84–87, 141–143.

Levitt, S. D. & Venkatesh, S. A. (2000). An economic analysis of a drug-selling gang's finances. *Quarterly Journal of Economics* 115(3), 755–789.

Los Angeles County Sheriff's Department. (1992). *L.A. Style: A Street Gang Manual of the Los Angeles County Sheriff's Department*. Los Angeles, Los Angeles Sheriff's Department.

Los Angeles Police Department. (2014). What gangs do? Accessed February 15, 2014, at: http://www.lapdonline.org/get_informed/content_basic_view/23469.

Martínez, J. F. E. (2008). Bloods. In L. Kontos and D.C. Brotherton (Eds.), *Encyclopedia of gangs*. Westport, CT: Greenwood.

Martínez, J. F. E. & Ramos, M. A. (2008). Crips. In L. Kontos and D. C. Brotherton (Eds.), *Encyclopedia of gangs*. Westport, CT: Greenwood.

Maxson, C. L. (1995). Street gangs and drug sales in two suburban cities. In *Research in Brief*. Washington, DC: National Institutes of Justice Research.

Maxson, C. L. (1998, October). Gang members on the move. In *Juvenile Justice Bulletin*. Washington, DC: Office of Juvenile Justice and Delinquency Prevention, Office of Justice Programs, U.S. Department of Justice.

Maxson, C. L. (1999). Gang homicide: A review and extension of the literature. In M. D. Smith and M. A. Zahn (Eds.), *Homicide: A sourcebook of social research*. Thousand Oaks, CA: Sage.

McDaniel, D., Egley, A., Jr. & Logan, J. (2012). Gang homicides: Five U.S. cities, 2003–2008. *Morbidity and Mortality Weekly Report* 61, 46–51.

Miller, J. (1998). Gender and victimization risk among young women in gangs. *Journal of Research in Crime and Delinquency* 35(4), 429–453.

Miller, J. & Decker, S. H. (2001). Young women and gang violence: Gender, street offending, and violent victimization in gangs. *Justice Quarterly* 18, 126.

Morganthau, T. (1988, March 28). The drug gangs. *Newsweek* 20–27.

Morris, D. J. (2008). *War of the Bloods in my veins: A street soldier's march toward redemption*. New York: Scribner.

Morselli, C. & Décary-Hétu, D. (2013). Crime facilitation purposes of social networking sites: A review and analysis of the "cyberbanging" phenomenon. *Small Wars and Insurgencies* 23(5), 152–170.

Mydans, S. (1990, January 29). Life in a girls' gang: Colors and bloody noses. *New York Times*, 1, 12.

National Drug Intelligence Center. (1996). *National gang survey report*. Johnstown, PA: Author.

National Gang Intelligence Center. (2013). *2013 national gang report*. Washington, DC: Federal Bureau of Investigation.

National Institute of Justice. (2011). What is a gang? Definitions. Accessed April 12, 2014, at: http://www.nij.gov/topics/crime/gangs-organized/gangs/definitions.htm.

National Public Radio. (2005, December 7). Tookie Williams and the history of the Crips.

Office of Juvenile Justice and Delinquency Prevention. (2013). *Highlights of the 2011 national youth gang survey*. Washington DC: Author.

Operation Safe Streets. (1995). L.A. style: A street gang manual of the Los Angeles County Sheriff's Department. In M. W. Klein, C. L. Maxson, and J. Miller (Eds.), *The modern gang reader*. Los Angeles. Roxbury.

Oxford English Dictionary. (2013). Subculture. Accessed November 10, 2013, at: http://oxforddictionaries.com/us/definition/american_english/subculture.

Padilla, F. (1992). *The gang as an American enterprise*. New Brunswick, NJ: Rutgers University Press.

Papachristos, A. V. (2009). Murder by structure: Dominance relations and the social structure of gang homicide. *American Journal of Sociology* 115, 74–128.

Patton, P. L. (1998). The gangstas in our midst. *Urban Review* 30(1), 49–76.

Peralta, S. (2009). *Crips and Bloods Made in America*. Docuramafilms.

Pfautz, H. W. (1961). Near-group theory and collective behavior: A critical reformulation. *Social Problems* 9, 167–174.

Pitts, J. (2012). Reluctant criminologists: Criminology, ideology and the violent youth gang. *Youth and Policy* 109, 27–45.

PoliceOne. (2014). Gangs: East Coast Crips. Accessed September 12, 2014, at: http://blutube.policeone.com/gang-videos/3222043850001-gangs-east-coast-crips/.

Porché-Burke, L. & Fulton, C. (1992). The impact of gang violence. In R. C. Cervantes (Ed.), *Substance abuse and gang violence*. Newbury, CA: Sage.

Quicker, J. C. & Batani-Khalfani, A. (1998). From Boozies to Bloods: Early gangs in Los Angeles. *Journal of Gang Research* 5, 15–21.

Randle, J. B. (2014). *Los Angeles County's criminal street gangs: Does violence roll downhill?* Electronic Theses, Projects, and Dissertations. Paper 10.

Reckless, W. C. (1961). A new theory of delinquency. *Federal Probation* 24, 42–46.

Reiner, I. (1992). *Gangs, crime and violence in Los Angeles: Findings and proposals from the district attorney's office*. Arlington, VA: National Youth Gang Information Center.

Rodriguez, L. (2005). The end of the line: California gangs and the promise of street peace. *Social Justice* 32(3), 12–23.

Sanders, W. B. (1994). *Gangbangs and drive-bys: Grounded culture and juvenile gang violence*. New York: Aldine De Gruyter.

Sanders, W. B. (2001). Drive-bys. In J. Miller, C. L. Maxson, and M. W. Klein (Eds.), *The modern gang reader, second edition*. Los Angeles: Roxbury.

Savelli, L. (2009). *Gangs across America and their symbols*. Flushing, NY: Looseleaf.

Schneider, J. (2001). Niche Crime: The Columbus gangs study. *American Journal of Criminal Justice* 26, 93–107.

Shakur, S. (1993). *Monster: The autobiography of an L.A. gang member*. New York: Penguin.

Shelden, R. G., Tracy, S. K. & Brown, W. B. (2001). *Youth gangs in American society, second edition*. Belmont, CA: Wadsworth.

Simmons, D. & Moses, T. (2009). *Bloods and Crips: The genesis of a genocide.* Bloomington, IN: Authorhouse.

Simpson, C. & Pearlman, A. (2005). *Inside the Crips: Life inside L.A.'s most notorious gang.* New York: St. Martin's Griffin.

Skolnick, J., Bluthenthal, R. & Correl, T. (1993). Gang organization and migration. In Scott Cummings and D. J. Monti (Eds.), *Gangs: The origins and impact of contemporary youth gangs in the United States.* Albany: State University of New York Press.

Sloan, C. B. (2007). *Bastards of the party* [Motion picture]. New York: Home Box Office.

Smith, C. F. & Doll, Y. (2012). Gang investigators' perceptions of military-trained gang members (MTGM). *Critical Issues in Justice and Politics* 5(1), 1–17.

Southgate, D. E. (2008). Rap. In L. Kontos and D. C. Brotherton (Eds.), *Encyclopedia of gangs.* Westport, CT: Greenwood.

Spergel, I. (1990). Youth gangs: Continuity and change. In N. Morris (Ed.), *Crime and delinquency: An annual review of research,* Vol. 12. Chicago: University of Chicago Press.

Spergel, I., Curry, G. D., Chance, R., Kane, C., Ross, R., Alexander, A., Simmons, E. & Oh, S. (1996). *Gang suppression and intervention: Problem and response.* OJJDP Summary, Office of Juvenile Justice and Delinquency Prevention, Office of Justice Programs, U.S. Department of Justice.

Starbuck, D., Howell, J. C. & Lindquist, D. J. (2001, December 2). Hybrid and other modern gangs. In *Juvenile Justice Bulletin.* Washington, DC: Office of Juvenile Justice and Delinquency Prevention.

Stoltze, F. (2012). Forget the LA riots: Historic 1992 Watts gang truce was the big news. Accessed September 12, 2014, at: http://www.scpr.org/news/2012/04/28/32221/forget-la-riots-1992-gang-truce-was-big-news/.

Street Gangs. (2014). Rollin 60s Neighborhood Crips in Los Angeles, California–Hyde Park area. Accessed July 28, 2014, at: http://www.streetgangs.com/crips/losangeles/r60scrips.

Sullivan, M. L. (2006). Are "gang" studies dangerous? Youth violence, local context, and the problem of reification. In J. F. Short Jr. and L. A. Hughes (Eds.), *Studying youth gangs.* Lanham, MD: AltaMira.

Swift, R. (2011). *Gangs.* Toronto: Groundwork Books.

T, Ice. (1995). Foreword. In Y. Jah and S. Keyah (Eds.), *Uprising: Crips and Bloods tell the story of America's youth in the crossfire.* New York: Touchstone.

T, Ice. (1995). The killing fields. In M. Klein, C. Maxson, and J. Miller (Eds.), *The modern gang reader.* Los Angeles: Roxbury.

Taylor, S. S. (2009). How street gangs recruit and socialize members. *Journal of Gang Research* 17, 1–27.

Taylor, S. S. (2012). Why American boys join street gangs. *African Journal of Law and Criminology* 2(1), 56–68.

Thornberry, T., Krohn, M., Lizotte, A. & Chard-Wierschem, D. (1993). The role of juvenile gangs in facilitating delinquent behavior. *Journal of Research in Crime and Delinquency* 30, 55–87.

Thornburgh, A. G. (1988). *Blood and Crips street gangs: Briefing book*. Washington, DC: Office of Justice Programs.

Umemoto, K. (2006). *The truce: Lessons from an L.A. gang war*. Ithaca, NY: Cornell University Press.

United Gangs of America. (2010). Bounty Hunter Bloods. Accessed April 15, 2014, at: http://unitedgangs.com/2010/04/06/bounty-hunters/.

United Gangs of America. (2013). Crips. Accessed April 4, 2014, at: http://www.unitedgangs.com.

United Gangs of America. (2014). Rollin 60s Neighborhood Crips. Accessed April 4, 2014, at: http://www.unitedgangs.org.

United Gangs of America. (2014). Sylvia "Rambo" Nunn (gangster). Accessed October 24, 2014, at: http://www.unitedgangs.com.

U.S. Department of Justice. (2002, November). Crips. In *Drugs and Crime*. Washington, DC: U.S. Drug Intelligence Center.

Valentine, B. (1995). *Gang intelligence manual: Identifying and understanding modern-day violent gangs in the United States*. Boulder, CO: Paladin.

Vigil, J. D. (1988). *Barrio gangs*. Austin: University of Texas Press.

Vigil, J. D. (1990). Cholos and gangs: Culture change and street youth in Los Angeles. In C. R. Huff (Ed.), *Gangs in America*. Newbury Park, CA: Sage.

Vigil, J. D. (1993). The established gang. In S. Cummings and D. J. Monti (Eds.), *Gangs: The origins and impact of contemporary youth gangs in the United States*. Albany: State University of New York Press.

Vigil, J. D. (2002). *A rainbow of gangs: Street cultures in the mega-city*. Austin: University of Texas Press.

Vigil, J. D. & Yun, S. C. (2002). A cross-cultural framework for understanding gangs: Multiple marginality and Los Angeles. In C. R. Huff, (Ed.), *Gangs in America III*. Thousand Oaks, CA: Sage.

Vistica, G. (1995, July 24). Gangstas in the ranks. *Newsweek* 126(4) 48.

Walker, R. (2013). Crips and Bloods history. Accessed October 15, 2013, at: http://www.gangsorus.com/crips_bloods_history.htm.

Washington/Baltimore High Intensity Drug Trafficking Area (HIDTA). (2013). Bloods. Accessed January 18, 2014, at: http://www.hidtagangs.org/GangLibrary.aspx.

Washington/Baltimore High Density Drug Trafficking Area. (2013). Crips. Accessed January 18, 2014, at: http://www.hidtagangs.org/GangLibrary.aspx.

Weems, E. L. & Lowe, C. (2013). *America's most notorious gangs.* Dixon, CA: Universal Publishing.

Williams, S. & Cottman Becnel, B. (1998). *Life in prison.* San Francisco: Chronicle.

Williams, S. & Smiley, T. (2007). *Blue rage, black redemption: A memoir.* New York: Simon and Schuster.

Zatz, M. (1987). Chicano youth gangs and crime: The creation of a moral panic. *Contemporary Crisis* 11, 129–158.

Index

About the Author

HERBERT C. COVEY, PhD, is deputy director of human services for Adams County, Colorado. His published works include *What the Slaves Ate: Recollections of the American Foods and Foodways from the Slave Narratives* and *How the Slaves Saw the Civil War: Recollections of the War through the WPA Slave Narratives* (both with Dwight A. Eisnach); *African American Slave Medicine: Herbal and Non-Herbal Treatments*; *The Methamphetamine Crisis*; *Youth Gangs*; and *Street Gangs Throughout the World*.